Bernard Lonergan's Philosophy of Religion

Bernard Lonergan's Philosophy of Religion

From Philosophy of God to
Philosophy of Religious Studies

Jim Kanaris

State University of New York Press

Published by
State University of New York Press, Albany

© 2002 State University of New York

All rights reserved

Printed in the United States of America

No part of this book may be used or reproduced in any manner whatsoever without written permission. No part of this book may be stored in a retrieval system or transmitted in any form or by any means including electronic, electrostatic, magnetic tape, mechanical, photocopying, recording, or otherwise without the prior permission in writing of the publisher.

For information, address State University of New York Press,
90 State Street, Suite 700, Albany, NY 12207

Production by Michael Haggett
Marketing by Anne M. Valentine

Library of Congress Cataloging-in-Publication Data

Kanaris, Jim, 1964–
    Bernard Lonergan's philosophy of religion : from philosophy of God to philosophy of religious studies / Jim Kanaris.
        p. cm.
    Includes bibliographical references and index.
    ISBN 0-7914-5465-7 (alk. paper) — ISBN 0-7914-5466-5 (pbk. : alk. paper)
    1. Lonergan, Bernard J. F. 2. Christianity—Philosophy. 3. Experience (Religion) I. Title.

BR100 .K3 2002
210'.92—dc21
                                                  2002002512

10 9 8 7 6 5 4 3 2 1

*In loving memory
of my parents
Stergios Kanaris
(1934–1995)
and
Maria Panagiotidis
(1934–1999)*

Contents

Acknowledgments	ix
Abbreviations	xi
Introduction	1
1 The *Kehre* of *Philosophy of God, and Theology*	9
Making Room for Religious Experience	10
Deliberately Bracketing Religious Experience	17
2 The Philosophical Aspect of the Concept of Experience	23
The Reader's Experience in *Insight*	24
The General and Specific Notions of Experience in *Insight*	29
Self-Appropriating the General Structure of Experience	38
The Technical Aspect of Self-Appropriation and the Problem of the Relation of Concept to Experience; or, Lonergan, Kant, and Hegel	40
The Existential Aspect of Self-Appropriation	57
3 Religious Experience, Reflection, and Philosophy of God	61
Religious Experience in pre-*Insight* Literature	61
A Necessary Diversion: The Nature-Grace Distinction	69
The Ascendency of Love	72
Religious Experience in pre-*Method* Literature	80
Religious Experience: Emergence of the Expanded Viewpoint	89
4 From Philosophy of God to Philosophy of Religion	101
The Model of Religion: The Point of Departure	102
Lonergan's Philosophy of Religion	118
What Is It? What Does It Do?	123
Conclusion	147
Notes	151
Bibliography	179
Index	193

Acknowledgments

I am indebted to so many people who have contributed in one way or another to this book either in its development, its subject matter or in my personal or professional development. Just as one's work is never one's own, one's person is never one's own work.

I must begin by thanking two colleagues in particular. Maurice Boutin of McGill University has been a great source of inspiration, contributing significantly to my philosophical formation. Never have I left discussions with him unenlightened by some valuable anecdote or detail of history, philosophy, or theology. He has been a Virgil to me, pointing the way through the often inhospitable and rough terrain of learning with remarkable insight: "chi m'avria tratto su per la montagna?"* Patrick Byrne of Boston College has also been a great support during this and other ventures. Whatever insight I may have into Lonergan is owed in no small measure to Dr. Byrne, whose knowledge of Lonergan is as incisive as it is formidable. For the times he has taken the time to engage me on my ideas, I am truly grateful.

Also providing an invaluable service has been the team at the Lonergan Research Institute in Toronto, especially Robert Croken, Michael Shields, and Frederick Crowe. Making sure I promptly received whatever manuscripts and articles I requested and even offering their facilities for research one cold winter weekend in 1998 are only a few of their contributions that spring to mind. The assistance of the Social Sciences and Humanities Research Council of Canada must be duly acknowledged here as well.

Others who have not had a direct hand in this study but have nevertheless contributed significantly to my personal and professional life include, most notably, Sean McEvenue, Eric Christianson, Joseph McLelland, Louis Roy, and Todd Blayone. The interest they have taken in the direction of my work has been a source of great encouragement. To Stephen Gaudet I owe a special word of thanks. His editorial skills came to my aid on countless

---

* "Who else but he could take me up the mount?" (Dante, *The Divine Comedy, Volume II: Purgatory*, trans. Mark Musa [London: Penguin Books, 1985], 29 [iii. 6]).

occasions in earlier drafts. Whatever clarity I chanced upon in expressing a thought, his input was doubtless behind it. For remaining lapses in style or form I take full responsibility. Also valuable were the comments of anonymous readers of the State University of New York Press, the concrete guidance of whose editorial team is also appreciated.

To my family I owe more than words can tell. They alone have borne, without complaint (I'm continually startled by saying), the necessary evils of a long and often agonizing journey. The bloody entry of knowledge Lonergan talks about is, evidently, an enduring event and of a multifaceted nature. Thank you Birgit, Maria, and Sophia, my constant reminders of grace.

Finally, I dedicate this work to the memory of two very loving and hardworking individuals, my parents. They supported me in my decisions in both measurable and immeasurable ways. Unfortunately they were unable to see this project finally come to fruition. You are dearly missed. Αἰώνια ἡ μνίμη σας.

Abbreviations for Works by Lonergan*

BeLR	"Bernard Lonergan responds," in *Language, Truth, and Meaning: Papers from The International Lonergan Congress 1970* (1972)
CAMe	*Caring about Meaning: Patterns in the Life of Bernard Lonergan* (1982)
CWL	*Collected Works of Bernard Lonergan* (1988–)
CWL 2	Volume 2 of *CWL*: *Verbum: Word and Idea in Aquinas* (1997 [1946–1949])
CWL 3	Volume 3 of *CWL: Insight: A Study of Human Understanding* (1992 [1957])
CWL 4	Volume 4 of *CWL*: *Collection* (1988 [1967])
CWL 5	Volume 5 of *CWL*: *Understanding and Being: The [1958] Halifax Lectures on* Insight (1990 [1980])
CWL 6	Volume 6 of *CWL*: *Philosophical and Theological Paper 1958–1964* (1996)
CWL 10	Volume 10 of *CWL*: *Topics in Education: The Cincinnati Lectures of 1959 on the Philosophy of Education* (1993)
FBe	"Faith and Beliefs" (Paper presented to the American Academy of Religion, Newton, MA, October 23, 1969)
LoE	"Lectures on Existentialism" (Boston College, 1957)
MIT	*Method in Theology* (1972)
OPCC	"On the Ontological and Psychological Constitution of Christ" (1987; *De constitutione Christi ontologica et psychologica*, 4th ed. [1964])

OSB	"On Supernatural Being: A Schematic Supplement" (*De ente supernaturali: Supplementum schematicum*; Collège de l'Immaculée Conception, Montreal, 1946–47)
PGT	*Philosophy of God, and Theology* (1973)
PHRP	"A Post-Hegelian Philosophy of Religion," in *3C* (1985 [1980]): 202–23
PRP	"Philosophy and the Religious Phenomenon," *Method: Journal of Lonergan Studies* 12/2 (1994): 125–46
RCo	"Religious Commitment," in *The Pilgrim People: A Vision With Hope*, ed. Joseph Papin (Villanova, PA: The Villanova Press, 1970), 45–69
SRe	"The Scope of Renewal," *Method: Journal of Lonergan Studies* 16/2 (1998): 83–101
UM	"Understanding and Method" (first draft of Lonergan's 1959 course notes *De Intellectu et Methodo*, revised in 1997)
VFT	"Variations in Fundamental Theology," *Method: Journal of Lonergan Studies* 16/1 (1998): 5–24
2C	*A Second Collection* (1974)
3C	*A Third Collection* (1985)

---

*Dates in square brackets indicate original publication date. Other abbreviations are indicated in Siegfried M. Schwertner, *International Glossary of Abbreviations for Theology and Related Subjects*, 2nd ed. (Berlin and New York: Walter de Gruyter, 1992), pp. xli and 488.

Introduction

Bernard Lonergan (1904–1984) is a thinker many should read but never manage to do so. That he wrote large technical books is doubtless a factor. Scholars are industrious people. If they are going to labor over a work filled with technicalities, it better be short or hugely popular! Lonergan's books are neither. The mere mention of a projected twenty-two volume *Collected Works of Bernard Lonergan* suffices as a demonstration of this. The first major scholarly publication to gain him some notoriety was *Insight: A Study of Human Understanding* (1957). As the title suggests, the work is largely philosophical, although catalogued as a work of twentieth-century theology. In *Insight* Lonergan unveils what he feels is one of the most significant yet woefully neglected operations of human consciousness: insight. Analysis of it promises to answer the age-old questions that have plagued philosophy since Descartes— one could argue since Plato and Aristotle. *Insight* is a curious work, for it aims to advance or occasion "insight into insight." It doesn't aim to impart knowledge of the various fields invoked nor, curiously enough, does it aim to impart knowledge of insight per se. It is a book in aid of self-knowledge, that is, knowledge of one's own experiencing, understanding, judging, and deciding. If one grasps what insight is but fails to identify and hone the process in oneself, the point has been sadly missed. *Insight* gives a modern twist to the old saying inscribed on the temple of Apollo at Delphi: *gnōthi seauton* (know thyself). We will look at *Insight*'s meaning in greater detail in chapter 2.

The reputable Stephen Toulmin once described *Insight* as "a masterly work, whose importance reaches far beyond the boundaries of theology and Catholic philosophy."[1] This rings true to anyone who has bothered to read *Insight*. Why many overlook its importance is doubtless because Lonergan writes as a theologian and as a Catholic. He taught theology in Catholic institutions of higher learning in North America and Europe, interrupted, as it were, by a brief appointment as Stillman Professor at the multidenominational Divinity School at Harvard. Philosopher of religion David Burrell once observed that *Insight* "[r]eminds one of the relentless questioning of Wittgenstein's *Philosophical Investigations* or the polymorphic self-critical inquiry carried on by Kierkegaard."[2] But whereas Wittgenstein and Kierkegaard command universal interest, Lonergan's name continues to inspire quizzical looks. I don't hope to offer an answer as to why this might be. Personally I often wonder whether his being a religious and Jesuit to boot hasn't something to do with it. Timing is another factor. Lonergan describes his account of cognition as foundational. Today the slightest hint of a foundation makes people nervous. The issue is a complex one, about which I have said a few things.[3] In this study such matters are relegated to an endnote if at all. What concerns me here is how Lonergan, the theologian and methodologist, conceives the task of thinking about religion today. It is a question of philosophy of religion but not in the usual sense. Lonergan's version is unique, owing to his vocation as a theologian who is deeply philosophical and intensely methodical. However one feels about these issues, one thing is certain: Lonergan's philosophy of religion demands closer scrutiny than afforded it in the past. What I hope to show is that his ideas stand toe-to-toe with "systems" as elaborate and profound as Wittgenstein's and Kierkegaard's. If this book rectifies even minutely the present situation, it has served its purpose.

What *Insight* did for Lonergan's reputation as a philosopher-theologian, his second great work, *Method in Theology* (1972), did for him as a methodologist. Actually both works establish him in these roles. But *Method in Theology* brings out his methodological intentions more clearly. *Insight* is, or was originally intended as, a prolegomenon for doing theology in the theoretic turn of the scientific revolution and the philosophic turn to the subject. *Method* extends this vision by concentrating on the concerns and expressions of "existential" consciousness; developments in the human sciences are relied on for methodological direction. *Method* is particularly relevant to Lonergan's philosophy of religion, and much energy has been expended on it in secondary literature. However, neither *Method* nor *Insight* contain Lonergan's full-blown theory of philosophy of religion. One needs to look at lesser-known writings for that, both early and late. In works contemporaneous with *Method* Lonergan brusquely states what he understands more or less by philosophy of religion. Later, in public talks and published articles, he focuses his attention on developing these ideas more explicitly. The early writings, both pre-*Insight* and pre-*Method*, provide important clues as to this development, incidentally alongside which Lonergan amplifies an earlier form. In fact, this earlier form is a different "philosophy of" altogether. Understanding Lonergan's philosophy of *God*, and the various adjustments made to it by Lonergan, is crucial for understanding the development and dynamic of his philosophy of religion. And so in this study much time is spent sorting through what I take to be the relevant issues in his philosophy of God. The disclaimer, then, is that this study is not about communicating basic knowledge of Lonergan's philosophy of God. So much has been written on it already.[4] The extent of our discussion of his philosophy of God is limited to ascertaining the general structure of his philosophy of religion as a whole. In a word, this study aims at being comprehensive, not exhaustive nor introductory, which cannot be said without something approximating an apologia.

The question being tackled is, like it or not, a technical one. What does Lonergan conceive philosophy of religion to be? One would think that the introductory issues should be tackled before launching into technical issues in an individual few know. Philosophy of religion also poses certain problems. No one today entertains the view that philosophy of religion is a monolithic field. As Stephen Crites observes, it is more accurately described as "a zoo, with each enclosure exhibiting yet another exotic species."[5] And yet philosophy of religion is still recognized as something of an autonomous field of research. Standard, even if peculiar, means of scrutinizing the religious phenomenon attend its application. Placing the terms "philosophy of religion" and "Lonergan" side by side seems to demand some outline of the field and Lonergan's relation to it. These are valid points I struggled with while preparing this book.

Even if Lonergan is relatively unknown this is not due to any sluggishness on the part of Lonergan scholars. There has been a steady stream of introductory works on Lonergan since before the publication of *Method*. The first truly authoritative work of this kind is David Tracy's *The Achievement of Bernard Lonergan* (1970). Of Tracy Lonergan speaks rather glowingly in the forward: "In our many conversations he has let me experience Schleiermacher's paradox, namely, that an intelligent interpreter will know the process of a writer's development better than the writer himself."[6] Many have followed Tracy's lead by producing equally illuminating books of Lonergan's highly specialized thought. Mention might be made of Hugo Meynell's introductions to Lonergan's philosophy and theology, and more recently books by Joseph Flanagan, W. A. Stewart, and Terry Tekippe.[7] Lonergan's long-time friend and disciple Frederick Crowe, affectionately dubbed the "grandfather of Lonergan studies," has also provided a succinct biography of Lonergan.[8] The book is astonishing for its accessibility and the insights it provides into the life and thought of Lonergan. Introductory chapters also appear in numerous books treating Lonergan vis-à-vis some topic in a related field. This book might have fallen into that category, were it not for my quirky writing habits. All authors have their reasons for carrying out research the way they do, even if finally unknowable. Even so, allow me a meager attempt at an explanation in this particular case.

As I said, this study aims at being comprehensive. As I set out to address the issue of Lonergan's philosophy of religion, I bracketed questions of an introductory nature for strategic reasons. I wanted to avoid reducing what requires careful development to a short chapter or two, owing to meaningful introductory segments. Besides, this ground has been amply covered, and in a far more competent manner than I am capable. Although most of what I say is given a context, the focus throughout remains Lonergan's philosophy of religion. Indeed, even in those places where I discuss points covered thoroughly in the literature, it is always with this aim in view. A trajectory is provided to help the reader decipher the development in Lonergan's philosophizing about God and religion, which requires paying attention to painstaking detail. Part of my claim is that the extant literature on the topic though overwhelming in one way is nonetheless incomplete. This induced me to go beyond introductory matters to make something of a plausible case. Thankfully there is precedence for this. J. Michael Stebbins, for example, in his remarkable study of Lonergan's early writings,[9] bypasses issues of an introductory nature and goes into far greater detail than I in making his case. Far be it from me to compare the present work to Stebbins'; the two couldn't be more different. And yet the point, I trust, is clear. We stand on the shoulders of those on whose work we build our analyses, and must to a certain extent assume.

To reiterate, there has been a steady stream of studies of Lonergan's thought on God and religious experience. However, I have not seen detailed in them its various stages, how, for instance, religious experience in his early thought differs from that in his later thought, giving him a whole new basis for conceiving the relation of philosophy to matters religious in one way or another. The fact that religious experience entered into his philosophizing about God at a particular point in time and that it changed the tenor of his thinking often does receive attention. Concerns like the one I just mentioned, however, are not very high or even on the agenda. It is a question deserving of research not solely for the sake of research, although clarifying some point in paramount thinkers like Lonergan is always a worthwhile endeavor and is usually welcomed. It also furnishes a broader picture of the dynamics of the whole of his philosophizing relevant to the data of religion and its thinking that I, for one, fail to see in the literature.

The issue of religious experience in Lonergan is paramount to answering the question that guides this study, hence, our immediate jump in chapter 1 to the period in Lonergan's thought where he attributes more to its influence in our philosophizing than at any time prior in his career. In this chapter, I pursue some reasons that have been given for the tardiness of his response, intimating its nature and what it meant for his controversial "proof" for God's existence. And so I am not concerned with his proof per se. The notion of religious experience, its fabric for the whole of Lonergan's philosophizing, is central. It is the linchpin binding his early philosophy of God to his late philosophy of religion. And it is the latter and its relation to the former that remains the sole objective of this study. Readers unfamiliar with chapters 19 and 20 of *Insight* might want to review as they read chapter 1 of this book (i.e., the section "Making Room for Religious Experience"). If the issues discussed in that section are not a concern to the reader, he or she is encouraged to proceed to the section "Deliberately Bracketing Religious Experience." Specialists will doubtless want to make the stop, unwilling, as I was, to grant what needs argument.

Reminiscent of the great debate in Martin Heidegger studies, many describe the transition from Lonergan's early to late development in terms of a *Kehre* or "turning." This serves as our point of departure in chapter 1, the significance of which is detailed in chapters 3 and 4. Something of a detour is taken in chapter 2 since any discussion of the concept of religious experience in Lonergan must grapple with what he means by "experience" in general. I have deciphered three senses to the term integral to his concept of consciousness, which I distinguish from a contemporary model, that of philosopher David J. Chalmers. Since Lonergan is emphatic about distinguishing between consciousness and its concept—indeed, that it is possible, necessary even, to do this—I trace this aspect of his philosophical claim against the background of Kant and Hegel. They are Lonergan's main dialogue partners on the question. This brings out elements that are unique to his concept abridged in his chosen term "self-appropriation." Self-appropriation has been the focus of much discussion in Lonergan studies—enough to produce a philosophical genre particular to the work of Lonergan scholars. Few discuss Lonergan without some reference to it. My main objective in discussing it is to examine one of its fundamental premises: the relation of concept to experience. Chapter 2 may have just as well been entitled "The Relation of Concept to Experience" with the added qualifier "in Lonergan." For straightforward expositions of the notion readers are advised to turn to introductory works such as those cited above.

In chapter 3, I return to the specifically religious dimension of the notion of experience in the early Lonergan. The significant pre-*Method* literature is examined in which religious experience receives mention, touching in some way on issues pertinent to his philosophy of God. Here we track the development of his category of religious experience as it moves from the periphery to the explanatory basis of his thought. The transition occurs without collapsing the distinction he wishes to maintain between loving religiously and an explanatory thinking about such loving and its objects. Lonergan's concept of the differentiations of consciousness, evolving out of his concept of the patterns of experience, allow for this possibility. It goes without saying that his appreciation for the level of decision, qua level, undergirds this whole process.[10]

In the fourth and final chapter the relevant *Method* and post-*Method* literature is examined in which is seen the emergence of what is technically philosophy of religion to Lonergan. His interest in philosophy of God is overtaken by issues of fundamental theology. This merges with a new-found appreciation for philosophy of religion, "the foundational methodology of religious studies" (*PRP*:128). Among the distinctions I have introduced is the difference between his model of religion and what he calls "philosophy of religion." They are not equivalent concepts in Lonergan. Conceiving it historically, I see the former, his model of religion, as the point of departure for what in his philosophy of religion he sets out to do. They are related, of course, but not one and the same thing. Also, to avoid confusion with the field of the same name, my recommendation is that we refer to his philosophy of religion as it is literally, as a *philosophy of religious studies*, distinguishing it firstly from his philosophy of God and secondly from his model of religion. I understand the term "philosophy of religion" in Lonergan to encompass all of these elements, whether it is philosophizing about God, God's existence and attributes, or about religion methodology.

Besides providing what I hope is a clear and comprehensive understanding of a very complex thought form, outlining the matter this way also aids in identifying precisely what are the points of contact between Lonergan's thoughts on God and religion and philosophers of religion as commonly understood today. This brings us full circle to the second factor mentioned earlier originally complicating this endeavor.

In the embryonic stage of this study, I had planned to relate Lonergan's philosophy of religion to the field of the same name. My task was quickly made more complex by the intricacies that are part and parcel of grasping Lonergan's philosophy of religion alone. I decided to follow a helpful bit of advice Lonergan often gave researchers; Patrick Byrne of Boston College was kind enough to remind me of it upon hearing an overly ambitious early draft of this project. The advice is to limit research questions simply to "What does X have to say about Y?" otherwise one would find oneself writing three studies: one on X, one on Y, and one on the relation of X to Y. Understood in the present context, a relation of X to Y question, which is what I set out to do originally, would involve a treatment of Lonergan's philosophy of religion (X), philosophy of religion as a field (Y), and the relationship of the two. Now this might be manageable if studies were available detailing each of the components upon which one could rely in relating X to Y. My research led me to believe, however, that treatments of X were incomplete for my purposes or not of a nature that allowed for a comprehensive analysis of the relation question. For instance, some stop, for legitimate reasons, with Lonergan's philosophy of God or, when going on to his philosophy of religion, relate it to issues and concerns that I admit are far more exciting than charting the various aspects of his philosophy of religion. My work was cut out for me as I waded through literature that left issues unresolved pertaining to the simple yet enormous question, What does Lonergan say about philosophy of religion? The present represents my answer to this question. Since this book went to press, some preliminary steps were taken to address these other issues, which require a work of equal length to treat adequately. Presently, all I can do is point the reader to my initial efforts.[11]

Chapter One

The *Kehre* of *Philosophy of God, and Theology*

Like every good philosopher Lonergan never tires of exploiting the meaning of terms for his own purposes, to be his "little self" as he once remarked (*PRP*:126). The term "philosophy of religion" is no exception. If introductory textbooks on the subject are any indication of what philosophy of religion is, then Lonergan's meaning differs substantially. The fact that his initial etchings of it are traced in a short paper that looks to social ethicist Gibson Winter for inspiration is illustrative of this (*2C*:189–92). In other words, one is not going to find arguments for God's existence or solutions to the "problem" of evil in Lonergan's philosophy of religion, technically so-called. Complicating matters somewhat is the fact that Lonergan does offer his own peculiar answer to such questions endemic to philosophy of religion, but under the guise of "philosophy of God," sometimes called "natural" or "philosophical theology." Bracketing the larger issue whether Lonergan's philosophy of God is accurately understood as philosophy of religion in the generic sense, we simply note for the time being that his philosophy of God is not his philosophy of religion. His philosophy of religion seeks to provide a critical ground for the relation of religious studies and theology, both functions of which he treats positively. His philosophy of God, on the other hand, particularly in its late stage, seeks to resituate or reclaim for theology (i.e., systematics) the activity of philosophizing about God. Much more will be said about these different types of philosophizing. Here this particular distinction is mentioned as a basic characteristic of their diverse functioning. It is also a convenient means of indicating the general framework within which Lonergan's philosophizing takes place.

MAKING ROOM FOR RELIGIOUS EXPERIENCE

Prior to the 1980s, scholarly discussion of Lonergan's philosophizing about God and religion is for the most part limited to his proof for the existence of God and his proposed solution to the problem of evil, although the former tends to dominate the discussion.[1] Both aspects are detailed in the last two chapters of his philosophical masterwork *Insight* (1957). Around the mid-1970s attention shifts from Lonergan's proof for the existence of God to his theological method prompted by the publication of *Method in Theology* (1972). Except for scattered contributions on his post-*Insight* emphasis on religious experience, discussion of topics in Lonergan relevant to philosophers of religion begins to peter out.

This doubtless owes itself to the fact that around this time Lonergan shifts his attention from his controversial argument for God's existence to what he came to see as its basis, that is, religious experience or, more generally, the religious phenomenon thought through theologically and analyzed historically through various methods produced by the human sciences. Is it any wonder that the philosophical community accustomed to analyzing truth in propositional terms evidences little interest here? Assigning logic a less perennial role than it has received in the West contributed to Lonergan's cultivation of extra-logical concerns, which some philosophers of religion think legitimate, yet merely assume or ignore in their candid admissions about the limits of logic.

It is tempting to think of Lonergan's mid-1970s shift as representing a radical break in his thinking. To push the issue of logic further, one might make the case that Lonergan freed himself from the alluring benefits of logic, which is so integral to his early work especially.[2] For instance, in his St. Michael's Lectures on *Philosophy of God, and Theology* (1973), Lonergan complains about the treatment of God's existence and attributes in *Insight*—no doubt prodded by the steady stream of criticisms that followed its publication. He notes disapprovingly that God's existence and attributes are treated there "in a purely objective fashion" predicated by an acceptance of intrinsically necessary first principles and a monist view of culture, that there is only one right culture (*PGT*:13). On this basis alone, it is difficult to avoid drawing the conclusion that Lonergan abandoned the rather bloodless categories that adorn his early Latin treatises, vestiges of which may be seen in that notorious chapter on God in *Insight*, chapter 19. Add to this that following *Philosophy of God, and Theology* Lonergan stops writing and lecturing about God's existence altogether as the conclusion to an argument. What he does instead is to develop, among his many other interests, what just a couple of years earlier he announced as the task of philosophy of religion, to "bring to light the conditions of the possibility of the [*sic*] religious studies and their correlative objects" (*2C*:191). Little concern is evidenced with regard to establishing the existence of God and removing the obstacle evil poses to religious faith. Other circumstantial evidence, however, confounds a clean break hypothesis. There is Lonergan's now famous statement in *Philosophy of God, and Theology* that while his proof in *Insight* suffers from a kind of scholastic objectivism he has no intention of repudiating it "at all" (*PGT*:41). There is also his admission that a shift in emphasis from logic to method "does not, by any means, involve an elimination of logic: for it still is logic that cares for the clarity of terms, the coherence of propositions, the rigor of inferences" (*3C*:139). In fact, one could make a convincing case that Lonergan never attributed more to logic than the role of ordering systematically what understanding grasps commonsensically or intellectually, to borrow a distinction from *Insight*. In his important study of Lonergan's early writings, for instance, J. Michael Stebbins points out that logic in the early Lonergan has both a weak and a strong function. When understanding is said to proceed inferentially, from effects to causes, logic plays an incidental role, similar to that mentioned above. When understanding proceeds deductively, from causes to effects, logic takes on a more commanding role. And yet "even in this latter case," Stebbins quickly interjects, "the controlling element is understanding rather than logic, for only insofar as one understands the principle or starting-point can one grasp its implications. Hence, understanding is a condition of demonstration, and not the other way around."[3] Besides being significant evidence for the relativization of logic in the early Lonergan, this foreshadows the preeminence he later attributes to method. As the seasoned reader of Lonergan knows, understanding is but a basic element of the method one is.

As for Lonergan dropping all references to proofs, one finds something of an analogy in Carl Sandburg's poem "Fog." After he says what he wants to say about the existence of God; after he has surveyed the various complaints against what he has said, Lonergan "moves on" like the fog in Sandburg's poem unperturbed by the contrivances of harbor and city. This idea of moving on captures well what happens to Lonergan in the early 1970s, in the *Kehre* that *Philosophy of God, and Theology* represents. The first thing to note is that it is merely a reorientation of, and not a break with, a traditional concern. One way of interpreting this is to make some imaginary, though pertinent, connections between Lonergan's *Insight*, *Philosophy of God, and Theology* and part one, question 2, article 3 of Aquinas's *Summa Theologiae*, "Whether God Exists?"

Chapter 19 of *Insight* functions more or less like the main body of Saint Thomas's *respondeo dicendum*, his solution to a series of contrary answers to a particular question. Notions are defined, concepts are invoked to convey a sense of intelligibility to the claim that God exists. While Lonergan's use and development of Aquinas far exceed in ingenuity Aquinas's application of

Aristotle in this instance, the level at which both proceed is almost identical. In *Philosophy of God, and Theology,* Lonergan seeks to include what he excludes in *Insight.* In it he may be seen as latching onto the significance of the cryptic sentences in the *respondeo,* which many think reveal the true ingenuity of Aquinas's Five Ways. I am referring, of course, to the formulaic inclusions that appear at the end of each of the ways: "and this everyone understands to be God," "this all speak of as God," "and this being we call God," and so on.

These little sentences provide insight into the presuppositions that underlie the genius of Aquinas's work. I might abbreviate them as his earthly awareness that belief is wedded to a context. The utilization of the best available systems of thought, then embodied in the widely circulated Peripatetic corpus, is encouraged for understanding systematically what believers hold matter-of-factly. Mark D. Jordan has recently emphasized this, modeling Aquinas's manner of conduct after that of Augustine in *De doctrina Christiana,* where Augustine condones the confiscation of philosophers' goods by theologians.[4] While Jordan overstates his case that Aquinas merely changed philosophical materials into theology, his point that "no single work was written by Aquinas for the sake of setting forth a philosophy" illustrates well the point I am making here.[5] Aquinas enlists categories from Aristotle to render systematically explicit what his contemporaries held implicitly, namely, a notion of God. This lends a different air to the notion of proof in Aquinas, often mitigated by an age that limits itself to observational paradigms of demonstration. It also underlines the foundational role of religious experience, broadly conceived, in supplying philosophical clarity to beliefs. Aquinas was no stranger to such an assumption.

Insight is built on the premise that Aquinas has it right concerning experience and rational reflection. The problem, Lonergan has diagnosed, is that Aquinas's perspicacity is couched in metaphysical terms that strike many today, weaned on J. R. R. Tolkien, as a glorified description of life on Middle-earth. Granted, Lonergan is not nearly as irreverent about the archaic form of Aquinas's account of cognition, but the point is clear. Aquinas's insights require translation into terms more apropos in a world, our world, having undergone the theoretic turn of the scientific revolution and the philosophic turn to the subject. The relative approval with which *Insight* has been met bears witness to Lonergan's achievement in carrying this out.[6] His translation comes to a head in chapter 19, the chapter on God, but without any consideration given to that implied in the tiny sentences of Aquinas noted earlier. Since what he does with Aquinas in *Philosophy of God, and Theology* is more discreet than in *Insight,* the fact of his reorientation is, when noticed, usually affirmed but without much in the way of explanation.

Lonergan never questions Aquinas's classic distinction between the truths that reason can know and those that surpass it. The titles of chapters 19 and

20 of *Insight* are in a way his own expression of this distinction. "*General* Transcendent Knowledge" refers to knowledge of God that lies within reason's reach, "*Special* Transcendent Knowledge" to knowledge of God, in the objective genitive sense, that eludes reason as the moon eludes an outstretched hand. In general transcendent knowledge the issue is knowing that God exists. Lonergan builds on the previous chapters of *Insight* to demonstrate the intelligibility of the affirmation of God. In particular he expands on the notion of being, introduced in chapter 12, and involves the reader in an exposition of causality in the context of intelligibility, which is crucial to his argument. The bulk of chapter 19—indeed, one could argue, all the previous chapters—is a prolegomenon for understanding the syllogism: "If the real is completely intelligible, then complete intelligibility exists. If complete intelligibility exists, the idea of being exists. If the idea of being exists, then God exists. Therefore, if the real is completely intelligible, God exists" (*CWL* 3:696). Since our primary concern is the shift in perspective from *Insight* to *Philosophy of God, and Theology*, I will reserve further comment on Lonergan's proof until chapter 3.

Having dealt with the affirmation of God, Lonergan moves on to the issue of special transcendent knowledge in chapter 20 of *Insight*. The issue there is one of acquiescing and enacting God's revelatory solution to the problem of evil. Basic is the view that humans neither originate nor preserve this solution; it is *specially* transcendent for this reason. Human intelligence and reasonableness, which is required in acknowledging the solution and carrying it out, accounts for the knowledge factor.[7] Little concern is expressed about providing the solution with determinate content. Incidentally, Lonergan believes "many possible solutions" exist. In *Insight*, however, precedence is given to the heuristic structure of these solutions, which means "we must remain content to affirm hope only in a generic fashion" (*CWL* 3:724). Notwithstanding this, metaphoric phrases such as "self-sacrificing love of God" (722, 748), "good news of the solution" (743), "love of God" (passim), not to mention simple assertions as "God is a person" (720), quickly mark Lonergan's generic offering as characteristically Christian. Still, if one reads Part V of Lonergan's *De Verbo Incarnato* (1964), in which the solution is identified with the redemptive activity of God in Christ and the Law of the Cross, one will doubtless gain a better appreciation of the generic venture of *Insight*. Comparatively, what is offered in chapter 20 is significantly generic, certainly generic enough to include at least the monotheistic traditions. To relate the structure to Asian and other religious traditions would be a trickier matter.[8]

What is significant for us is Lonergan's discussion of the notion of belief in chapter 20. It is significant not for the reason we may have originally, erroneously surmised, that belief is excluded from knowledge that is humanly attainable. Lonergan is clear that belief, assent to knowledge that is not immanently generated, is integral to all types of knowing.⁹ Belief in the truthfulness of scientific hypotheses is just as much a part of the scientist's life as belief in the truthfulness of doctrines is to the theologian's, unless of course there is reason to bring their "truthfulness" into question. The significance for us of belief in *Insight* hinges on the peculiar species Lonergan reserves for knowledge that transcends reason as if it were of no consequence to the kind immanent in reason.

To be sure, belief in chapter 19 involves what Lonergan calls a "higher integration" of the structure of human consciousness culled through the generalized empirical analysis of the preceding chapters. But there is no mention in it of the still higher integration outlined in chapter 20. This higher integration transcends both the interpersonal collaboration assumed in the first nineteen chapters of *Insight*, concerning the advancement and the dissemination of knowledge, and the horizon within which such collaboration is forged. By contrast, the collaboration outlined in chapter 20 consists principally in that of humankind with God, the former assenting to and incarnating divinely communicated truth—in a word, confronting the surd of evil with the mystery of God. This distinct function of belief explains why Lonergan thought it more fitting to treat the notion in chapter 20 than in chapter 19. It involves a particular understanding of belief to be discriminated from that assumed in previous chapters. A more daring conjecture, inferred from the foregoing, is that Lonergan, at this stage, did not think such belief contributed much if anything to the sort of undertaking he attempts in chapter 19. Belief in that chapter culminates in knowledge at which a general or ordinary collaboration of human beings can arrive (*CWL* 3:742). In chapter 20 belief remains in a sense belief, *special* transcendent knowledge, by virtue of its distinct manner of collaboration. It touches on "truths that man never could discover for himself nor, even when he assented to them, could he understand them in an adequate fashion. For the greater the proper perfection and significance of the higher integration, the more it will lie beyond man's familiar range, and the more it will be grounded in the absolutely transcendent excellence of [God,] the unrestricted act of understanding" (*CWL* 3:746). As Thomas Aquinas taught and Lonergan echoed, knowledge of this kind, fittingly proposed to humans for belief, is in a class of its own way beyond the pale of reason.[10]

Returning now to my earlier comparison of *Insight* with the particular question in the *Summa*, whether God exists (*an Deus sit*). I do not wish to make the absurd claim that the Lonergan of *Insight*, a first-rate interpreter of Aquinas, was unaware of the pithy sentences that appear in probably the most discussed question of the *Summa*. It would be truly remarkable if he were, given that he detected far greater subtleties in Aquinas in a book reputed to be among the most illuminating in the field.[11] In any case, it is in *Philosophy of God, and Theology*, not *Insight* or *Verbum*, where he plays on their significance (*PGT*:41), that religious experience, very generally conceived here, contributes greatly to the art of formulating proofs and rendering them meaningful. Why he does this in the 1970s and not the 1950s or the 1960s is open to conjecture. I will offer some thoughts on this below. Presently we need only note *that* he does and that he does so in continuity with, while adding to, what he says in *Insight*.

The fact of continuity is seen in Lonergan's candid admission that he has no intention of repudiating what he does in chapter 19 of *Insight*. As far as I know, he never retracted statements like the following, which still found supporters in the 1970s but slowly lost their grip as Nietzschean and Heideggerian critiques of ontotheology became part of the common sense: "I do not think it difficult to establish God's existence" (*PGT*:55). Mindful that what he establishes is not some concept of God, but a notion of the epistemically unattainable God implied in our intending of complete intelligibility, Lonergan states that while *Insight* may not be the best expression of this he nonetheless expressed it there as best as he could.[12] It is similar to what he says about a decade later concerning *Insight* and its terminological affinities to faculty psychology. "Although in *Insight* I am still talking as if it were faculty psychology, what I am doing is not faculty psychology" (*CAMe*:43). Likewise, although in *Insight* he establishes the existence of God scholastically, objectivistically, what he says is still valid, he believes, despite the antiquarian form in which he says it. It is a special case of cognitive dissonance where one's performance is thought to override one's choice of terms.

Still, this positive reassessment applies to the argument as an argument and not to the context it presupposes. The argument's context, Lonergan obliged his critics, does require some rethinking. To put it in the terms of our earlier analysis, general transcendent knowledge includes something of the collaboration at work in special transcendent knowledge. Even if what is achieved by general transcendent knowledge comes about without the aid of beliefs that feed special transcendent knowledge, usually those who hold such beliefs are the ones who can affirm what general transcendent knowledge concludes. Bernard Tyrrell, who has written a definitive study of Lonergan's philosophy of God, observes similarly that "for Lonergan such things as 'proofs' for the existence of God are not generally worked out by the unconverted but by those who are already believers and are seeking a deeper understanding of what they believe and an intelligent grasp of the meaningfulness, reasonableness and worthwhileness of their religious conversion."[13] However, this was not always the case. Despite his pre-1970s appreciation of religious experience, which I discuss in chapter 3, Lonergan did effect a genuine transformation in his thought at this stage. While it did not involve a complete ideational overhaul, it did involve a change in emphasis and direction.

His desire in *Philosophy of God, and Theology* to reclaim for systematics the activity of thinking philosophically about God accounts for the change in emphasis: "[W]e should put an end to the practice of isolating from each other the philosophy of God and the functional specialty, systematics" (*PGT*:55), a practice rooted in the eighteenth and nineteenth centuries. Elaborating on this by contrasting it with what he says in *Insight*, not only would it seem that the problem of evil demands "the transformation of self-reliant intelligence into an *intellectus quaerens fidem*" (*CWL* 3:753), but affirming the existence of God seems to as well. Not that believing in God's existence is solely a matter of faith for Lonergan. He never veered from Aquinas's position that we can *know* that, not what, God is. Nevertheless he did come to emphasize the "believing" that finally grounds the "knowing" that God is or, melding his terms with the punch line in Aquinas, that the intelligible term of our unrestricted intending is what we mean by God. It is a shift from the proleptic answer his proof provides to the prepredicative question driving it: *an Deus sit*. "Proof" gives the impression that the question coercing it is fundamentally philosophic, which Lonergan rejects. Answers to the question of God, subsequently developed into proofs and, incidentally, disproofs, begin at a far more basic level and touch on matters that are religious. "One cannot claim that their religion has been based on some philosophy of God. One can easily argue that their religious concern," of which proofs are an important aspect, "arose out of their religious experience" (*PGT*:55). Hence, his wish is to see theologians, who commonly have firsthand knowledge of religious experience, sharing again in this particular form of proof making.

What accounts for the change in direction in Lonergan, besides detaining himself from further addressing matters of proof, is his growing preoccupation with philosophy of religion, forging one that is. In *Insight* he had expressed, among many other things, his understanding of how reflection on cognitional theory irons out the many wrinkles of classical proofs for God's existence. *Insight* furnishes us with one based on their hidden premise, namely, that the world is intelligible.[14] Incidentally, in Lonergan's scheme of things, God is glimpsed in every Archimedean cry of discovery (*CWL* 3:706).

Insight's proof attracted disproportionate reactions bounded by the usual extremes of uncritical acceptance and uncritical rejection. Lonergan did address himself to many of these concerns but stopped suddenly with the publication of *Philosophy of God, and Theology*.[15] He did so unannounced, there being nothing in the record to suggest it was a momentous event. A few years earlier he began speaking about a different "philosophy of" that would bring some nuances to his understanding of religious experience. At first it bore many of the marks of his philosophy of God—indeed, in certain respects it was indistinguishable from it. But by 1975/6 it had developed into the full-blown program he made intimations toward in 1970, its purpose being to bring to light the conditions of the possibility of religious studies. In *Philosophy of God, and Theology*, Lonergan turns the page on that aspect of his philosophical theology that argues for the existence of God implied in the intelligibility of the universe and our continual intending of it. The time had come for him to "move on," to treat other relevant issues capturing the imagination of his contemporaries. In the future his philosophy of God would consist in theological reflection on religious experience and its contents, which his emerging philosophy of religion would approach more differently still.

DELIBERATELY BRACKETING RELIGIOUS EXPERIENCE[16]

Many have been led to believe that Lonergan's underscoring religious experience in the 1970s marks its debut in his thought. More careful readers might point to the early 1960s, say, to a paper entitled "Openness and Religious Experience" (1961), which he submitted in absentia to a congress in Italy.[17] Others might want to opt for the early 1950s as the more likely date, with chapter 17 of *Insight*, for instance, in which Lonergan makes clear references to the dynamics of religious experience in his analysis of myth and mystery. Indeed, one could go as far back as 1943, to a paper entitled "Finality, Love, Marriage" where he provides an extended treatment of love, later to become his signature term for religious experience. *Method* itself does not parallel in breadth the treatment of love in "Finality, Love, Marriage."[18] The fact is that Lonergan as a religious was always preoccupied in one way or another with religious experience. We may note a high degree of hyperbole on his part when he says in *Insight* that he does not know what a mystic experiences (*CWL* 3:348). This is quite out of character with one who in 1977 could speak of "twenty-four years of aridity in the religious life" that were canceled out by over thirty-one years of spiritual joy in it, that is, since before 1946.[19]

The view that Lonergan began his treatment of religious experience in the early 1970s is simply an error in judgment. In addition to the works cited above, one could also invoke as evidence to the contrary his 1946 course on grace, in which he deals with the question under the cognate term "awareness of the supernatural," or "mystical experience" as in *Verbum*.[20] In any case, this leaves intact the widespread assumption that religious experience in Lonergan receives considerably more attention in the early 1970s than at any time prior in his career. Except the minor alteration it introduced into his philosophy of God (i.e., general transcendent knowledge), the function of religious experience in his thought remained relatively unchanged up to this point. It is abbreviated in *Insight* in a way stripped of, while remaining faithful to, the Aristotelian language governing the little he does say about the topic in his early work: "a dimension to human experience that takes man beyond the domesticated, familiar, common sphere, in which a spade is just a spade"

(*CWL* 3:557). The interesting question is why Lonergan waited almost three decades to acknowledge the centrality of this dimension in fundamental theology.

The reasons are predominately political. As the editors of the *Collected Works* state: "the concentration on doctrine that characterized the Roman Catholic Church during the modernist scare inhibited development on religious experience, and Lonergan got round late to the question."[21] During and following that crisis the notion of experience was approached with extreme reserve under the threat of excommunication. Ironically, it would be this very crisis that demanded critical reflection *with recourse to experience*. Under the leadership of Pope Paul VI (1963–1978), Roman Catholic theology rediscovered the existential dimension without which it dries out into theological rationalism or else becomes diluted into a piety of ill-repute.[22]

At the turn of the century Pope Pius X (d. 1914) summarized and condemned the opinions of Catholic intellectuals, commonly called "modernists," who were attempting to reconcile the Catholic faith with modern rationality. Running through these opinions, thought to be particularly damnable, was an immanentism. Immanentism rendered superfluous so-called objective philosophical inquiry into the supernatural and, because the supernatural was rejected, led to the denigration of Roman Catholic dogma, said to derive solely from religious experience. Many Catholic theologians are of the opinion that the encyclical *Pascendi* (1907), in which Pius X categorically rejects modernism, was something of a pastoral and, needless to say, political necessity. The developments that followed in its wake, however, are usually regarded by these same theologians to be theologically stultifying and detrimental to the many legitimate concerns of a Church that John XXIII later described as constantly in need of renewal (*aggiornamento*).

The picture is a bleak one. Clerics, for example, were required to take what was popularly known as an oath against modernism. At an event surrounded by pomp and circumstance, ordinands were expected to affirm certain anti-modernist propositions and to assent to the relevant official Church documents on the matter, that is, to the formerly mentioned *Pascendi* and the *Lamentabili* (1907), a decree listing some sixty-five modernist errors. The practice lasted fifty-seven years and was brought to a felicitous close in 1967, one of the expeditious effects of the Second Vatican Council. More serious was the alarmist tendency to brand as modernist Catholics whose ideas bore the slightest hint of concord, real or imagined, with those condemned by the Holy See. For a time theologians now considered pillars of the Church such as Yves Congar (1904–1995) and Karl Rahner (1904–1984) suffered an unsure fate as such at the hands of Vatican officials. Held in the balance, too, were the works of Henri de Lubac (1896–1991) and Jean Daniélou (d. 1974) whose later appointments as cardinals is another admirable if embarrassing piece of church history to add to a growing list. Also thought unhelpful, though well intentioned, was the creation of an unofficial group of zealous theologians known as Integralists or *Sodalitium pianum* (Solidarity of Pius) whose job it was to report to Monsignor Benigni, its director in Italy, those whose teachings smacked of modernist conviction. J. J. Heaney well describes the aftermath of *Pascendi* as a period in which "[t]hinking and nuance were rejected in favor of polemics. Modernism became a slogan to be applied to whatever was disliked in liberal Catholic thought, theology, literature, and politics."[23]

Lonergan's theology can hardly be pegged "liberal," even by the standards of early twentieth-century Catholic thinking. His method in theology, on the other hand, deemed radical by some,[24] might be viewed this way, however misguidedly. Were he in the 1940s and 1950s to have given the place he did in the 1970s to taboo subjects like religious experience—a pivotal element of his method in theology—it is more than likely that Lonergan would have undergone the strain of cross-examination. For someone whose mission was to provide Catholics with the needed background for understanding the modern world (*CAMe*:262) this could only be seen as counterproductive.

There would have been no grounds to discredit Lonergan as a modernist. We already saw that he openly declared, even in his so-called *Kehre* stage, that reason could attain to knowledge of God and that such pursuits, despite growing distaste for them, were entirely in keeping with the demands of historical consciousness, thought by "modernists" to have flattened such philosophical concerns. It would be difficult to imagine *Insight* receiving its imprimatur had Lonergan reasoned otherwise, had his conclusion in chapter 19, for instance, been equivocal or made contingent upon the type of self-validating exercise of the previous chapters—precisely what Lonergan later admitted it should be. Even so, a scare is a scare. Underscoring something as touchy as religious experience came at a price, one that a noncontroversialist like Lonergan would rather avoid paying. When asked late in his career if he was deliberately careful treating sensitive issues in the modernist crisis, he responded: "Well, you never want to be stupid. . . . In other words, you don't deliberately mislead people who are not bright, or allow them to mislead themselves" (*CAMe*:123), especially if they hold positions of power. Lonergan was in no hurry, it seems, to suffer the professionally turbulent fate of some of his colleagues whose "new theology" Pius XII condemned in *Humani Generis* (1950) for its supposed ideational links to modernism.

Are we to limit Lonergan's cunningness to the level of the strategic, a case of political know-how pure and simple? We could, of course, but that would give us a very skewed picture of him: a conniving individual who is both disingenuous and lacking in courage. An early autobiographical remark to the effect that he is orthodox but thinks a lot sums up his disposition more adequately.[25] Lonergan saw no reason to sacrifice shrewdness or intelligence on the altar of orthodoxy and vice versa. As Qoheleth would counsel (Eccles. 7:16b), Why destroy oneself and others along with one? If the witness of consciousness is to be trusted, Lonergan could be heard saying, the two can be mutually compatible, though it is a life's work of self-transcendence to strike a serviceable balance. What this means in the present context is that he doubted partisan support of either side of the modernist issue led one very far in this direction. While he could side with many on the Right that modernists had several philosophical and theological blind spots, he could not condone the Right's ignorance of history and what it is (*CAMe*:123). Not unlike the wiser among us, he was not prepared to put his career on the line for the sake of ignorance. "You never want to be stupid."

What probably gained Lonergan some immunity from needless interrogation is that he lived and moved, especially in his earlier work, in the language praised by Pius X, Scholasticism. That "much of Lonergan's creative genius lies doubly buried in his Latin Scholastic works"[26] worked, in this instance, to his advantage. Genius the Roman Curia of pre-Vatican II could accept. Creativity, genius' bedfellow, was another matter entirely. It pinched a very sensitive nerve. While their lying "doubly buried" in Lonergan's work does not serve the average reader, it did Lonergan at a time of crisis. Scholasticism was a powerful instrument in his hands. With it he could reform the Catholicism that gave him the intellectual tools with which to think but had itself forgotten how to think.[27] The catch is that he could do this without pulling the rug from under him, thinking in a language from which he could not escape but to which he refused to be shackled. Thought could be had in and by a language that threatened thoughtlessness.

Did this insure Lonergan's good standing with those in the upper echelons of the Roman Church? It did not guarantee it, but it did not hurt either. Few would doubt that his career would have taken a different turn had he interpreted Aquinas in, say, the language of Martin Heidegger, whose thought he could appreciate but had certain reservations toward (*LoE*:2, 13, 32, 69, 70–71; *CWL* 6:242). But Lonergan did not do his doctoral studies in Freiburg, where he would have had a chance to participate in the seminars of Heidegger and thus fall under his direct influence. He did them in Rome, where taking Heidegger seriously meant flirting with the dangers of idealism. In certain respects Lonergan never outgrew this kind of suspicious evaluation of philosophers, many of whom, chiefly modern philosophers, he admits to not having a direct or thorough knowledge of.[28] Thus, some sympathizers such as Francis Schüssler Fiorenza have been led to ask "whether major authors and positions in the history of philosophy (Hume, Kant, or Hegel) or in the history of theology (Tertullian, Origen, Athanasius) can be reduced to abstract epistemological categories such as materialistic empiricism, idealism, or critical realism, as Lonergan has often done."[29] The simplest answer is: probably not. Yet despite what he held in private or confided to students and colleagues, he did temper these kinds of claims in his public lectures and later writings. To contextualize one of his comments he made in an interview, he wrote "positive stuff" in which he referred people back to argue with the author whose views he was outlining or quoting.[30] His primary task was, in his own words, "to provide Catholics with the background for understanding something about the modern world—without giving up their Catholicity" (*CAMe*:262). He could do this effectively by appropriating the insights of others without sacrificing his early center of meaning, scholasticism, or capitulating to the views he personally found unacceptable both within and without that center. In *Insight* and *Method in Theology*, Lonergan emphasizes the importance of beginning what he would regard as the source of personal and corporate reform where one is. After all, that is where one is. Not only, then, did he have to begin with the mind he wanted to reform just where it was with its own presuppositions, as Quentin Quesnell rightly observes. But he himself could only do this where he was with his own presuppositions. Because he was there.[31] It may not have been where someone like Karl Rahner was, but it is where Lonergan was.

Implied, too, in Lonergan's deliberate bracketing of religious experience is his dissatisfaction with the move to make religious experience all-important. The philosophical issues of truth could not be so easily pushed aside, particularly in the Christian tradition where they have commanded such serious attention since the second century. Hence, he is made exceedingly uncomfortable by what he recognizes as the modernist tendency (in the above sense) of devaluing truth by valuing it merely as symbolically worthwhile. In the first of a series of discussions that followed each of his 1958 Halifax lectures on *Insight*, Lonergan, after making the Catholic's case clear, according to which truth is decisive, satirically articulates the modernist position as follows:

> [I]f you want to be a modernist, you will say that what counts is religious experience. Truth, well, it has a certain symbolic value, and the propositions—such as the two natures in one person in Christ— no doubt helped the Greeks of the fifth and sixth centuries in their religious experience, but they aren't very helpful today, and so we can forget about them. Truth is not the decisive thing in the modernist, it is religious experience—intense religious life—and you adapt these propositional symbols to the exigencies of the age. (*CWL* 5:279)

He saw this as a principal failure of pragmatist and existentialist approaches to religion as well, whether the religious phenomenon was targeted as something worthy of cultivation or not. Whatever their many insights, he doubted that they could make a positive contribution to the task of faithfully translating into modern terms ancient truths of faith and to do so congruent with the whole of church history and not just a part of it. So, for example, he could spot an equivalence between the existentialist pattern of thinking and that of Christ in the Gospels, arguing in his 1957 lectures on existentialism that the former serves as a good basis for biblical theology.[32] But he is hard-pressed to find any equivalence between existentialist thought and conciliar-type thinking. Actually he is quite adamant that with an existentialist basis one cannot go on to Nicea and Chalcedon, Trent and the other councils. Conciliar thinking grapples with the propositional nature of the truths held in faith, not ontologically or experientially fundamental issues like "being a man," time, and liberty. In a fashion typical of the times, that is to say before the Second Vatican Council, he pinpoints as one of its main objectives the ability to clearly decipher the opposition between Catholics and Protestants on the nature of faith. The former, he states, cannot bring themselves to agree with the latter that faith is simply confidence in God (*fides fiducialis*). Faith also involves assent of the intellect to truth (*intellectus in verum*) (*LoE*:13–14). Faith, in other words, has a basis in our experience; it must correspond in some way to the truths attained via insight into presentations. For Lonergan, reliance on existentialism alone could never bring the good Catholic existentialist this far.

Insight presupposes this context. One might express its overarching aim as seeking an answer to the question: How can a thinking individual, a Catholic no less, hold truth to be decisive in an age where temptation rages high to view it as an outmoded idea (a relic of the past) or as the sole possession of endeavors bearing directly on the objectively verifiable or, lastly, as the unattainable reward and/or punishment of the solipsistic wayfarer? Looking at the structure of the work alone, the whole of *Insight* may be seen as pivoting on this truth theme expressed in the middle chapters on judgment and objectivity. To them the initial eight chapters lead; on them the last seven chapters hang. But rather than minimize that which seemingly threatens truth in its propositional form, Lonergan grants it (the reader's experience) such a high function in *Insight* that it becomes the linchpin of the book's argument. Unique to his position is the way he does this without making truth our captive or contributing to the widespread illusion that our concepts of truth can be so objective that they are independent of the mind that thinks it. His is a phenomenological case for truth minus the need for absolute certainty or apodicticity, the cradle, he believes, of skepticism (*LoE*:50–51, 54).

Chapter Two

The Philosophical Aspect of the Concept of Experience

Up to now I have been analyzing religious experience in Lonergan's philosophy of God in a general way, providing the necessary background for understanding the shift he effects in the early 1970s. Among our more important finds is what that shift does not imply. First, it does not imply that Lonergan abandons his proof in his later writings. Second, it does not imply that he overlooks religious experience in his early writings. Neither is denied as the other comes up for reflection. What may look like a denial of the logistics of proof is but an admission of its subtext of meaning. Where proof and religious experience pass each other by in *Insight* as though complete strangers, in *Philosophy of God, and Theology* they embrace like long-lost relatives. The implication of this union is that both can coexist with the different concerns by which they exist. If the modernist crisis delayed the full budding of religious experience in Lonergan's early philosophy of God, its cessation did not eradicate his personal concerns that made keeping it at bay tolerable during the modernist scare. It is not purely accidental that the last chapter ends with remarks about the centrality of truth in *Insight*, propositional and otherwise. This Lonergan never abandoned even in the twilight of his philosophy of God.

That is why we must now delve more deeply into Lonergan's concept of experience before even beginning to think about greeting the dawn of his philosophy of religion. The generalities of the previous chapter lead us only so far. They merely hint at a union concerning whose dynamics we are left largely in the dark. In the next two chapters, then, I attempt to cast light on that dynamic, ironing out some of the details I have mentioned *en passant*. This should help us ride the incoming tide of his philosophy of religion more adeptly. Because Lonergan in *Philosophy of God, and Theology* recognizes *Insight* to be the terminus a quo of the problematic, I begin my treatment there. We are thus discharged from the task of having to trace the history of the concept from the early 1940s to the early 1950s. I, for one, have failed to detect anything radically different in that body of literature to warrant such an undertaking here. Except for the obvious advantage of equipping us with a comprehensive knowledge of experience in Lonergan, I have serious doubts that this kind of endeavor would contribute anything to our discussion bordering on the revolutionary.

THE READER'S EXPERIENCE IN *INSIGHT*

The term experience has more than one meaning in *Insight*. Experience can be either noematic or noetic. An experienced quale in Lonergan counts as experience every bit as much as the conscious experience that receives or acts upon qualia. More emphatically, experienced qualia are as experiential as the experience that allows for qualia to emerge in consciousness. If I am unconscious, I do not experience the activity about me. Something may bring me out of my unconscious state, say, intense heat, but as unconscious I am oblivious to data that are extraneous and happen to be non-intrusive for whatever reason. Once I become conscious of that activity, in its sheer presentedness, it enters the conscious flow of my experience. This accounts for the noematic sense of experience, which is very much a part of Lonergan's vocabulary. In this study I bracket the noematic, particularly as it pertains to the data of sense. I focus rather on the noetic, which strikes me as more crucial for understanding Lonergan's philosophical intentions.

One can detect at least three meanings to this noetic aspect of experience in Lonergan: a general and a specific meaning as well as one available only to the reader.[1] My including the latter may seem spurious since all writers assume their audiences interpret what they read in the light of their manifold experiences. Some writers forge better approximations than others. But the "successful" fusion is the business of the reader. Undergirding this process is an often tacit and necessary rhetoric of persuasion to lessen the initial gap between a text's affirmations and a reader's horizon. *Insight* falls in a branch of writing that makes this implicit framework explicit. The reader's experience is focused on as primary, although Lonergan takes pains to emphasize that he, in his ruminations about the nature of that experience, cannot impart an understanding of it. What he does instead is provide readers with personalizable examples and an avenue through his own thinking to effect this for themselves. Since the aim is insight into insight, which for Lonergan is synonymous with insight into oneself, the playing field he selects are those areas of inquiry in which insight is given the clearest expression, namely, mathematics and physics.

Such is the burden under which Lonergan labors in *Insight*. Its readers are constantly reminded not to lose sight of this as they work their way through its contents. Doing so would be to miss the point entirely. Although peppered with numerous examples taken from mathematics, physics, and psychology, *Insight* is not intended as a contribution to these fields of research. "Our ambition," he states, "is to reach neither the known nor the knowable but the knower" (*CWL* 3:91), the knower who knows vis-à-vis his or her experience of knowing. *Quidquid recipitur ad modum recipientis recipitur* (whatever is received is received after the manner of the receiver).

All this is stated several times between the covers of this rather unwieldy book. Among its most succinct expressions is in the introduction, a significant portion of which is worth quoting here on account of its relevance for the whole of our study.

> [M]ore than all else the aim of the book is to issue an invitation to a personal, decisive act. But the very nature of the act demands that it be understood in itself and in its implications. What on earth is meant by rational self-consciousness? What is meant by inviting it to take possession of itself? Why is such self-possession said to be so decisive and momentous? The questions are perfectly legitimate, but the answer cannot be brief.
>
> However, it is not the answer itself that counts so much as the manner in which it is read. For the answer cannot but be written in words; the words cannot but proceed from definitions and correlations, analyses and inferences; yet the whole point of the present answer would be missed if a reader insisted on concluding that I must be engaged in setting forth lists of abstract properties of human knowing. The present work is not to be read as though it described some distant region of the globe which the reader never visited, or some strange and mystical experience which the reader never shared. It is an account of knowledge. Though I cannot recall to each reader his personal experiences, he can do so for himself and thereby pluck my general phrases from the dim world of thought to set them in the pulsing flow of life. Again, in such fields as mathematics and natural science it is possible to delineate with some accuracy precise content of a precise insight; but the point of the delineation is not to provide the reader with a stream of words that he can repeat to others or with a set of terms and relations from which he can proceed to draw inferences and prove conclusions. On

the contrary, the point here, as elsewhere, is appropriation; the point is to discover, to identify, to become familiar with, the activities of one's intelligence; the point is to become able to discriminate with ease and from personal conviction between one's purely intellectual activities and the manifold of other, "existential" concerns that invade and mix and blend with the operations of intellect to render it ambivalent and its pronouncements ambiguous. (*CWL* 3:13–14)

To this experience Lonergan accordingly appends the term "self-appropriation," which conveys a sense of the personal nature of the event. "No one," he writes just a few lines above the passage just quoted, "can do it for you" (*CWL* 3:13). Because it is epistemic in nature, he supplies the correlative cognitive contents to occasion in willing readers a firsthand awareness of the act allowing them to understand, if indeed they are understanding, that content. This bears an uncanny resemblance to what goes on in psychotherapy. Lonergan himself has drawn the parallel. But where in psychotherapy the main objective is to increase a person's emotional capacity and self-sufficiency, in self-appropriation it is a person's epistemic capacity and self-sufficiency that are at issue.[2]

Insight assumes an audience relatively familiar with or simply affected in one way or another by a wide array of ideas. Due to their sheer polymorphicity and conflicting nature, these ideas often inspire stances ranging from disillusioned and learned skepticism to naive and erudite dogmatism. The so-called median fails to convince, not least because some of its own proposals are discordant, but more notably because those in the skeptic camp are either too disillusioned to believe that another idea will deliver them from their current plight or, ironically, too convinced to abandon their *knowledge* that ideas merely extend the mirages of perception. Those in the dogmatist camp, to complete this finally fanciful generalization, are wary of the median for fear of sacrificing absolute certainty for something less, which is surely a slippery slope into the tangles of skepticism. Yet if we are permitted to believe, if only for this one instance, what Bruce Duffy calls "the Devil's proposition," that people are, on the whole, more reasonable than they are unreasonable,[3] there are only medians, medians that, for reasons of performative consistency, gravitate toward the epistemically viable in extremist positions.

The median upon which Lonergan settles accedes to levels of probability and, when obtainable or appropriate, relative certainty. But he does not vie for such a stance by prioritizing the conceptual and doctrinal questions of epistemology, which have long preoccupied philosophers questing after the foundations of science.[4] Prior to questions about the status of knowledge, how what we presume to know is meaningful or true, is the knowing that generates the knowledge about whose status epistemologists are concerned. Unless we address this prior issue, Lonergan argues, answers concerning the status of knowledge are bound to be truncated, as in logical positivism, or exaggerated, as in Edmund Husserl's phenomenology.[5] Thus, we read in the opening lines of the introduction that the question is not "whether knowledge exists," which is an epistemological question in ontological dress, but "what precisely is its nature" (*CWL* 3:11). As a way of determining this Lonergan offers an intensely personal phenomenology of cognition. What it is said to deliver is an understanding of the condition of the possibility of knowledge based not on the epistemologist's definitions and laws of what constitutes knowledge. That, for Lonergan, is of secondary importance philosophically. Rather the condition of the possibility of knowledge is based on, is one with, the structure of consciousness implied in and thus revealed by existing forms of knowledge, which are read in a certain way. Epistemologists, who understand their science to be foundational, approach this the other way around. There the attempt is made to secure and, as often happens, exclude certain forms of knowledge by appealing to an elaborate set of criteria brought to that knowledge from the outside, as it were. The aim, of course, is to insure the objectivity of what is claimed to be known.

Lonergan is not one to dispute the need for criteria. But he is suspicious of criteria deduced from a combined gradation of purportedly self-evident truths and obvious laws. Here the hope is that such criteria would bring us one step closer to truly veridical knowledge as though such knowledge would have to finally come from the object itself. If this is not intended in the quest for maximizing certainty, it is implied. Also implied in it, according to Lonergan, is a faulty notion of objectivity, according to which in its crudest form reality is ready-made "out there now" susceptible to the glance that will unravel its mysteries. Lonergan deems this a vestige of our animal consciousness whose extroverted realism never fails to work its way into an understanding of ourselves and the world. However, while constitutive of all forms of sentient life, such realism does not fashion the worlds of meaning human beings inhabit through reflective judgment. For the adverse effects and evanescent blessings of these worlds only we can assume responsibility.

What is happening when we know? is the question proposed in the first part of *Insight* to disengage the reader from the quandaries of object-constitutive discourses as epistemology, whether they examine questions of human agency or objectivity. In other words, the emphasis in Lonergan's question is on the knowing that knowers do, rather than specific concepts and categories to which they are to adhere in order to know. In this way our anticipations of what knowledge should be can be tempered or canceled by what our knowing actually does. The place to begin is where one is, confused or over confident or simply indifferent. Readers must decide this for themselves. The rhetoric is subtle but apparent. John Angus Campbell, working from the perspective of rhetorical theory, has pointed out that Lonergan's rhetoric is "constitutive rather than persuasive," by which he means to distinguish it from modern forms of rhetoric that use argument and style as "a psychological inducement to persuasion devoid of cognitive import."[6] Modeled after the natural sciences, they build on the traditional scientific model of objectivity, according to which human beings passively mirror nature, simplistically known as reality. Assuming the so-called facts of this reality, mirrored by perception and ideas, the modern rhetor sets out to motivate the audience to believe those facts on a psychological or emotive plane. "The distinctly rhetorical aspect of this process is to make one's case so vivid that one's arguments will rival the force of sense perceptions and thus motivate belief. Argument, in the modern rhetorical tradition, is thus not understood as a matter of intellectual apprehension, but as a psychological process in which feeling is transferred from 'sensation' to 'ideas' through association."[7]

The traditions of rhetoric with which John Angus Campbell associates Lonergan put less of a premium on persuasive tactics, viewing persuasion as a proximate aim of rhetoric. With Aristotle, Giambattista Vico, John Henry Newman, and Kenneth Burke, to name only a few, Lonergan affirms a rhetoric of human action, his own contribution being "a specialization of human intelligence."[8] Where the modern rhetor assumes a passive notion of the human person as someone to be persuaded of mirrored facts or apodictic truths, Lonergan is earnest in emphasizing the active role of the knower in discovering truth. Notions of a mirrored reality and mirroring agent are, for him, simply a mistake of intelligence, an intelligence negligent of its cognitive operations. In having discerned a congruency between Lonergan's rhetoric in *Insight* and that in classical and humanist thinkers, Campbell goes on to characterize the rhetorical element of the former as one that puts "the audience in a frame of mind where they may intelligently grasp a potential good and reasonably affirm it as prudent or just in the particular case."[9] Postponing discussion of the larger issues shaping the context of Campbell's statement, that is, Lonergan's notions of "common sense" and "theory," of principal interest for us is the fabric of this rhetoric.

The fabric of Lonergan's rhetoric is persuasive in the general pedagogical sense of trying to evoke in one's audience, through illustrations and whatnot, the needed insight that will enable them to catch onto what one is saying. Insights, at root, cannot be transferred. One cannot impart them as one imparts gifts. The needed insight that will render intelligible the mathematical solution to a problem is something to be grasped for oneself as is the punch line of a joke. One can explain these things to someone, but one must have the insights oneself if one is to understand what is being explained. The insight Lonergan seeks to communicate to readers is incommunicable in a qualified or heightened sense. There the insight to be had is into oneself and not some mathematical formula or joke, painting, or philosophical paradox. The data is oneself and the only one privy to that information is oneself. Thus, both data and insight into that data are the reader's own. What Lonergan offers in the pages of *Insight* is an odyssey of self-understanding, where "self-understanding" means understanding the data of oneself for oneself. The only thing of which he can finally persuade readers is to brave the journey. The task is to intelligently grasp and reasonably affirm for oneself who one is as one is in the midst of a manifold of concerns "that invade and mix and blend with the operations of intellect to render it ambivalent and its pronouncements ambiguous" (*CWL* 3:14).

Elsewhere I expand on this element in Lonergan in terms of a philosophical pragmatics of language.[10] I only note it here as a distinct aspect of his thinking on experience. It is the truly original component of his thought. It makes good the claim that self-appropriation is not a ready-made theory about who one is but a means of discovering in oneself who one is (*2C*:213).

THE GENERAL AND SPECIFIC NOTIONS OF EXPERIENCE IN *INSIGHT*

Besides this remote functioning of experience, which Lonergan as an author does not venture to pronounce on but repeatedly draws his readers' attention to, are his technical designations of the term. I might put this otherwise as his own, more general mapping of the dynamism of experience he invites readers to check against their own experience of it.

Insight is not, accordingly, written in the "geometrical form" where one's definitions are clearly determined at the outset of an investigation followed by axioms and propositions; and so the shift in its meaning of terms, chiefly that of experience, can be confusing. Still, Lonergan is consistent. I mentioned earlier that experience, namely, as noetic, has basically a specific and general meaning in *Insight*, confusion over which may arise due to the integral relationship of the former to the latter. Thus, experience can be a reference either to the sensate operations of consciousness (seeing, hearing, touching, smelling, and tasting), what I call the "specific meaning of the term," or the combined levels of consciousness Lonergan identifies as experience, understanding, and judging, the "general meaning" (see fig. 2.1). Both specific and general meanings have their correlative contents. To hear is to hear something, to touch is to touch something, and so on.[11] What later becomes the distinct level of decision, which is the level particularly relevant to religious studies and theology, is spoken of in *Insight* simply as a corollary of the judgment. Complicating matters further is his notion of the patterns of experience, which determine the different ways in which the data in the specific

Fig. 2.1
Specific and General Notions of Experience (Noesis)

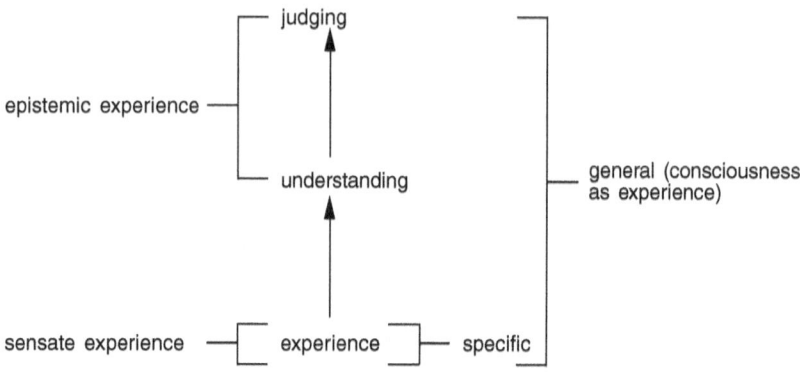

and general modes of experience are approached, arranged. Most grant that listening to a symphony is not like listening to a lecture on sound waves. Though the operation is the same, the manner in which it operates is not.

Consider the experience of reading this page. We are presented with series of marks on a white sheet of paper that are arranged according to the rules of syntax and meaning in the English language. The marks are given not only through the elaborate programming of software that transmits them to a printer, but also in our experience of seeing them (specific). Were we blind, experiencing these marks through other sensate means would be necessary to glean their significance. Yet there is another sense of experience in addition to this one, the experience of understanding these marks wrought through a lifetime of familiarity with the language along with an ability to judge correct and incorrect usage (general). Moreover, following the marks on this page, in this study as a whole, requires that attention be given to their particular pattern of expression rather than the perhaps more intriguing sonata playing in the background, the hunger rumblings of one's stomach, or the myriad other distractions that vie for one's attention. It requires the type of experience similar to that which diverted the Milesian philosopher Thales' attention from the well into which he fell, because of his wonder at the stars, though maybe not so excessively. The Thracian servant girl, whose derisive remarks about Thales' impracticality are not altogether unwarranted, typifies its absence, oblivious as she was to the stars.[12]

The example Lonergan gives in chapter 1 of *Insight* concerning the nature of the circle is as good a place as any to concretize further his concept of experience. He begins by asking us to imagine a cartwheel with its constituent parts, its hub, spokes, and rim. The episode is imagistic and hence of the experiential order for Lonergan. The image, in other words, is formed in one's experience and is occasioned by one's experience, mediate or immediate, of a body named "cartwheel." The question Lonergan invites us to raise about this datum of experience, Why is it round?, edges us toward an understanding of it, not of the datum per se but its nature, its circularity. The datum as experienced does not provide us with this, for we cannot conclude that the wheel is round because the spokes are equal. "The spokes could be equal yet sunk unequally into the hub and rim. Again, the rim could be flat between successive spokes" (*CWL* 3:31). From the datum we only glean clues as to its nature, which eludes experience (specific). The clue is that the roundness of the wheel cannot be accounted for by the wheel. An equality of distance "must"[13] obtain between the hub and the rim. So we decrease the hub to a point and thin out the spokes and rim into an infinity of equidistant lines. Does this solve the nature question? It does, in so far as we recognize that the points and lines of which we speak are unimaginable; they are not of the order of experience (specific). "One can imagine an extremely small dot. But no matter how small a dot may be, still it has magnitude. To reach a point, all magnitude must vanish, and with all magnitude there vanishes the dot as well. One can imagine an extremely fine thread. But no matter how fine a thread may be, still it has breadth and depth as well as length. Remove from the image all breadth and depth, and there vanishes all length as well" (32). Where the stuff of experience (specific), into which insights are had, can be either sensed, perceived, or imagined, the stuff of intelligence, concepts like points and lines, cannot. So the geometer would have us *suppose* that a dot has only position, a line only length. One does not see, feel, or picture concepts, one thinks them.

With this act of supposing, defining, formulating, we have "transgressed" the boundaries of experience in the specific sense. Both datum and its correlative conscious operations transmogrify, as it were, from imagined percept to conceptual content. The operation of supposing or thinking, however, is still one of experience, though in a broader sense. In our waking life we are constantly and spontaneously raising and answering questions, unless our waking life resembles a zombie's. The qualitative distinctions that hold in the question and answer process, too, need not avert us from the experiential fact that thinking occurs, however differently.

Equating this many-named activity with experience, in the general sense, seems so obvious that we are left wondering whether Lonergan contributes much to what we already know. Everyone knows that thinking and understanding are an integral part of conscious experience. Did not Descartes teach us that doubting this, as radically as we see fit, merely confirms it? But Lonergan's identification of thinking with experience contains subtleties that can and often do elude even the most careful of thinkers. It centers on his analytic demarcations between sensate experience and epistemic experience, where epistemic experience denotes distinct levels of understanding and judgment consisting of correlatively distinct conscious operations. A convenient catalogue is supplied in *Method*, among which are the operations of understanding, conceiving, formulating (level of understanding) and reflecting, marshaling and weighing evidence, judging (level of judgment) (*MIT*: 6; *CWL* 3:299). The awareness immanent in these operations, Lonergan invites us to corroborate in part one of *Insight*, is unlike, though ontologically interwoven with, that immanent in visual, auditory, tactile, olfactory, and other kinds of experiential operations in the specific sense outlined above. In circles where people bother about these questions, these distinctions are habitually overlooked, as are their qualitatively distinct awarenesses. Philosopher David J. Chalmers, for instance, now noted expert on and author of the remarkable book *The Conscious Mind* (1996), lists "thought" in his catalogue of conscious experiences. But no sooner than we look do we find that Chalmers means by the term something equivalent to what earlier we described as imagination. "When I think of a lion," he observes, "there seems to be a whiff of leonine quality to my phenomenology; what it is like to think of a lion is subtly different from what it is to think of the Eiffel Tower."[14] Note how, to be considered a conscious experience, the awareness is identified with the olfactive, the sensate. If this assumption is not stated clearly enough here, perhaps the sentence with which Chalmers opens his categorical entry brings it into sharper focus. "Some of the things we think and believe do not have any particular qualitative feel associated with them, but many do."[15] Would Chalmers include in his list those things that do not? It is hard to tell. But the list of experiences he notes at the end of his catalogue, which are supposed to compensate for experiences he has not considered like dreams, arousal, fatigue, and intoxication, suggests that he thinks of consciousness in predominately sensate terms.

Chalmers represents a wing in current philosophy of mind that is critical of the functionalist concept of consciousness, the view that consciousness is to be examined in terms of the causal role it plays in explaining behavior. Theirs, the functionalists', is an objective study of conscious experience, limiting colloquies on subjective mental processes to "late-night discussion over drinks."[16] Granting more to so-called internal states of consciousness is, to these siblings of behaviorism, mystery-mongering and not true science. Chalmers has no intention of joining the ranks of "mysterians." His quibble with the functionalist type of approach is that in its reductionism it limits itself to what he calls the easy problems of consciousness concerning the causal efficacy of human behavior. It is one thing to explain how, say, the brain integrates information and quite another to explain why such integration produces the subjective experience it does. The latter Chalmers identifies as a hard problem reductive theories of consciousness cannot explain because it goes beyond questions concerning the mechanics of conscious functions. The shapes and colors I see or the feelings I get as I look at the computer screen in front of me are doubtless caused by a peculiar firing of neurons in my brain. But the experience I have as I gaze at the screen is quite unlike what a third-person explanation would make of it. "Why is the performance of [that function] accompanied by conscious experience? It is this additional conundrum that makes the hard problem hard."[17]

One does not have to read too far into Chalmers to discover that his notion of consciousness is thought out on the conceptual playground of functionalism and eliminativism, albeit as their alter ego.[18] Thus, we see him driving a conceptual wedge between consciousness as subjective and immaterial and awareness as objective and physical. This is meant to guard against the reduction of the former to the latter, a basic manner of conduct in functionalist and eliminativist circles. Chalmers here gladly invokes the moderate concession of physicist Steven Weinberg. Consciousness is one of those fundamental components in the universe that escapes materialist explanation. Contrary to what most materialists hold, consciousness does not derive from physical laws. Its laws are of the psychophysical order, still unknown to us, that supervene on those of the physical. Where physical laws tell us about the way nature behaves, psychophysical laws tell us about the way nature is related to conscious experience, "how experience arises from physical processes."[19]

This is not the place to get into the issues of dualism Chalmers' position raises. Nor need we address his acceptance of the controversial belief that machines may one day be capable of consciousness by duplicating our neurons with silicon chips, the very stuff science fiction novels and motion pictures are made of. The physicalism he offers is softer than that espoused by typical AI theorists, but it is a form of physicalism nonetheless that many would doubtless find as disturbing. In any case, our concern is more specific. It is with his phenomenal concept of mind qua conscious experience, which poses as an auspicious contemporary example of what Lonergan does *not* mean by the concept, at least not fully. "On the phenomenal concept, mind is characterized by the way it feels."[20] It itself is not a conglomerate of physical components but eventuates itself in and through these components because of the way in which they are structured. Lonergan could, I think, go along with this model of the irreducibility of consciousness, but he would have difficulties with the notion that consciousness is characterized by feeling. This is for him the case, not because feelings are rejected as integral to our conscious life. He would be the first to admit that it is and that without it our conscious experience would be paper-thin. "The whole mass and momentum of living," he states, "is in feeling" (*2C*:221). Rather, his difficulties center on equating consciousness with feeling, which betrays a sensatism that marginalizes other components in the spectrum of consciousness.

The experiences Chalmers catalogues as conscious Lonergan views as first-level experiences, experiences in the specific sense. Were we to think of a lion as a biologist does, a qualitatively distinct experience would result unlike that mentioned in Chalmers' lion example. It may not be of the sensate variety, but it is no less conscious. Returning to our earlier illustration. When inquiring into the nature of the circle, presuming we never gave it much thought before, we may have experienced a given number of things. Some might report the peculiar sense of consolation that occasionally follows upon the "aha" of insight, that the nature of the circle is unimaginable. Others might be less jubilant in the light of what always seemed obvious. Our experiences may not have been predominately olfactive or ocular, but they, too, were sensationally constituted. Lonergan contends that besides this sensate awareness is the subtle yet recognizably distinct—let us call it—epistemic awareness germane to thinking. Because consciousness is a unity of diverse operations, this awareness is not without its correlate sensate awareness so that when thinking about a lion (in the technical sense of thinking, say, about its complex physiological structure) "a whiff of leonine quality" may indeed be present. But the awareness immanent in imagining a lion is as different from thinking about one as seeing is from conceiving. Part of the problem resides in the close association of awareness with the sensible. Chalmers attempts to correct this by sharply distinguishing consciousness from awareness, the latter being "objective and physical."[21] Vestiges of this association, however, can be detected in his frequent characterizing of the irreducibly conscious in sensate terms. According to Lonergan, consciousness eventuates itself sensationally, but also epistemically, which involves sensations but is not itself a sensation. Chalmers has probably undermined the confidence of his functionalist colleagues who are quick to identify phenomenal concepts of consciousness as occultist. But his account of it, though commendable at one level is incomplete at another.

Awareness, for Lonergan, is not fundamentally "awareness of," which is what drives Chalmers to distinguish it from consciousness as its objective feature.

> If seeing is an awareness of nothing but color and hearing is an awareness of nothing but sound why are both named "awareness"? Is it because there is some similarity between color and sound? Or is it that color and sound are disparate, yet with respect to both there are acts that are similar? In the latter case, what is the similarity? Is it that both acts are occurrences, as metabolism is an occurrence? Or is it that both acts are conscious? (*CWL* 3:345)

The answer Lonergan is trying to solicit, of course, is that both acts are conscious, the awareness of which differs in kind. But isn't this tantamount to saying that consciousness amounts to looking at a look, hearing hearing, and other such nonsense? Lonergan responds: "One may quarrel with the phrase 'awareness of awareness,' particularly if one imagines awareness to be a looking and finds it preposterous to talk about looking at a look. But one cannot deny that, within the cognitional act as it occurs, there is a factor or element or component over and above its content, and that this factor is what differentiates cognitional acts from unconscious occurrences" (*CWL* 3:345–6). This factor is, as we have seen, what Chalmers also regards as consciousness, but Lonergan offers a more differentiated understanding without having to distinguish between consciousness and awareness to insure the subjectivity of the former.

In thinking about the circle, in following the lead of clues prodded by my questioning of its image, I am conscious, I am aware, in a way in which I am not when I am imagining the circle. I am conceiving a nature I can neither perceive nor imagine, nor is the operation by which I am doing this similar to my perceiving and imagining, although it involves them. It requires that I follow clues and entertain concepts that will yield an understanding of circularity, which is unattainable at the level of experience (specific) as I experience thinking of it (general). In other words, awareness is present "but it is the awareness of intelligence, of what strives to understand, not as a schoolboy repeating by rote a definition, but as one that defines because he grasps why that definition hits things off" (*CWL* 3:346). Needless to say, yet evidently necessary to say, the awareness immanent in conscious operations such as perceiving and sensing are unlike that immanent in this conscious intelligent grasping. When I think about what it is that makes images materialize on my television screen and reach my eyes, I am not perceiving the intelligibility of that nexus of events. I am conceiving that nexus as I search for a possible explanation of an occurrence given—I am lucky enough to say—in my experience (specific). Because of the irreducibly subjective nature of conscious awareness only the reader can corroborate its different eventuations. Although we can and do speak of it, and speak of it differently, our words do not bestow the awareness of which we speak.

However, a possible explanation, even an excellently formulated and believable one, is not the terminus of our intellectually patterned conscious striving. We want to know whether there is more to our explanation than brilliance or hints of it. We want to know whether it accounts for what is actually or probably the case. It consists of an awareness, "judgment" Lonergan names it, that follows upon understanding, that seeks to confirm whether the conditions of understanding are met in experience. Judgment is as distinct from understanding as understanding is from experience (specific). Knowing that a circle is "a round plane figure whose circumference is everywhere equidistant from its center" requires an understanding of each term in the definition and why the absence of one of them would render it deficient. With the circle the conditions to be met are definitional, whether the terms and relations of the definition adequately capture what the image cannot supply; with my example of the television the conditions are empirical in that the explanation to be affirmed or denied concerns the experiential conjugate of sight. Nevertheless the awareness immanent in both types of understanding operates on the same level. A similar form of question carries the awareness: have the conditions of my definition of circularity or my theory of picture transmission and reception been met in experience, have they been met in that which I am trying to explain?

Lonergan directs the reader's attention to these distinct modes of awareness through concrete instances of knowledge. Whether that knowledge through advancements in a particular field has been superseded by more adequate forms (Newton's notions of absolute space and time by Einstein's special theory of relativity springs quickly to mind) is besides the point in *Insight*. Acts of understanding and judgment whose contents may be flawed are still acts of understanding and judgment. Besides, if the operations of consciousness are embodied, one expects that the more prudent of ways to them would be via the route paved by the knowledge they evidently occasion. Mental exercises are fine for Lonergan as long as they have a basis in fact, that is, actual instances of knowledge. Otherwise our theories about consciousness or mind would be as ahistorical as the possible worlds we can cleverly conceive or be puzzled by. This may be a logical necessity perhaps but not very this-worldly.

The way to consciousness, its structure, is through the instantiations of consciousness, biological, aesthetic, commonsensical, intellectual, religious, or whatever. The pattern Lonergan develops in *Insight*, indeed in most of his works, is the intellectual. It is the pattern of conscious experience that represents most literally the outworking of the desire to *know*. As such it is not what many today, congenial to this kind of query seeking, would describe as an existential outworking of that desire in terms of a calculated letting-things-be. Nor, obviously, is it an artistic outworking of the desire in terms of expressing oneself, one's view of the world, through art, music, or other creative means. Nor for that matter is it a religious outworking of the desire in terms of seeking or attaining spiritual enlightenment. The outworking of the desire to know in the intellectual pattern of experience is any potentially theoretical endeavor preoccupied with the nature or state of things, where by the nature or state of things is meant any differently patterned act or content of experience whose peculiar intelligibility, or lack thereof, we seek to bring to understanding. I say potentially theoretical because it begins in untheoretical child consciousness with the incessant "why" question and, if encouraged, begins, through osmosis, to resemble something of the theoretical in adult, practical consciousness. There is a world of difference between being interested in or repeating a theory about the nature or state of things and understanding or concocting one based on a personal apprehension of it. The former Lonergan views as intelligent without necessarily being intellectual.[22]

Our earlier wrestling with the nature of the circle is an example of intellectually patterned experience in the technical sense. Children, generally, do not think about such things. When they have to it is a matter of repeating a definition whose significance they cannot really explain. Adults themselves, even those with pretty good recall of high school geometry, usually struggle to explain what it is that makes a circle a circle and why our images, though invaluable, do not supply its definition. These are technical questions, the source of which is the desire to know immanent in what Lonergan would call the untutored mind. Commonly the adequate answer will be provided by the mind with a native aptitude for such questioning and the needed training that usually goes with it. What about its role in relation to other patterns, its difference from and service to them?

Earlier I made reference to the aspect of difference in terms of competing patterned experiences that constantly vie for our attention. The example of Thales and the Thracian girl represents a general disposition that separates one person's interests and concerns from those of another. However, as we all know, a human life is made up of several overlapping patterns of experience that complement and interrupt the flow of each other's movement. One can be curled up on a couch absorbed in the unwinding plot of a novel (aesthetic) while snacking (biological) without interrupting the flow of events. Writing a novel while giving into biological urges, of a more forcible nature of course, can yield a completely different set of results. Doing so runs the risk of having that eminently perfect word or phrase slip one's mind, an experience most writers prefer to do without. And so precautions are taken that many a non-writer would consider extreme. Lonergan gives the apt example of Sir Isaac Newton incarcerating himself in a room for weeks while trying to figure out his theory of universal gravitation. "A bit of food was brought to him now and then, but he had very little interest in it, and he slept only when necessary, but as soon as that was over he was back at work. He was totally absorbed in the enucleation, the unfolding, of his idea. Insofar as it is possible for a man, he was living totally in the intellectual pattern of experience" (*CWL* 10:86).

I might further explain the differences between the patterns by means of a personal encounter not too long ago with Vivaldi's *L'Estro Armonico Op. 3*, no. 9. This should place us in a better position to discuss the relevance of Lonergan's self-appropriating venture in the context of other patterns of experience, which are not necessarily intellectual.

I certainly cannot boast of any musical training of worth, but the first time the rapturous sounds of the "Larghetto" fell on my ears I can distinctly remember feeling drawn to the somber, melodious notes of the recorded violin, as other objects of thought and sense receded to the periphery of my consciousness. As soon as I took note of this—restrained myself, as it were—no longer did the violin exercise its musical authority over me. I had stepped out of a particular way of being to a reflective one detached from the immediate experience of inadvertent participation. Although a number of factors probably evoked the synchronistic enchantment of aesthetic and affective pleasure—about which I am not ready to comment, nor am I qualified to—the unprecedented experience of transitional awareness was as vivid as tripping on a flight of stairs while deep in thought.

What I have just described is a shift from one pattern of experience (aesthetic) to another (commonsensical-intelligent). Suppose I were a classically trained musician sensitive to obtuse and skilled interpretations of the concerto in question. Would this constitute a drastic change in circumstance? In a sense it would, for the disciplined ear becomes accustomed to the odious and the laudable, reacting courteously (it is hoped) to the object meant to instill aesthetic delight. As in all fields theoretical instruction and years of practice tend to segregate lay responses from those of the specialist. However, the character of the experiential pattern doesn't change no matter what the scale of participant expertise. The degree of elation doubtless varies, but reflective awareness introduces another dimension to the experience no longer simply aesthetic. Whether the content of the pattern is later abhorred as aesthetically unpleasing does not alter the fact that the initial experience was what it was and that the reflective reflex added something different to it. Relative changes in aesthetic taste leave the pattern functionally unharmed, if not enriched.[23]

SELF-APPROPRIATING THE GENERAL STRUCTURE OF EXPERIENCE

In Lonergan self-appropriation in the intellectual pattern of experience is a coming-to-oneself, one's conscious self, to make of that self, whatever the predominate pattern, something more attentive, intelligent, reasonable, and responsible. As such it does not provide the musician, the artist, the scientist with the specific skills of their craft. What it provides, rather, is a means by which to mediate the subject and object of those skills rationally self-consciously. This doubtless has an effect on the way in which those skills are consequently thought out. Showered with compliments about an extraordinary stage performance one evening, Sir Laurence Olivier is said to have nodded in compliance while adding that he did not know why. His remark, probably an outburst of irony concerning the unpredictable nature of an audience's reaction from performance to performance, indirectly supports a point I wish to make here. It hinges on noting the difference between being in a pattern of experience, reflecting on it commonsensically, intelligently, and objectifying it in general, theoretical terms. In his memoirs, for instance, Olivier dilates on the qualities that make for a successful actor. The "equal trinity of contributing qualities" he describes (talent, luck, stamina), immediately following which are pithy precept-like explanations, is advanced by Olivier as the outcome of thinking "more deeply" about the issue.[24] Few would doubt that Olivier is among this century's finest actors and that his summary of the qualities of a successful actor is sound. Whatever he says is borne by years of experience and profound insight. But few, including Olivier himself, would be willing to vouch for such summaries being a theory of acting or serving as a basis for one.

To answer essential problems in acting such as whether actors "feel" or merely imitate or whether they should speak "naturally" or rhetorically requires a familiarity with the history of acting, its various schools and philosophies. Susanne K. Langer has written a mammoth three-volume work entitled *Mind: An Essay on Human Feeling*.[25] One suspects that a thorough analysis of the dispositions just mentioned would require an analysis comparable to hers, if not in scope, then in design.[26] While in-depth analysis of the conditions of acting and audience participation may not completely allay the perplexity underlying Olivier's ironic outburst, it might bring him, were he alive, a step closer to doing so. At the very least it would place his hunches about (un)successful performances on a securer footing.

What contribution does self-appropriation make to this consciousness-raising endeavor? Is it merely an acquisition of theoretical knowledge about a particular way of being? Were I to have stopped with the last paragraph, this inference might be called for. But there is more. To continue my discussion of Olivier, acquiring a knowledge of the history, concepts, and methods of his aesthetically patterned field would contribute firstly only to his understanding of the field and secondarily, if at all, to his near-perfect qualities as an actor. What does not follow necessarily from such an acquisition is the ability to critically mediate one's own experience of whatever pattern in the light of and in critical dialogue with such broader knowledge. This is what Lonergan's program of self-appropriation principally aims to serve. Garnered is the ability to identify the difference between reacting negatively or positively to a view and knowing why while developing one's own view. The absence of this arguably practical element is usually that which inspires the widespread animosity frequently, and often deservingly, voiced against theory and method.

The Technical Aspect of Self-Appropriation and the Problem of the Relation of Concept to Experience; or, Lonergan, Kant, and Hegel

The critical mediation of multipatterned experience in the light of and in critical dialogue with the ideal of knowledge—this captures the objective of self-appropriation. In *Understanding and Being*, his 1958 Halifax lectures on *Insight*, Lonergan speaks of self-appropriation in terms of an answer to a problem having a technical and existential aspect. The technical aspect follows upon a "natural ideal," the pursuit of knowledge, which is the pursuit of an unknown. Since nature does not supply the conception, humans, yielding to the ideal, feel compelled to as the sciences and philosophy concretely demonstrate. The problem arises on account of the ideal of knowledge having been severely and, in certain respects, irreparably criticized. Lonergan mentions Kant's critique of pure reason and contemporary scholastic objections to "essentialism," which he summarizes as having undermined the view that philosophy is a movement "from self-evident, universal, necessary principles to equally certain conclusions" (*CWL* 5:13). In the same breath he mentions "the Hegelian difficulty," which recognizes every explicit ideal of knowledge to be an abstraction of a former one fraught with similar inadequacies. As a new emergent form takes shape, it too will suffer from the same inadequacies, presumably by association, and so on indefinitely. Mention could be made of other thinkers far more critical of reason than Kant and Hegel ever dreamed of being. Some Lonergan knows, others he doesn't. Nevertheless, the relevance of his point suffers little. Can there be a true ideal of reason even if variously conceived ideals of pure reason have been abandoned? Stated otherwise, If reason is not pure, then what is it? What can we expect of it? The assumption, of course, is that reason exists, which Lonergan argues is implied in all our questioning. Arguing against this would be to prove it.[27] For Lonergan this is not the real issue, as he candidly states in the opening lines of *Insight*: "The question is not whether knowledge" or reason "exists." It is "what precisely is its nature" (*CWL* 3:11). That, as philosophers of consciousness would say, is the hard problem.

Lonergan conceives the nature question, the ideal of knowledge, in terms of a dynamic self-presence in acts of experiencing, understanding, judging, and deciding. It is a being present to oneself in a way that chairs being present in a room or individuals being present to one another is not (*CWL* 5:15). Self-appropriation begins by adverting to this conscious self-presence, not as awareness of the other, the other's presence to me, but as the condition of the possibility of the other being present to me. "If I were unconscious, you would not be present to me.... If you were unconscious, I would not be present to you." *That* the other is present to me, whatever the ontological constitution or epistemological form of that other, is made possible by my being present to myself. "[I]t is not being entirely absorbed in the object; rather, it is adverting to the fact that, when you are absorbed in the object, you are also present to yourself" (*CWL* 5:16). This is in keeping with the objective of the first part of *Insight*, in which readers are immersed in the objects of knowledge. The aim is to elicit the structure of that knowledge, which is the reader's self. By fumbling over questions of a classical and statistical nature, questions that evade most of us or most of us would like to evade, readers are given the opportunity to witness the functioning of that structure in act, in their experience, loosely so-called. Wanting to know or refute what Lonergan is saying, whatever the case may be, whether it is about probability or one's self-presence, is the self-validating means Lonergan offers readers to experience this structure in and for themselves. Handing them the concept would practically insure they avoid experiencing the structure.[28] This would be to change the meaning of self-appropriation into an appropriation of another self and his ideas, namely, Lonergan's. While this is inevitable in the communication process, it is handled explicitly, pedagogically, in *Insight* as a means to a greater cognitional end.

It is important to be clear about this conscious self-presence, which Lonergan conceives as four-tiered. Objectifying it is not equivalent to being conscious on all four levels. "[T]here follows at once a distinction between consciousness and self-knowledge. Self-knowledge is the reduplicated," objectified "structure: it is experience, understanding, and judging with respect to experience, understanding, and judging. Consciousness, on the other hand, is not knowing knowing but merely experience of knowing, experience, that is, of experiencing, of understanding, and of judging" (*CWL* 4:208), what I have called the "general structure of experience." In later writings, Lonergan introduces the terms infrastructure and suprastructure as a convenient means of indicating this same distinction. Infrastructure refers to consciousness, to the subject as subject, as present to herself experiencing, understanding, judging, and deciding. Suprastructure refers to accounts of consciousness, possibly of the self-knowledge variety, to the subject as object, as an encapsulation of the infrastructure "within a suprastructure of language and knowledge" (*3C*:117; 55–73). The aim of self-appropriation is to get people to experience this infrastructure for themselves so that they may effect a suprastructural account of it in their own terms, vis-à-vis their own life experience. Noticing this four-tiered infrastructure, adverting to it, is "to move into self-appropriation" (*CWL* 5:17). To affirm one's understanding and judgment of this structure, to "suprastructuralize" it, is, presumably, to bring the self-appropriating venture to a close. Once the subject is appropriated the venture is taken up again in relation to a more developed self-knowledge and in greater openness to a fuller realization of it.

How this is supposed to resolve the problem raised and answered by Kant and Hegel in their own distinct ways is an interesting question. In effect, Lonergan accuses the whole history of epistemology of having forgotten the essence of subjectivity (*Subjektvergessenheit*) much like Martin Heidegger accuses the whole history of metaphysics of having forgotten the essence of being (*Seinsvergessenheit*). They are distinct accusations and, I believe, mutually compatible, although their theses, that is, the manner by which they are reached, are irreducible to one another.[29] As for Lonergan's accusation, the implication is not that subjectivity has been ignored per se. He recognizes the issue to have been a prominent one, particularly in the twentieth century due to the influence of thinkers like Hegel, Søren Kierkegaard, Friedrich Nietzsche, Heidegger, and Martin Buber. The issue, he holds (as do many others), goes back to Kant whom he believes "brought the subject into technical prominence while making only minimal concessions to its reality" (*2C*:70, n. 2). Although Lonergan does not explicitly state why he believes Kant makes only minimal concessions to the reality of the subject, the reason he thinks this doubtless owes itself to his transferal of the Kantian problematic as regards knowing the object to knowing the subject. Just as our judgment and reasoning give us only mediate knowledge of what intuition (*Anschauung*) "knows" immediately—and what intuition knows immediately is of a sensitive nature, phenomena, not noumena (reality in itself)—so too our judgment and reasoning about the human subject reveal only a phenomenal subject, a representation of a representation. Lonergan views the subsequent history of epistemology "as a series of attempts to win for the subject acknowledgment of its full reality and its functions."[30]

Much of the history concerned with the Kantian problematic Lonergan regards as haunted by a picture-thinking presupposed in Kant's attempt to unveil the workings and limits of empirical reason. The Kantian argument, he acknowledges, is a valid one if by "object" one means what one can settle by representational, picture-type thinking. " 'Object' is what one looks at; looking is sensitive intuition; it alone is immediately related to objects; understanding and reason can be related to objects only mediately, only through sensitive intuition" (*2C*:78). In *Insight* he believes he has shown that this type of thinking is fundamentally mythic, in the negative sense. What is related to the object immediately, he counters, is questioning. So-called sensitive intuition (for Lonergan experience in the specific sense), consciousness (i.e., general structure of experience), and suprastructural accounts of these are what is related mediately to the object "inasmuch as they are means of answering questions, of reaching the goal intended by questioning" (78–79). The goal Lonergan has in mind is the universe of being, the notion of which precedes, penetrates, and transcends the answers given to our questions in experience, understanding, and judging. By arguing that it is questioning that relates us immediately, nonrepresentationally (that is, nonpictorially) to objects of sense Lonergan relativizes the fundamental role often attributed to "sensitive intuition" in epistemology. In this way he reinstates judgment, supported by understanding of what is given in experience (specific), as constitutive of the knowing process. In knowing we mediately yet really, noumenally, know what is immediately, phenomenally, given in our questioning initiating the process. To put it otherwise and to render more accurately one of Lonergan's statements on the issue, to know that an object is not noumenal but phenomenal is just as much a matter of judgment as knowing that an object is not phenomenal but noumenal. Sensitive intuition gives us neither phenomena nor represented noumena. "Both are matters of judgment."[31]

In so far as one conceives the antithetic as a subject "in here" representing a finally unknowable reality in itself "out there" ("in here" even)—a representation based, moreover, on an immediate yet nevertheless representational intuition—it is hard to imagine how Kant's problematic could be answered convincingly. Not only that, it would be hard to imagine how one could affirm the so-called noumenal reality of the subject intending a noumenally real world of being, one which could be known incrementally, partially, really. With Hegel's response to Kant Lonergan is far more satisfied, at one level anyway.

> Hegel's dialectic has its origins in the Kantian reversal both of the Cartesian realism of the *res extensa* and of the Cartesian realism of the *res cogitans*; but where Kant did not break completely with extroversion as objectivity, inasmuch as he acknowledged things themselves that, though unknowable, caused sensible impressions and appeared, Hegel took the more forthright position that extroverted consciousness was but an elementary stage in the coming-to-be of mind; where Kant considered the demand of reflective rationality for the unconditioned to provide no more than a regulative ideal that, when misunderstood, generates antinomies, Hegel affirmed an identification of the real with a rationality that moved necessarily from theses through antitheses to higher syntheses until the movement exhausted itself by embracing everything; where Kant had restricted philosophy to a critical task, Hegel sought a new mode, distinct from Cartesian deductivism, that would allow philosophy to take over the functions and aspirations of universal knowledge.[32]

Comments in his 1960 lecture on "The Philosophy of History" suggest that for Lonergan philosophical reflection on the subject proper begins with Hegel. "It is said of Hegel, or he said it himself, that he transferred philosophy from the *substance* to the *subject*; Spinoza wrote about the substance, Hegel wrote about the subject."[33] Lonergan uses this as a springboard for his own reflection on the subject and so we do not glean much information from the lecture as to his understanding of Hegel's meaning. Something of relevance crops up in his 1963 lecture on "The Mediation of Christ in Prayer" with regard to the notion of mediation qua the *Begriff*—rather: mediation as aspiring after the *Begriff*, the universal concept. But by far his most relevant comments for us are in *Understanding and Being*, which tie in with his assessment of the Hegelian system in *Insight*.

Part and parcel of Hegel's turn to the subject is a problem that is difficult to surmount outside of his solution, his dialectical system. Although Lonergan recognizes a legitimacy in the concerns of Karl Marx and Kierkegaard against the system, he appears to be unconvinced that their alternatives adequately or directly address the equally legitimate philosophical problems raised by Hegel. In fact, with regard to Kierkegaard he baldly and, one suspects, overgeneralizingly states that "[h]e couldn't refute Hegel. When he said 'I exist, and I have to live, and I have to be a man, and I have to be a Christian,' and so on, that affirmation of the subject in Kierkegaard is blind, it ties in with faith as confidence, the Lutheran tradition of faith, not faith as believing [propositionally formulated] truths"(*CWL* 6:239)—that is, the Catholic tradition of faith. With regard to Marx he is slightly less pungent, arguing that Marx's concern with the dialectic of community, external human affairs as they concretely happen, is "just a matter of the symmetries" (*CWL* 5:299). The toppling of the system outward into the factualness of Marx and inward into the factualness of Kierkegaard, to use the familiar description in *Insight* (*CWL* 3:398), did involve distinct moves of getting beyond Hegel but without, in Lonergan's opinion, really getting beyond him philosophically, epistemologically.

The problem, or why it should be considered a problem, is hard to put a finger on. We met it earlier in "the Hegelian difficulty" of abstraction and the ideal of knowledge. It regards the process of appealing to some sort of ideal that accounts for the event of knowledge, the pursuit of an unknown to-be-known. From Hegel or Hegelians (probably a combination of both) Lonergan gleaned that this involves a process of abstraction in which one extracts from an operative ideal, an ideal that is not itself the ideal being appealed to. An alienation ensues that a consequent, reconciling concept means to resolve that is itself an abstraction, and so on indefinitely. What Lonergan tries to surmount through self-appropriation is the relativist reading of this notion of abstraction that finds support in Hegel's philosophy, which Lonergan judges to be "unrestricted in extent" yet "restricted in content, for it views everything as it would be if there were no facts" (*CWL* 3:398). What he means by this is that so-called facts in Hegel are concepts of incomplete understanding, because of which or in the face of which contradictions arise. This is said to necessitate a fuller understanding that is itself a limited viewpoint to be subjected (that *is* subjected) to the same process over and over again. The objective of the desire to know in Hegel is clearly unrestricted. Lonergan insists, though, that this objective is not identified "with a universe of being, with a real factual existents and occurrences. For being as fact can be reached only insofar as the virtually unconditioned is reached; and as Kant ignored that constitutive component of judgment, so Hegel neither rediscovered nor reestablished it. The only objective Hegel can offer the pure desire is a universe of all-inclusive concreteness that is devoid of the existential, the factual, the virtually unconditioned" (*CWL* 3:397). The virtually unconditioned pertains to any state of affairs whose conditions happen to be fulfilled (hence *virtually* unconditioned). What the notion does is guard the other as other, connecting us to the other through judgment.[34] It is Lonergan's way of emphasizing the centrality of the subject without concluding that everything is subjective or that objectivity is subject-free. Hugo Meynell has expressed this very thing in contrasting Lonergan, Kant, and Hegel. "The concept of the virtually unconditioned is of cardinal importance in Lonergan's philosophy, enabling him to avoid Hegel's conclusion that thought ultimately has nothing to think of but itself, without embroiling him with Kantian 'things in themselves' such as somehow exist in utter transcendence of our cognitional processes."[35]

In Lonergan's estimation, what separates his contribution from that of Hegel is Lonergan's recognition of the epistemically determinative function of the virtually unconditioned. Key to understanding this is Lonergan's pronouncement in *Insight* that, unlike himself, "Hegel endeavors to pour everything into the concept" (*CWL* 3:447). Whatever it is that we know is a concept of the concept "that unfolds itself in the Logic, and forms the essence both of the world and of the I."[36] For Lonergan concepts are "byproducts of the development of understanding" (*CWL* 3:447), the fruition of inquiring intelligence. The debate is an old one, but from Lonergan's self-designated *critical* realism we are to gather that the issues have changed. No longer is it a question of concepts being appended to a world, like stamps to an envelope, by a self-sufficient or concept-independent understanding. The idea is that concepts are sharply distinct from understanding and its objects. This is supposed to insure the world's independence of the mind as well as the mind's ability to know this independently of the concepts it brings to bear on the world. Granting concepts a more fundamental role, it is felt, paves a way into the monistic trap of idealism from which there is no escape. Lonergan is not in the least bit convinced by certain realist alternatives to this obviously caricatural snapshot of idealism. The most notable is from his fellow Catholic thinker, Étienne Gilson (1884–1978). Before turning to the issue as Lonergan conceives it, it would be good to pause briefly and look at Gilson. His answer to the Hegelian supposition that "the concept overreaches what is other than itself"[37] should help us appreciate Lonergan's arguably more nuanced position.

Relying on Lonergan's reading of Gilson, we see in his (Gilson's) reaction to idealism something resembling what we may tentatively refer to as "basicalism," namely, the view now in vogue that there are certain properly basic beliefs that, while rational, cannot be bolstered or undermined by argumentation, nor, incidentally, do they require argumentation to uphold. Usually included among such beliefs is the existence of the self and an external world. Belief in God is another. Alvin Plantinga, its more recent proponent in Anglo-American circles of philosophy of religion, adds to the list beliefs such as the existence of other minds and the past.[38] Lonergan is able to go along with this—tolerate it, I should say—up to a certain point. Once it becomes a dogmatism, as he believes it has in Gilson's realism, he is quick to engage its premises, which for him usually, if not always, means its implicit and presumably faulty cognitional theory.

The reason Gilson offers for what I have described as basicalism is that once one argues from critical premises, the conclusions reached via that route will only give one mere postulates or mere predicates. On that basis the best available realist conclusion is only as good as its idealist rival. Something more universally evident, something more indubitable must be appealed to that will decide the issue. That something more in the realist's favor, Gilson feels, is a truth that is immediate and does not belong to the intellect. What he wants is a veridical whole to be affirmed prior to its predicative parts. Gilson gives a realist twist to Berkeley's "truth" that the real is perceived. "Thus, no matter what way we may put the question to realism, no matter how profoundly we may inquire of it, How do you know a thing exists? Its answer will always be, By perceiving it."[39] Lonergan agrees with Gilson that his is a dogmatic realism, which is a blunt reaffirmation of a truth whose validity Kant denied. But Lonergan evaluates Gilson's dogmatism negatively for being uncritical in a way in which Kant is not. Lonergan's comment in *Collection* about Gilson's position bristling with difficulties (*CWL* 4:197) is a subtle yet evident jab. Gilson's claims are not made without philosophical argumentation or, needless to say, in ignorance of the history of philosophy. But as a dogmatism Lonergan is not persuaded by it. The givenness and universal accessibility of Gilson's immediate realism is all but given and universally accessible. In fact, Gilson's realism is vague and restricted, restrictive even. "That is why in the last analysis"—Lonergan quotes Gilson disapprovingly, insinuating that his answer to idealism is not really an answer—"you do not accept any part of realism as long as you do not accept it whole and entire."[40]

For the same reason Lonergan opts for Hegel over Kant he opts for Hegel over Gilson. (That Lonergan opts for the critical component of Kant's idealism over Gilson's dogmatism goes without saying.) Kant admits the indispensability of the noumenon yet leaves it alone in the sense that it completely transcends our understanding. The noumenon is invoked, in other words, as a limit concept (*Grenzbegriff*). Gilson tries to bridge this (for Kant) unbridgeable gap by simply affirming the "knowability" of the noumenon through immediate intellectual perception. With Gilson, then, it is not a matter of engaging the problematic of noumenal objects completely transcending our experience. That is a problem of critical philosophy. It precludes the dogmatic affirmation of a thing's existence through, to use Kant's terms and assumptions, "the representations which their influence on our sensibility procures for us."[41] Rather it is, as we saw, a matter of bluntly reaffirming the existence of noumenal reality, despite what Kant tells us, whatever name we may choose to give it. Kant's response is simple and direct. What Gilson affirms as real and immediate is but the phenomenal content of a sensitive intuition understanding reflects upon. What Gilson affirms, in other words, is a representation (his affirmation) of a representation (what appears to us in intuition, in sensation), not the thing or reality to which he thinks we have direct access.

The key notion here is mediation. Knowledge of a thing, in the critical sense of knowledge, is always mediate. Immediate knowledge is typically reserved, interestingly enough even by those who *reflect* on the issue, to perception, the perceiver perceiving a given. We saw Kant's answer to this in terms of his bifurcation of things-in-themselves and as they appear to us. Immediacy of self to thing is qualified as mediate immediacy[42] at best, which the logical function of the mind organizes through various a priori categories and conditions. Hegel extends the notion of mediation to Kant's things-in-themselves with the result that they, too, along with their appearances, are seen as mediated *by the concept*. "Hence it comes to pass for consciousness that what it previously took to be the *in-itself* is not an *it-self*, or that it was only an in-itself *for consciousness*."[43] It is in consciousness and by consciousness that the in-itself is posited, which means for Hegel that the in-itself is not a reality apart-from-self but a concept of the self, for the self. Not only are noumena mediately related to us through sensibly intuited phenomena, they themselves, conceived as apart-from-self, in alienation from the self, are mediately related to and by us through the concept. Hegel pushes the logic of Kant for all its worth and thereby brings to light its self-contradictory nature. As long as humans are the ones positing an in-itself, it cannot be viewed as other than an in-itself in, of, and for the self.

Hegel's argument is not an argument for solipsism. Solipsism for him is one of several deficient or incomplete reactions to direct realism and Kantian idealism. Actually a good bulk of part one of the *Phänomenologie* is spent critiquing solipsism. In this connection Robert B. Pippin's summary of the first three chapters of the *Phänomenologie* is very incisive.

If the question is how we account for the directness of conscious experience, for the fact that we think this, not that, thought and thereby successfully refer to this, not that, fragment of the world, Hegel tries to show the incompleteness and inadequacies of any account that maintains that the answer to such a question is: it is the world itself which, by impinging on our senses or mind, draws our attention to it in this or that way, given this or that feature of the object. Along the way in this account, he also tries to show why not much is gained by postulating different, nonsensible, sorts of external entities [i.e., noumena] by apprehension of which a discriminating reference to the sensible world is possible: universals, abstract objects.... Any relation to objects, even nonsensory objects, is, it is argued, inexplicable, or at least radically underdetermined, by any *direct apprehension or causal influence or the object itself.* Such a possibility is said already to presuppose some way of *comporting oneself toward* the world, some active attending and discriminating that cannot be a simple result of our encounter with the world, since the world offers up too many different ways for such a taking up and holding together.[44]

By chapter four, we see Hegel writing about the other being preserved in the unity of self-consciousness with itself. As Pippin remarks, this has nothing to do with Hegel "shifting the focus from the what's 'Out There' as the guarantor of truth claims to what's all 'In Here.'"[45] What the shift to self-consciousness and ultimately to Absolute Spirit involves, rather, is a reconceptualization of the mind-world relationship beginning with the mind itself, our world within the world and what it reveals about the relationship. It does not involve assumptions about objects "out there" that the mind "in here" can or cannot know for whatever reason.

By concept as mediation in Hegel we are not to understand the setting up of another dichotomy, say, between the concept and that of which it is a representation. A fundamental feature of the notion is that what we think is bare, conceptually untainted immediacy, is relative to the concept that allows us to think it so. In other words, it is a mediated immediacy, not in the sense of Kant, where what is immediate is a mediating appearance of noumena. The immediacy here is one borne by or "lifted up" into the concept. The concept as our individual and corporate references of meaning open up the very possibility of what is present to consciousness as immediate, as *significantly* immediate. For Hegel the concept, which, generally speaking, I understand to consist of an undifferentiated hybrid of our systems of meaning, is, as Charles Taylor notes, "an active principle underlying reality, making it what it is."[46] Thus, that which one is given spontaneously to view as merely regulative Hegel recognizes as constitutive and universal.

Lonergan's acceptance of mediation is a qualified one. Although he rejects the understanding that the mediating concept through its various stages of development is constitutive, he does admit to its universality. He uses the word "in a broad sense, in a universal way, as did Hegel," but not "on Hegelian presuppositions of an idealism" (*CWL* 6:162). He agrees with Hegel that Kant goes wrong when identifying the concept as a tool of our knowing, the means by which we grasp reality "without prejudice to the nature of reality itself."[47] But he does this for different reasons guided by a different method of inquiry. Indeed, in many respects Lonergan is in great sympathy with Kant. Kant's desire to maintain nature's independence from our systems of thought is certainly something Lonergan appreciates. But he is as certain as Hegel that putting a wedge between reality and that which can be objectively, phenomenally, known raises more problems than it solves. At the same time, Lonergan is far from convinced that Hegel's stress on the concept preserves the other as other within the unity of self-consciousness, although it does indicate, even if incompletely, the close relationship between objectivity and thought. He is even less persuaded that the concept is an efficient cause, an active principle, underlying and hence making reality what it is. What this garners is a self-enclosed conceptual system in which "the relations of oppositions and sublation between concepts are pronounced necessary; and the whole dialectic is contained within the field defined by the concepts and their necessary relations of opposition and sublation" (*CWL* 3:446). There is little room here, Lonergan contends, for the heuristic anticipations of consciousness, awaiting "from nature and from history a succession of tentative solutions," not bound by the necessary relations of concepts. For the same reason that the German historical school of the nineteenth century and its offshoot the history of religions school found Hegel's dialectical logic untenable Lonergan does as well: it is not conducive to contemporary methods of inquiry where one begins with research and reaches conclusions only when one's position is verified empirically (*3C*:202).

Grasping the nature of insight as a preconceptual act of understanding, distinct from and serving as the basis for the concept, is Lonergan's ticket, so to speak, out of the Hegelian circle of meaning. As an operation of the subject, such an act is merely one among several distinct conscious operations forming the spectrum of our experience (general). However, through phenomenological analysis of insight we come to understand not only the function of this act, but also that through which presentations are had (experience in the specific sense). We also come to understand that under the constraint of which we gauge our understanding to be either probably true or false, incomplete, or inconclusive. In other words, what insight into insight reveals is a preconceptual structure providing for the determinate conceptual content upon which Hegel relies to extract a structure he views as fundamental. Where Kant underestimates the role of the concept, on Lonergan's view, Hegel overestimates it. Kant underestimates it by granting ontological supremacy, albeit a relative ontological supremacy, to sense intuition, "the place" where reality is immediately apprehended. A gradation of mediation follows further removing us from the mediate immediacy of the intuited object. "[I]f knowledge can have an immediate relation to the object only through a sort of intuition, then *Vernunft* [reason, judgment] as tendency towards the unconditioned, will resemble intuition even less than *Verstand* [understanding], as faculty of the intelligible, resembles it."[48] This has only a descriptive bearing on the performance of objects of intellect. By viewing it as such Kant in no way wants to undercut the importance of intellect and its object. However, for Hegel and Lonergan, Kant's approach betrays a lingering sensatism or intuitionism burdened by needless aporia.[49] And yet Lonergan finds Hegel's radical reversal of Kant to be conceptually incarcerating, even if enormous in range of vision. A recurrent complaint is that Hegel "does not and cannot regard the factual as unconditioned" (*CWL* 3:398), which owes itself fundamentally to his "fixing the concepts that will meet the anticipations" of consciousness (3:446) rather than the other way around.

For Lonergan what intuition gives us is presentations, not reality, noumenal or phenomenal. One does not arrive at these distinctions by intuiting them; they are concepts of the understanding. As concepts of the understanding they are constitutive of what we *think* presentations are, providing the very space within which we think them. What the concept does, according to Lonergan, is mediate a world of understanding apart from which presentations (are) merely present, experience (specific) as experience (specific). The hope that one can "ground belief in an extramental material world in data given prior to any knowledge of such [a] world" Lonergan would regard as fundamentally misguided—as would Kant and Hegel, but for different reasons and with different results.[50] But the concept itself depends on the insight of which it is an expression, and the insight of which the concept is an expression is garnered through inquirers who care to conceive the anticipated intelligibility of that into which they inquire. Whether or not that anticipation can be fulfilled is beside the point. Without the inquirer, then, the concept, as well as the insight, could never be; without the insight the concept could never be understood in its being. Following the logic of the former claim is easy enough. I might simplify the latter merely by pointing to the familiar experience of repeating something, a definition or theory, without understanding. That there will always be concepts as long as there are humans to think them is pretty well guaranteed; that those who repeat them understand them is not.

The concept for Lonergan arises on account of a process of questioning that culminates, at one level of inquiry, in insight. "When you have an insight, you are given certain data, and you ask, 'Why are these data a man?' You grasp form, soul, and then you form the concept. You combine these data with this intelligible unity as you [formulate] a concept."[51] The concept is then subjected to another process of questioning that aims at determining the concept's veracity level. The conditions that allow for judgment to finally determine this will be relative to the type of concept in question, whether, for instance, it is analytic or empirical. Reflective understanding is that which grasps whether an insight has adequately dealt with the "what," "why," and "how often" questions of intelligence,[52] and whether the conditions of the insight are met in present or remembered data, or in the meanings or definitions of terms.[53] Like insight it, too, is a preconceptual grasping but of a qualitatively distinct sort. Where insight pivots between the concept and experience (sensation, perception, and the free flow of images), reflective understanding pivots between the concept and the "yes" or "no" or "probably (not)" of judgment. "The function of reflective understanding is to meet the question for reflection ['Is it so?'] by transforming the prospective judgment from the status of a conditioned to the status of a virtually unconditioned; and reflective understanding effects this transformation by grasping the conditions of the conditioned and their fulfilment" (*CWL* 3:305). Important to note, in the light of what has gone before, is that what is grasped is not given in or outside intuition, which the understanding then re-presents; nor is it contained in and by the concept, making it one and the same thing as the concept, a conceptual content. What insight grasps is a presentationless form in the presentation or image. It is culled through questioning and is formulated in the concept. The concept is something added to the presentation whose intelligibility is coterminous with the understanding, not sensation or perception. In this way what is immediate to us is acknowledged as immediate but not under the assumption that that immediacy constitutes reality, intuitively mediate or otherwise. This also dispenses with the notion that the concept gives us reality in its being as that reality. The concept "merely" mediates forms grasped through insight that are subsequently confirmed or disconfirmed through reflective understanding. Reality is mediated on the level of judgment, not on that of understanding or its concepts. In the notion of mediation Lonergan wants to hold on to a distinctness between what is mediated and what is doing the mediating. The virtually unconditioned is that which secures this for him. It is not of our own making; it is attained, connecting us with the absolute (*CWL* 5:119). And yet there is a sense in which *the grasping* of the virtually unconditioned puts us into immediate contact with reality, where "immediate" is stripped of perceptionist connotations

Fig. 2.2

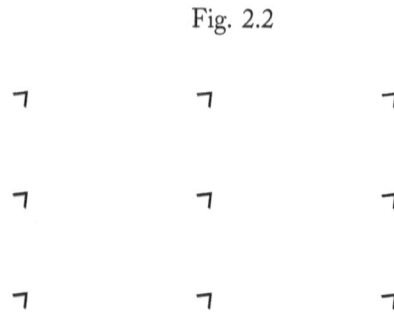

Source: CWL 5:109 (n. 4)

and "the real" is what is known in judgment. This constitutes Lonergan's critical realist relativization of the subject-object distinction.

In chapter 5 of *Understanding and Being,* Lonergan refers to a diagram that spells out in more detail the schema of the dynamism I have been describing. The diagram consists of nine arrows as disposed in fig. 2.2.

The arrows represent each cognitional act in its dynamism as it is "sublated" by subsequent acts and levels. This Lonergan identifies with "the pure question" (*CWL* 3:34) and "the pure desire to know" (*CWL* 3:372–5). Making the precise correlations would render a diagram that looks something like fig. 2.3. Keep in mind that these acts and their correlational contents pertain to what Lonergan calls "the subjective field" (*CWL* 3:204), our noetic experience.

Fig. 2.3
Levels and Operations of Consciousness

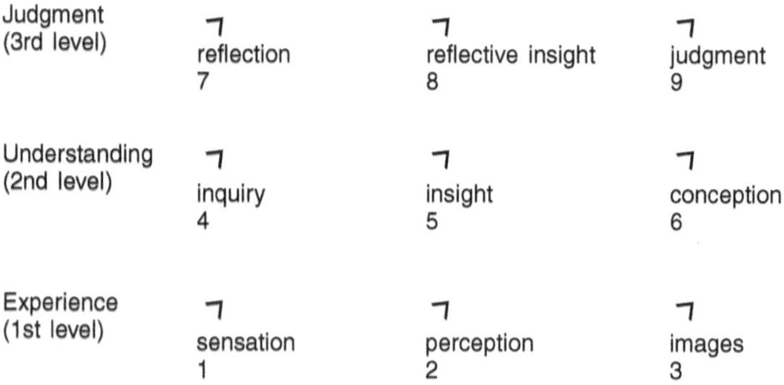

Judgment (3rd level)	⏋ reflection 7	⏋ reflective insight 8	⏋ judgment 9
Understanding (2nd level)	⏋ inquiry 4	⏋ insight 5	⏋ conception 6
Experience (1st level)	⏋ sensation 1	⏋ perception 2	⏋ images 3

The virtually unconditioned is the point of contention Lonergan sees between himself and Hegel. He pinpoints Hegel's notion of the concept as symptomatic of his unacceptable view. By basing the concept on the preconceptual insight, by identifying reflective understanding as that which grasps and thus attains to the status of the virtually unconditioned, Lonergan believes he has discredited the supposed Hegelian propensity to reduce the virtually unconditioned to the status of the concept. Virtually unconditioned here can refer either to consciousness (experience in the general sense), the bodies it encounters (the content of experience in the specific sense), or the things it conceives (the content of an act of insight). I find myself as puzzled by Lonergan's assessment as Jon Nilson is. Nilson argues that Lonergan's interpretation of Hegel in *Insight* is based on a stereotype "which is not only inaccurate but downright bewildering in view of the affinities between *Insight* and the *Phenomenology*."[54] In my view, at least as regards the notions of the concept and the virtually unconditioned, it is a question of semantics. Lonergan notes that what Hegel understands by concept he is apt to interpret quite differently (*CWL* 3:447). There is more to this rather innocent remark than what first meets the eye. Lonergan interprets Hegel in such a way that what Hegel is said to espouse and what he actually espouses become indistinguishable from what Lonergan takes the concept to be. Instead of understanding Hegel's position about the concept as an affirmation that knowing the other depends on the knowing self, Lonergan interprets this as stamping out the other, the factual, reached through judgment. Does this not force Hegel into a paradigm in which concepts are judged as merely conceptual? The content of a second-level operation, which Lonergan takes Hegel's *Begriff* to be, can only be incomplete without a third-level grasping of its fulfilled conditions. Thus, "restricting" reality to the level of the concept fails to put us into contact with what is other than ourselves. It is no wonder, then, that Lonergan sees Hegel as advocating, finally, something of an incarceration of the self and the other in a self-enclosed, even if infinitely expanding, world of concepts. This is the case even though Lonergan is greatly appreciative of Hegel's attack on empiricism and his notion of *Aufhebung*.

Nilson is right when he argues that the only thing Hegel destroys is precisely that which Lonergan also wants to destroy, "that view of knowing which sees objects as existing independently of the process of knowing."[55] The issue for Lonergan, though, which Nilson incidentally does catch, is that knowing is not a matter of conceiving, whether it is conceiving the necessary relations between concepts or being "aware" of the concepts that constitute our understanding of knowing. Rather, knowing involves grasping the conditions of something and whether those conditions are met in experience, specific or general. The aim is to disentangle the subject from the concept, securely identifying the former with the preconceptual. The result is that both knower and known are preserved in their irreducibility, notwithstanding that Lonergan would be the first to admit that it is through concepts that we come to knowledge of both. I am not so sure, however, that attacking Hegel's system as conceptualistic, oblivious to the virtually unconditioned, adequately targets the problem or pinpoints what really distinguishes Lonergan from Hegel. Expanding on Nilson's argument, we may state that if the proper target of Lonergan's criticism is not what Hegel diagnoses as self-consciousness (*Selbstbewußtsein*), particularly in the opposing modes of Stoicism and Skepticism, the former retreating from the actual world, the latter extinguishing world and self with literally "unhappy" results (*unglückliches Bewußtsein*); if the proper target is not self-consciousness, Hegel's negative comment on it strongly suggests, to put it in the language of Lonergan, that he affirms the factual, even though he does not speak of it in terms of grasping the virtually unconditioned.

> Hegel's analysis of the "unhappy consciousness" and of him who wishes to be a world unto himself shows that the loss of the world of facts existing independently of the self is at the same time the loss of the self. For the self is known and actualized through its relations with the world and with the other selves with whom it lives. The destruction of the self without a world can be regarded as an Hegelian argument for the world of fact.[56]

That the concept in Hegel determines the structure of reality is indisputable. Not even the most ardent realist readings of Hegel can change this. But it is, quite simply, a mistake to extrapolate from Hegel's *absolute* idealism the reduction of "reality" to the concept, whether we are talking about the insightful subject or the insightful insight. We have seen already that by the claim he is issuing an attack on empiricist understandings of the subject-object relation. What I have not mentioned is that Hegel is also attacking idealist assumptions about the source of the world's ideality, namely, the objects and events we experience (in Lonergan's specific sense), that source being the human mind and its forms. Hegel distances himself from this form of idealism, labeling it "subjective." (Incidentally, Plato's version of it he thinks superior to that of Bishop Berkeley and Kant.) Lonergan's negative assessment of Hegel seems to involve a mixture of the latter's thought with contemporary versions characteristic of European idealism.[57]

In arguing for the centrality of the concept, Hegel is not denying that there are operations of consciousness. What he is arguing for is a simultaneity, an "equiprimordiality," between the concept and the various operations of consciousness, although he does not use these terms or enumerate the operations as precisely as Lonergan does. On more than one occasion Lonergan himself has admitted to the integral nature of the relationship. After his first

1958 Halifax lecture on "Self-Appropriation and Insight," when confronted by a questioner about the questionability of getting behind the concept to the insight, or rather the one having the insight, Lonergan openly states that there is a sense in which one cannot do this (*CWL* 5:271). He goes on to add, of course, that there is a sense in which one can, noting the "complicated" nature of the delineation. This ties in with what he says about abstraction in Hegel's sense, how in our thinking we are implicated not only in the framework of concepts we think, but also in the implicit framework of those enabling us to think them. "[T]here is no eliminating an element of abstraction" in our formulation of ideals, which in Lonergan's philosophy happens to be self-appropriation.[58] And so we might interpret the sense in which one cannot "get behind" the concept as an affirmation of the unity of mind and its contents. In direct opposition to what he perceived to be the subjectivisms of his day, Hegel understood this unity to be one grounded in the rational structure of what is other than the self. The idea (*Idee*) as the self-determining and self-differentiating whole is this other.[59] The sense in which one can get to the preconceptual we ought to view as an affirmation, not of Hegel's idealism, to be sure, but of the differentiable unity of mind and its contents. The unity in this instance is one grounded in the rational structure of the self detectable only by the self. Hegel emphasizes the unity and thus as a result the Logic in and through which it develops; Lonergan emphasizes the difference discerned in and through cognitional self-reflection, a difference he believes that cannot be reduced to the Logic. This is where the real difference lies. Thinking it a matter of who places their chips where, on insight or concept, is a misdiagnosis beset with interpretational oddities.

We see this element coming to the fore in Lonergan's later works as he writes more explicitly about method, even though the "conceptualist" accusation remains constant. Hegel's efforts are seen in the context of one replacing a static view of logic with a logic of movement. Lonergan more or less states that while this may have been an advance in an age constrained by a logical principle, it does not serve one like our own constrained by an empirical principle, "that there always is required some empirical element in any judgment of fact or of possibility or probability" (*PRP*:126). Since I have already treated the contentious claim that Hegel ignores or cannot deal with the factual—that he is ill-equipped to handle nonsystematic matters of fact Nilson is willing to grant[60]—I want to look at this element of the logical as the more feasible of Lonergan's proposals. It appears in an article in which he launches his programmatic for contemporary philosophy of religion. As an element of the formal component of his thinking, however, it also applies to, in that it is operative in, his philosophy of God.[61]

Lonergan would rather leave logic in its traditional role of determining the coherence and weakness of systems. More particularly, he would confine its relevance to single stages in the process of developing thought, assigning to method the guiding role of leading thought from a less satisfactory stage to one that is more satisfactory. "In brief, the relevance of logic is at the instant, when things are still" (*PRP*:128). Not even the more dynamic notion of Hegel, it is implied, can change this function of logic, this endeavor of dealing with what comes to rest in the concept. Out of this emerges a structure whose relations and conclusions are thought necessary dictated by the logic of movement itself. Elizabeth A. Morelli provides a convenient summary in her commentary on the article in question in terms Lonergan himself would use.

> [W]hat makes Hegel's "method" ultimately inadequate for Lonergan is that it remains under the domination of certain logical ideals, while Lonergan's approach is "under the constraint of an empirical principle"... Rather than the progressive and inexorable interplay of determinate, conceptual contents, Lonergan's philosophy of religion offers avenues of inquiry based on foundational methodology. In short, Hegel's approach is logical rather than methodical insofar as it is conceptualist rather than heuristic.[62]

In light of what has been said about Hegel and the concept, it might be more prudent to replace Lonergan's "conceptualist" with "logicist" since the issue centers on two distinct methodological approaches and not on specific questions of the progressions of conscious operations.[63] But as with all labels, this one too doubtless suffers many inadequacies. In any case, Lonergan, through an independent phenomenology of mind, believes he has pushed past the structure Hegel views as primary. As a result he has thwarted the necessitarianism that flows from it. In Lonergan's scheme of things there is no inner, self-developing necessity guaranteeing viewpoints that emerge, which in turn create the conditions for those yet to emerge; there is only a meeting of questioning minds and the events demanding their attention or soliciting their interest. Hegel comes to his conclusion because he underscores the content of thinking subjects rather than their performance. What counts is the result of questioning rather than the process of questioning itself. That process, we have seen, Lonergan objectifies in terms of a four-tiered structure of cognitional operations intending being. Like Emerich Coreth, Lonergan argues that the question is the basic mode of that structure's functioning. Unlike Coreth, Lonergan argues that the subjective pole, not the objective (being), is what is basic in the process of questioning.[64] While the formulation of this process involves an element of abstraction, from which one may infer a logic of movement, its functioning is conceptually implicit still as well as prelogical. Speaking of it in emancipatory language Lonergan states:

There is an escape from the abstraction insofar as I turn to the sources that are functionally operative in my inquiries, my investigations, my attempts to formulate. And insofar as the subject himself is a concrete being, in the measure that he has self-appropriation, in the measure that he has moved in on the basis as it operates, whence the ideals get expressed, he perhaps has a starting point towards meeting it. (*CWL* 5:298)

The Existential Aspect of Self-Appropriation

Besides being an answer to a problem that has a technical aspect, self-appropriation is also an answer to a problem that has an existential aspect. It is one thing to grasp in oneself the general structure of experience that is oneself through a performance-sensitive exercise; it is another to overcome the personal obstacles that keep getting in one's way. We came across this earlier in the medians gravitating toward what is epistemically viable in extremist positions. The existential concerns hinged on gradations of disillusionment that knowledge delivers what we think it does and on gradations of leeriness that would keep our doubts about what knowledge can deliver in check. Each disposition, however coolly displayed, involves a level of personal investment wrought by a complex interplay of personal (not always "conscious") and interpersonal conflicts. Professors trying to break new ground while maintaining their credibility as researchers are aware of the tug of this conflict. Students, too, are aware of it as they perpetuate arguments for positions they themselves are unsure about as they seek the approval of professors and fellow students. The adjustments to make in the event that one is in error make the task of affirming something terribly difficult. Contrary to what many think, discovery is not a painless affair. In fact, it causes a considerable amount of discomfort.

Self-appropriation, the breakthrough to the subject as subject, is beset by analogous adversities. A "dark struggle" with the flight from understanding, filled with "the half-lights and detours" in a slow development, was Lonergan's experience (*CWL* 3:9). It is not all that uncommon. Part of the problem consists in desiring an end, which as anticipated is unknown, in the horizon of that desiring. Speaking to the issue of self-appropriation Lonergan states, "We already have our ideals of what knowledge is, and we want to do self-appropriation according to the ideal that is already operative in us—not merely in terms of the spontaneous, natural ideal, but in terms of some explicit ideal" (*CWL* 5:17). Now it is true that the precondition of an as-yet-unknown is the horizon in which one sets out to know it, hence, Hans-Georg Gadamer's giving the notion of "prejudice" a positive meaning.[65] But what initially is an inescapable horizon, and its sometimes necessary prejudices, can preclude questions from even arising. Thus, one can insure that an unknown stays unknown. For every demonstration of the positive function of horizons, there exists a demonstration of the negative as well. This, in essence, is the complaint Jürgen Habermas levels against Gadamer, and one Lonergan could also be seen raising.[66] The term Lonergan uses is "bias," preconscious ("dramatic"), individual, group, and general. Each is said to contribute to our native disposition to avoid that which would disturb our psychic equilibrium and the pragmatic demands of our situation, individual and social. The problem is that our psychic equilibrium may be delusional and our situation too self-serving and intellectually stifling to reverse the aberrations of its own making. The prognosis of an aberrant world view creating the principles for its own reversal is not very promising (*CWL* 3:249).

Because Lonergan offers a cognitive therapy his discussion centers on the operation he deems central to cognition: insight. Thus, his discussion of bias is of a side to cognition that hampers its emergence, which is to hamper the "complete free play to intelligent inquiry" (*CWL* 3:246). And although his discussion does not exclude the average individual, its principal target is the person or group in whom the desire to know exercises considerable influence. Contrary to common persons going about their daily routines unreflectively, these individuals reflect on the structures in which they find themselves, either nurturing them or forging new ones. In other words, they actively participate in the world shaped by the insights of economists, novelists, journalists, scientists, philosophers, and theologians, and may themselves be the subjects of these and other professions. That world is the world of "common sense," which directly affects each one of us and none of us can completely control. This is not a comment on the mental abilities, resourcefulness, or influence of workaday people. It is merely an observation of the subtle forms of bias that shape the experience of the intended audience of *Insight*. The following is a simple test to determine whether one is part of that audience. If one finds oneself reading and understanding the arguments put forward in books like *Insight*, it is safe to conclude that one is part of that audience. If the one concluding this happens to be a secretary, an assembly line worker, an executive, he or she can pride him- or herself on being one of those rare statistics where the general rule does not apply.

The lines in so-called real life are not clearly drawn. "There are as many brands of common sense as there are villagers" (*CAMe*:204). The horizon of an individual or group admits of several distinctions. And yet there are those visionaries who, because of their influence and/or genius, carve out for the rest of us ways according to which we comport ourselves in the world. Lonergan recognizes, having written a number of things on the topic, that bias is not simply a question of the intellect and that its proper domain is of a moral, social, political, religious, economic, technological order.[67] He does, however, hold the unpopular view that the intellect, conscious experience in the intellectual pattern, exercises considerably more influence on our being in the world than we literally care to think. What we think is inherited and although a good deal of that inheritance is beneficial to our self-development and that of society, it is commingled with enough oversight and bias to make that development less than developmental.

One way to reverse the effects of this is to engage one's ideals with those of others that seem more agreeable than one's own. The downside in a best-case scenario is to miss the issues that are particular to oneself as they are replaced, eclipsed, or colored by the ideals of someone else. Not that one can rid oneself of biases once for all. The objective here is not complete emancipation. But it does complicate matters when one has to discover the biases in the viewpoints one appropriates when one has incompletely negotiated the biases in oneself.

Lonergan's approach in *Insight* is to get readers not simply to think about themselves; it is not simply to think through their emotions or thoughts or to correct their blind spots. He does not hold out much hope for this kind of introspective analysis.[68] Rather, he gets us to think about ourselves by thinking about the concepts put forward by mathematicians, scientists, philosophers, and theologians. This keeps the exercise from degenerating into a form of subjectivism, providing a touchstone other than oneself that leads back to oneself. And it leads back to oneself, not in the sense that it provides a route by which one may appropriate what concepts happen to communicate about selfhood. Lonergan's sense is that the exercise occasions a means by which one can revert to the operations in oneself that make such communications intelligible to one. Any bias that gets in the way of this realization has to be dealt with on a personal level. One is not simply disputing a proposed structure, but a structure evidenced by and in the dispute itself, in oneself. Two things are involved here: (1) bias and (2) the performance of the operational structure hampered (not obliterated) by bias. Both can be identified in general terms and it is in that sense that they are transcultural. Yet their workings are specific to one's context and experience, which makes the appropriation of (2) and the negotiation of (1) entirely personal. *Insight* offers signposts as to the general structure of these things. It is up to one to engage one's ready-made ideals of what they are and how they supposedly function or ought to function. "[S]elf-appropriation is something you do yourself" (*CWL* 5:19). Because this poses "terrific problems" in areas of inquiry like epistemology Lonergan feels that people are prone to skirt the issue by denying the legitimacy of such pursuits or that there is even a problem. That is something one finally has to decide for oneself.

In this chapter, we have scrutinized the philosophical underpinnings of Lonergan's concept of experience, which he would say pertains to the act of knowing. We have seen that it involves more than the sensate qualities that seem to preoccupy today's philosophers of consciousness. Moreover, experience (general) is patterned differently. The experience, understanding, and judging that produces works of art has a distinctly different momentum from that which produces theories of art. One can be instinctively at home in one without having the capacity or concern to cultivate a sense for the other. Lonergan offers self-appropriation as the means by which one can discover this general structure of experience in oneself, relative to one's life-experience and interests.

Our discussion of the technical aspect of self-appropriation further elucidated Lonergan's concept vis-à-vis that of other paramount figures who have aided him in his own formulation of conscious experience and how we might appropriate its general structure. Despite the challenges posed by the equiprimordial constitution of conscious acts and their contents, Lonergan is persuaded that one can distinguish between the two as they occur. "[T]here is a factor or element or component over and above its content, and . . . this factor is what differentiates cognitional acts from unconscious occurrences" (*CWL* 3:346). What may be serving as an obstruction to the experience is the bias of some logic, the ramifications of which extend far beyond logic or the inability to perceive this and other distinctions—hence, the need to address the existential aspect of self-appropriation. For Lonergan, only self-appropriation can finally relax the logic of such claims and the numerous biases that infiltrate our conscious lives uninterruptedly.

Chapter Three

Religious Experience, Reflection, and Philosophy of God

In chapter 1, we encountered a tension in Lonergan that would finally give way to a reorientation in his thinking about religious experience. The orientation is one regarding the fundamental role in philosophical questions about the existence of God. I developed the suggestion that the modernist crisis in Roman Catholicism is probably that which contributed to his late treatment of the topic. He does treat religious experience in his early writings, but his self-criticism about the underlying "objectivism" of his philosophy of God (i.e., his proof in chapter 19 of *Insight*) suggests that he was thinking about the notion differently at least as early as 1972. Casual reference was made to this in the first chapter, in my comparison of *Insight* and *Philosophy of God, and Theology* with certain aspects of question 2, article 3 of the *Summa*. Noted, too, was the different function of belief in special transcendent knowledge compared to that presupposed in general transcendent knowledge. The ruminations in chapter 2 have laid a basis for a more precise evaluation of this distinction, that is, what it is that distinguishes Lonergan's early treatment of religious experience from that which emerged around the 1970s.

RELIGIOUS EXPERIENCE IN PRE-*INSIGHT* LITERATURE

"One might claim that *Insight* leaves room for moral and religious conversion, but one is less likely to assert that the room is very well furnished" (*PGT*:12). Rephrasing this in line with our own concerns, Lonergan's pre-*Method* thinking leaves room for religious experience, treats certain aspects of it even, but one is less likely to assert that it reveals a concern for religious experience qua religious experience. Lonergan's early treatment of the notion is dominated by his discovery that "intellect is intelligence" (*CWL* 5:19) and that its primary function is to unearth the intelligible in the world and human experience. For him, even the nonsystemizable is intelligible, although its intelligibility is of a different kind from that conceived in classical investigation.[1] There are grounds for continuing to account for this as the intellectualist period in Lonergan's career, provided that we recognize that the affective is not excluded from it.[2] The point is one of emphasis and orientation based on what is perceived to be a need in matters of (theological) inquiry. Unwarranted, then, both by the data and a sound process of reasoning, is the move to divide his career into early and late periods, where in the former he is viewed as closed off to the affective and in the latter, wanting to rectify this, as undercutting the intellectual. The intellectual is as present in Lonergan's later work as is the point of view of the omniscient narrator in a novel. While it may not be as pronounced, it is nevertheless there, exercising considerable influence over the way things unfold.

Various distinctions proposed in an article Lonergan published in the journal *Gregorianum* in 1954, "Theology and Understanding," shed light on the preceding. *Insight* had been completed by this time, in which a basis had been laid for his discussion of the "two types of knowing" and "the patterns of human experience" in the article (*CWL* 4:127). The context of the passage below is the relation of speculative theology to the teaching authority of the church and "ordinary religious experience" or, as he also puts it, "religious feeling."

> Knowledge is involved not only in defining compunction but also in feeling it, not only in discoursing upon the Blessed Trinity but also in pleasing it. Still, these two types of knowledge are quite distinct, and the methodological problem is to define the precise nature of each, the advantages and limitations of each, and above all the principles and rules that govern transpositions from one to the other.... Just as the equations of thermodynamics make no one feel warmer or cooler and, much less, evoke the sentiments associated with the drowsy heat of the summer sun or with the refreshing coolness of evening breezes, so also speculative theology is not immediately relevant to the stimulation of religious feeling. But unless this fact is acknowledged explicitly and systematically, there arises a constant pressure in favor of theological tendencies that mistakenly reinforce the light of faith and intelligence with the warmth of less austere modes of thought. Morever, such tendencies, pushed to the limit, give rise to the intense and attractive but narrow theologies

that would puff up to the dimension of the whole some part or aspect of Catholic tradition or Catholic experience; and by a natural reaction such exaggerations lead traditional thinkers to denigrate all scientific concern with the experiential modes of thinking in living. (*CWL* 4:127–8).

This adequately captures Lonergan's understanding of what he took to be a paramount deficiency in modernist-type thinking. It makes a good case for the importance of experience in reflection. Its argument is vitiated, however, when it ignores the significance of theoretical knowledge against which it posits its own experiential knowing. An early respect for intelligence, fostered by an eleven yearlong study of the notions of grace and *verbum* in Aquinas, impressed upon Lonergan the need for preserving both. Writing *Insight* gave him the opportunity to delineate their "advantages and limitations"—that is, the dynamics of their relation—in greater detail. Chapter 2 provides an overview of the elements involved in the relation of knowledge to experience, with some thought given to differently patterned experiences. Now we will concentrate on the relation with the concept of religiously patterned experience in view. We will also be tracking in what way Lonergan's thinking on the subject would change in the 1970s, consequently giving rise to a different "philosophy of" than his earlier philosophy of God.

The editors of the *Collected Works* volume, in which the quotation cited above appears, append the following important remark to the last phrase in the passage, ". . . scientific concern with the experiential modes of thinking in living":

> [T]his phrase shows the three aspects we need to keep in mind for an adequate view of Lonergan—there is the experiential aspect of living which he shares with the human race, there are experiential modes of thinking, in which some have gifts denied to others (Lonergan was not a poet), and there is the pondering of these modes proper to one in the intellectual pattern of thinking (here we find Lonergan's favorite role). (*CWL* 4:281, n. m)

As stated earlier, Lonergan does not substitute his "favorite role" for that of another in his later career, although the vigor with which he assumed it appears to have waned.[3] The purpose of one operating in this function is to procure an explanatory understanding of the data of sense and consciousness, the objective and subjective fields of conscious experience. Knowing that an object will fall if I release it and understanding why that happens is a simple example of this disposition often associated with the scientific endeavor. It involves moving beyond descriptions, say, of a free fall in relation to an observer, to explanations as to the "nature of" that occurrence. Although the canons of empirical method require that one's explanations satisfy the determinations of observation, one does so by prescinding from strictly observed data.

> When Galileo made his measurements, he came up with a series of measurements of distance with corresponding measurements of time, and he found a similarity in the law relating the distance and the time.... Distance and time are related to one another by a certain proportion. When the distance is 1, the time is 1; when the distance is 2, the time is 4; and so on: $s = t^2$. What turns out to be common to all cases of the free fall is the relation $s = gt^2/2$. If one prescinds from interferences, this relation is found in every instance, and the similarity exists in the relation of the aspects of the free fall. In other words, all the relations to us of a free fall are forgotten. You forget about what happens when something freely falling hits you, or what you would lose if you dropped your watch or your glasses. Just as in the case of the circle we related the equality of the radii and the appearance of roundness, so here we are relating distance and time. By a rather complex dealing with distance and time, we arrive at something that is similar in every case of a free fall. That step by means of which we arrive, through measurement, at the relations of things to one another is the fundamental step in the whole of the development of science from Galileo to the present day.[4]

Although explanation functions differently in the human sciences, parallels are to be found there as well. We see this, for instance, in philosophy and theology (granted that juxtaposing the terms theology and science is a slippery affair) where a technical language is employed to explain what common usage assumes, overlooks, or shows evidence of indifference toward. Not even a philosophy emphasizing ordinary language can avoid speaking about ordinary language technically.[5] It may not communicate what we assume is the profundity or "life relationality" of that language, but it does bring a needed precision to it. In certain cases technical language may even contribute to the profundity of ordinary language.

The "experiential mode of thinking in living," which Lonergan makes passing reference to in "Theology and Understanding," is religiously patterned. In this article, however, he is not even pondering this mode "proper to one in the intellectual pattern." He simply presupposes it. Lonergan's concern is, as the title openly states, theology and understanding. Theology, more particularly, speculative theology, according to Lonergan, is not religious experience or spirituality, but an understanding of it. It presupposes what

Christians would call the experience of grace in its reflection upon what is held in faith (i.e., the truths of revelation). In the article Lonergan is contesting the thesis of Johannes Beumer who "inclines to the opinion that Aquinas does not represent a pure gain in the forward march of Catholic thought on the nature of theology from Clement of Alexandria to the Vatican Council."[6] Beumer's misgivings about Aquinas are supported, he feels, by the predilection of Thomists who restrict themselves to the science of faith (*Glaubenswissenschaft*) or the method of theology at the expense of the understanding of the truths of faith (*Glaubensverständnis*). The latter assigns to method its end and goal. On the flawed view, which Beumer views as stemming from Aquinas, the science of faith proceeds from revealed truths, shown to be free of inner contradiction by *Glaubensverständnis*, to newly deduced truths outside the realm of faith. He argues that the proper role of deduction in theology (i.e., in *Glaubenswissenschaft*) is a fuller understanding of what is held already in faith. Moreover, that understanding is to be a positive apprehension of the *intelligentia mysteriorum* and not simply a demonstration of the way in which deduced truths apart from faith are compatible with those held negatively or defensively in understanding.

Lonergan's dissatisfaction centers on Beumer's attribution of this very real problem to Aquinas. Aquinas's theology, Lonergan argues, is neither the understanding of faith nor the science of faith, conceived in typical Thomist or "Beumerian" fashion. "The subject of [Aquinas's] theology is not a set of propositions; it is not even a set of truths; it is reality. *Deus*," *ipsum esse*, "*est subiectum huius scientiae*."[7] His description of theology as a science deducing conclusions from the articles of faith must be interpreted in the light of what he does rather than what he seems to be saying.[8] Lonergan detects in Aquinas's theological practice a development of Aristotle's distinction between causes of knowing (*causa cognoscendi*) and being (*causa essendi*). The former regards what is prior in relation to us (*prior quoad nos*), which in theology involves moving from the sources of faith, revelation, and concluding to what is revealable on that basis. In Trinitarian theory, for example, this consists in moving from scripturally based dogmatic affirmations about the consubstantiality of persons in the Godhead to conclusions about their internal relations and processions. It is a manner of conduct Lonergan identifies as proper to one operating in the way of discovery (*ordo inventionis*), which he also refers to as the analytic way. The *causa essendi* regards what is prior to us in itself (*prior quoad se*), which is always the case with God about whom we cannot have any positive knowledge—only analogical. This involves moving from the conclusions of the way of discovery "to a systematic presentation of the truths that have been revealed" (*CWL* 4:121). Here we get the movement Beumer wants and rightly sees as missing in Thomists—yet wrongly associates with Aquinas: the move toward a positive understanding of the truths of faith and not just a negative or defensive demonstration of their compatibility with other truths. It is the way in which Aquinas proceeds in both *Summae*, the way of learning (*ordo doctrinae*),[9] which Lonergan also refers to as the synthetic way. In the *Contra Gentiles*, for example, he proceeds from extra-revelational premises, invoking Scripture to confirm and illustrate his conclusions. In the *Summa Theologiae*, which unlike the *Contra Gentiles* in which both ways are used, everything is set out in the synthetic way.[10] When treating of God, for example, he does not begin by asking questions about the Trinity. Rather, Aquinas begins by working out a notion of God grounded in questions about God's existence, simplicity, perfection, goodness, immutability, and so forth. Instead of discussing whether the Son proceeds from the Father, he discusses whether there are processions in God and in what sense we can speak of such processions. Next he moves on to the clarification of the divine subsistent relations, on the basis of which he advances to an (explanatory) understanding of the distinctiveness of the consubstantial persons (*CWL* 4:122).

In his as yet unpublished manuscript "On Supernatural Being" (1946–1947),[11] Lonergan describes the *ordo inventionis* as a sound pedagogy for children, seeing as it proceeds analytically and "children only learn from many repeated examples" (*OSB*:1). The *ordo disciplinae*, on the other hand, requires a more developed mind that can grasp the essence of a matter with fewer examples. "[T]he synthetic way is far preferable, wherein the memory is not overburdened and the task of learning is rendered effortless with the joy of understanding" (*OSB*:2). Understanding is the operative term here, both for getting at what Aquinas is up to in his theology and what Lonergan's early—and, to a certain extent, late[12]—attitude is toward religious experience. Aquinas wants an understanding of what is given in faith, not just any understanding deduced from Scripture or the Fathers but an illumination of the truths of faith by reason. The stated purpose is to procure an intelligent grasp of what is given, what is accepted as already true, rather than defend or add to its veridicality. Since the understanding of the mysteries is imperfect, argues Lonergan, it is incapable of doing more. Conversely, however, it must not be made out to do less, which Lonergan sees as one of the main dangers of positions like Beumer's. They run the risk of encouraging "merely enthusiastic nebulosity."[13] That is the fear echoed earlier in our initial quotation from this article, and it is a point he makes frequently, even in indirect comments about the task of theology, as in the following from his course notes on understanding and method: "Theology is not all the more theological the more assiduously it ponders revelation—that is rather the role of faith—but the more clearly it evinces an understanding of what has been revealed" (*UM*:10). To render it in the terms above, the former consists in a combination of the experiential aspect of living with the experiential mode of thinking, both typically identified as "religious." We might think here of the whole gamut of experiences and reflections covered by William James in his classic study *The Varieties of Religious Experience* (1902). Certain forms of theology may also qualify as experiential modes of thinking, depending on the extent to which they are descriptive or communicative rather than explanatory in character.[14] Religious scripture might also be included in this category, although as scripture it is revered as surpassing in excellence or "inspiration" mere experientially religious modes of thought. Theology as evincing an understanding of what has been revealed obviously relates to the pondering of these modes proper to one in the intellectual pattern. The way Aquinas exhibits and in certain sense initiates this pattern in theology is what "Theology and Understanding" is about. Religious experience is treated as ancillary to establishing the significance of scientific (read: explanatory) theological reflection. The importance of both is assumed. However, theological reflection is stressed not only because Lonergan perceives a widespread oversight about how it functions, but also because such oversight has led to misunderstanding and, as a result, to an overestimation of what religious thinking can deliver epistemically.

"Finality, Love, Marriage" (1943) is an earlier piece, published originally in the journal *Theological Studies*, in which Lonergan does treat certain aspects of religious experience more extensively and explicitly. People familiar with *Method in Theology* are automatically made aware of this if only for the appearance of the term "love" in the title.[15] And yet, as the editors note, not even in *Method* does Lonergan provide "the extended analysis he undertakes here" (*CWL* 4:261, n. h), which is why many are now coming to appreciate the presence of this element in his pre-*Method* works.

The mode in which he operates is the same, as the topic that interests us comes into sharper focus. He prefaces his ruminations, for instance, by stating that his will be a "brusque occupation of strategic theoretical points on finality, on love, and on marriage" (*CWL* 4:18). Noting that vertical finality has always been acknowledged, he adds that "its ground and nature have hardly been studied" (*CWL* 4:21). More significant in light of what was previously said is Lonergan's remarks about J. C. Ford's discussion of marriage. He describes Ford's contribution as "more positive and doctrinal than analytic and explanatory; and if the former approach is more important to us as Catholics, it is the latter that is more relevant to the solution of problems."[16] Needless to say, the methodological route Lonergan takes in the article is the *ordo disciplinae*. The understanding imparted is one of the Christian view of marriage based on a systematization of conclusions that are coincident with revelational sources.[17] The editors describe it as a mini-*Summa*, "a theology of creation in its outline of nature, civilization, and grace; a theology of history in its analysis of human process; a theology of culture and religion in its study of life, the good life, and eternal life; and finally, in the context of all this, a theology of marriage" (*CWL* 4:259).

The term 'religious experience' or 'feeling' doesn't appear in the article. It is an exposition of love from a Christian, specifically Roman Catholic standpoint. The notion of vertical finality, which I will explain momentarily, is developed and drawn upon for a systematization of what he sees as love's stratal instantiations. As in "Theology and Understanding," one is not going to find here Lonergan examining religious experience as present-day philosophers of religion might, as a datum of experience many claim demonstrates, independently of rational proofs, the existence of God non-revelationally. Actually, the thought never crosses Lonergan's mind in this or any of his writings. What is presented is something of an intellectual odyssey about the way in which love, in its various aspects in world process, ascends toward the beatific vision (*visio Dei*), namely, immediate or intuitive knowledge of the divine essence reserved for the blessed in heaven. While one might wish Lonergan elaborated on the notion of the beatific vision as, say, the ultimate religious experience—irrespective that it is recognized as a "knowledge"— what we find him doing instead is taking the notion for granted. That is, he uses it as a limit belief that sets parameters to his argument. Moreover, his argument is not about how mystical or "peak experiences" foreshadow the ultimate experience. Rather it is about the common experience of marriage and its religious significance, which is rarely thought to be on a par with peak experiences. What Lonergan is after, then, is an explanation of the institution of marriage, which is motivated and brought to perfection by the Spirit of Love God has sent into our hearts.[18] To this extent he is preoccupied with "religious experience," a very tangible aspect of it anyway.

The explanatory tool is vertical finality. It is a notion Lonergan develops more fully in *Insight* in terms of emergent probability, less burdened by the Aristotelian categories of this article. Still, essential elements of emergent probability are in "Finality, Love, Marriage," which assumes the explicit treatment in *Insight* of a world order that is dynamic and constantly evolving. Vertical finality may, as Lonergan says, be "of the very idea of our hierarchic universe" but, as he also says, such a universe is not to be conceived as "an aggregate of isolated objects hierarchically arranged on isolated levels, but a dynamic whole in which . . . one level of being or activity subserves another."[19] In other words, the universe envisioned is not the one held up until the Enlightenment, that the universe is constituted by a hierarchy of beings whose every possible form has been actualized, permanent and divinely ordained. We get this, too, in Lonergan's distinction between vertical finality and its horizontal and absolute counterparts. "Straightforward metaphysics suffices for a knowledge of absolute and of horizontal finality: the former results from the idea of an absolute good; the latter results from the theorem of essence as principle of limitation. But vertical finality seems to operate through the fertility of concrete plurality" (*CWL* 4:21). We came across the idea of the concrete in chapter 2 in the guise of "the factual," which Lonergan elevates to the level of a principle separating historical consciousness from classical consciousness given to logic: "that there always is required some empirical element in any judgment of fact or possibility or probability" (*PRP*:126). While classical laws and metaphysical principles aid in the apprehension of the abstract per se, they are inadequate for getting hold of the concrete *per accidens,* as the emergence of modern science amply shows.

Vertical finality like absolute finality, in Lonergan, is to God. It differs from absolute finality in that it is a contingent-sublimating upthrust from lower to higher horizontal ends, where by "contingent" I mean all aspects of development that need not be so. For example, in his discussion of the concept of love Lonergan notes how a coincidental manifold of dispositions[20] often decides the level of ascent from nature to the beatific vision. Not even in a truncated ascent is the end germane to that level even reached. Friendship may transcend strictly appetitive ends, but if it is egoist, then a desired end of friendship has been hedged: mutual self-love. Absolute finality, on the other hand, is "hypothetically necessary" (*CWL* 4:22). It is the logical inference of which vertical finality, as Lonergan expounds it, is the scientifically and historically sensitive explanation. Thus, Aquinas is commended for explicitating that which is logically and ontologically prior in Aristotle's ethical theory. The tendency toward an absolute good, luring us beyond the extremes of egoism and altruism (*CWL* 4:25), is implied though missing from Aristotle's theory. As is usually the case in Lonergan, it is a complementary relation of integral though different tendencies. The article's emphasis, however, shows that what is currently needed is a development of vertical finality upon which modern science has thrown much light (*CWL* 4:21).

A Necessary Diversion:
The Nature-Grace Distinction

The discussion of vertical finality in "Finality, Love, Marriage" is traced against the background of the familiar nature-grace distinction. Without explicit reference to it in this article, Lonergan rejects the view of a "pure nature" apart from grace propounded by Michael Baius (1513–1589) and Cornelis Jansenius (1585–1638) in their efforts to secure the gratuitousness of grace. The view was influential right up until the end of World War II, when it came under severe criticism by the so-called *nouvelle théologie*. While Lonergan's position seems to have been forged independently of this postwar movement, his denunciation of a double-decker universe, one with and one without grace, is definitely parallel to it.[21]

We do not speak of the supernatural as opposed to nature but rather as compared with it. "Supernatural" supposes a world order in which some beings excel others in perfection; it denotes an order or level that is higher or the highest; it does not at all deny to that higher or highest order the objective intelligibility, coherence, proportion and harmony that we customarily indicate by the words "nature" and "natural." But it does deny to that lower order or level the perfection proper to the higher, the very perfection that causes the higher to be truly higher. (*OSB*:9)

It is a question of proportions, not oppositions. What is natural to God is not natural to human beings; it is supernatural relative to what is natural to human and other beings. Stated otherwise, that which is natural to God is proportionate to the divine substance. The divine substance transcends that which is proportionate to human and other substances. Anything that transcends the natural proportions of one level or order of being is supernatural, whereas what is divinely supernatural is judged as being absolutely the case.

Thus, the three levels of being Lonergan posits, nature, reason, and grace (not simply nature and grace), "come from and return to God" (*CWL* 4:30). They constitute an undivided reality grounded in and oriented to God. This anticipates what Hans Küng says several years later, that "[t]here is . . . *no two-level reality*, consisting of a 'natural' substructure of truths of pure reason and a 'supernatural' superstructure of truths of pure faith; justifiable distinctions between nature and grace, reason and faith, philosophy and theology, must therefore be seen and made within the one, undivided reality."[22] Lonergan is not as emphatic as Küng, however, that "a 'pure nature,' not oriented to the vision of God, *does not exist*." That is because Lonergan believes that such a pure nature, a world order without grace, is a concrete possibility. In other words, no internal contradiction exists in the view that the God who wills this universe could will another in which there is no grace (*CWL* 4:90). If the option were not available to God, then God would have to give grace, which binds God from withholding grace. Notice that the question is not whether a pure nature apart from God exists. God is a presupposition of the distinction. Hence, although Lonergan is not as emphatic as Küng, his conclusion is virtually the same. The notion of a pure nature is a theological abstraction. In Küng's words, "It can at best be abstracted theologically from the existing order of grace (as an unclear and imprecise auxiliary theological construct)."[23]

While Lonergan does not appear to be as convinced as Küng that the notion is obscure, his choice of terms suggests that he, too, deems it something of an auxiliary construct at best. Lonergan's term for it is "marginal theorem," the suppositions of which he traces to post-Reformation scholasticism, not Aquinas (*CWL* 4:90). Why he considers it marginal centers on the nature of what it establishes, that is, a truth merely on a par with the truth of any other possibility. The upshot is that a truth established along these lines is not a truth worth elevating to the status of a central doctrine, as has been done with the pure-nature theorem. J. Michael Stebbins interprets this to mean that the theorem for Lonergan represents an abstract possibility, not a concrete one based on attentiveness to world order.

> Theologians with an essentialist bent try to deduce the possibility from the gratuity of grace or from divine liberality; to their way of thinking, then, the notion of a state of pure nature is a necessary consequence of central doctrines, and thus could itself be considered something of a central doctrine. But their approach betrays a lack of attention to the concrete order of things, a failure to recognize that the "*ordo universi* [order of the universe] is a whole and that the whole is prior to its parts" [*CWL* 4:89]. For Lonergan, however, the idea of a world-order without grace is a possibility only in the negative sense that it involves no internal contradiction.... Within this perspective the possibility of a state of pure nature is a theorem, not a doctrine; as such it may prove to have its uses for theological speculation; but it can have no more than a marginal significance.[24]

Of more consequence to Lonergan than the argument itself are the conceptual presuppositions of the mind arguing for its doctrinal centrality. The force of an argument varies in accordance with the presuppositions held. If one holds that finite natures are prior to world orders; if one holds that there are two parts to a world order—a necessary part, which meets the exigencies of finite natures dealt with by the natural light of reason (philosophy), and a contingent part, which may or may not be present since it regards the acceptance of that which completely transcends natural exigencies, dealt with by revelation-based, deductive reasoning (theology)—then the argument will carry the doctrinal weight it evidently carries with many. But if the world order is, as Lonergan holds, prior to finite natures; if the world order is an intelligible unity of lower natures that are intrinsically subordinate to higher ones, "as appears in chemical composition and in biological evolution" (*CWL* 4:85), then such presuppositions, which exclude the possibility of a natural tendency toward what is supernatural, need to be radically relativized.

The presuppositions are those of "static essentialism." Its corollary Lonergan takes to be "closed conceptualism," which is similar to static essentialism though differing from it in terms of emphasis. Where essentialists posit ideas of finite natures in the mind of God, "pretty much as the animals were in Noah's ark" (*CWL* 4:85), conceptualists posit ideas in the human mind acquired through "an unconscious process of abstraction over which we have no control; our conscious activity is limited to seeing which terms are conjoined by an objective, necessary nexus and thence to deducing the implications that are there to be deduced" (4:86). Lonergan is as sympathetic to conceptualism as he is to essentialism. His argument against both is grounded in his understanding of understanding outlined above in chapter 2. One does not arrive at an understanding of the structure of our world order through deductions of what is possible in an abstract world order. Nor does one arrive at an understanding of it through the interconnection of terms unconsciously abstracted from sensible data. If our concern is with this world order, then it is to this world order that our attention ought to be riveted. What this reveals, according to Lonergan, is a hierarchy of intrinsically constituted relations so that what is "higher" is not simply higher, nor "lower" simply lower, as posited in static essentialism. Stebbins articulates this in terms of a plurality of lower beings and activities entering into the constitution of higher beings and activities. It is something that holds for the relation of nature to grace as well.[25] What is being denied, in other words, are two world orders that run parallel to, being utterly distinct from, one another. For Lonergan, "the natural and the supernatural orders are intrinsically related parts of a single cosmic order."[26] Its apprehension, still constantly evolving of course, has come about through a development of understanding in fields such as science, philosophy, and theology. Careful consideration of their distinct methodologies will show that terms, from which principles and conclusions do result (as conceptualists rightly stipulate), are the expressions of acts of understanding. They are garnered, not through an unconscious process of abstraction (as conceptualists wrongly stipulate) but through a conscious and intelligent raising of questions. Hence, conclusions reached via insight into an actually existing world order ought to take precedence over those deduced from a so-called necessary nexus of terms about world order. The latter pertains to what may possibly be, but because such possibility is of an abstract nature, disengaged from what may possibly be concretely, Lonergan views the science from which it stems to be "closed to real development" (*CWL* 4:85).

The Ascendency of Love

According to Lonergan, love has three aspects that are operative on the levels of nature, reason, and grace: a passive aspect, inasmuch as love is a response to motive good, an immanent aspect, inasmuch as love is a perfection of the lover, and an active aspect, inasmuch as love produces further instances of the good (*CWL* 4:30). A fourth aspect is said to be superimposed upon the three on the level of reason, inasmuch as love rationally examines and selects its motives, wills its immanent perfection, and freely effects further instances of the good. Lonergan names it accordingly the aspect of reflection and freedom. Not surprisingly, the agency of God is recognized in all three aspects of love (passive, immanent, and active). The three levels of nature, reason, and grace, said to be realized in one subject, are attributed to God as their source and end. On the level of nature, appetitive love, God is described as implanting in nature love's proper mode of response and orientation. On the level of reason, God governs the self-governance of human beings through an antecedent spontaneity to goodness and truth. This antecedent spontaneity is "sublated" (to use a term Lonergan would himself later use to describe a similar process) on the level of grace, the highest level, "so that the truth through which God rules man's autonomy is the truth God reveals beyond reason's reach, and the good which is motive is the divine goodness that is motive of infused charity."[27] This sublational reinforcement of love's aspects, reason to nature, grace to reason, is what gives marriage a finality in the Christian context of meaning, a love whose consummation is had only in the vision of God.

The ascent is one in which Lonergan, following Aquinas, grounds in the notion of alterity implied in the Deuteronomic call to "love the Lord your God with all your heart, and with all your soul, and with all your might" (Deut 6:5; Matt 22:37 and pars.). The call is, among other things, to love God, the infinite other, above everything, including the no-thing of the self (*Summa Theologiae* 2–2.26.3). The test of such love is one's selfless love of (finite) others (1 John 4:12). Its initial stage, on the level of sensitive spontaneity (nature), Lonergan portrays as an aesthetically alluring tendency away from self to what is delightful in the other. Couched in this essentially erotic move is a deep-seated need for company. This takes one beyond "the merely organistic tendencies of nature to the rational level of friendship with its enduring basis in the excellence of a good person" (*CWL* 4:32). Marriage, as the unitive effect of the immanent aspect of this ascendancy, is isolated as the full expression of the reciprocating love of friendship with its basis in nature and reason. On the level of grace, this union represents a sacrament of the union of Christ and the church. "It is the efficacious sacrament of the realization of another self in Christ" (4:33). Regarding such matters Aristotle's *Ethics* contributes little or nothing, not simply because it predates Christian revelation, but because its goal is humanistic. Although a desired, horizontal end of reason and a partial fulfilment of nature's upthrust, by itself it is a truncation of vertical finality. For the true end of friendship—a good, Aristotle estimates, that surpasses all other goods, making life desirable—must have its basis in more than what is pleasurable or acceptable, that is, if it is not to be merely subjective.[28]

Through active love is to be attained the goal leading from eros to company, company to friendship, friendship to marriage, marriage to mystic union. It is active love looking back to the motive good, actuating its own immanent perfection and moving it toward its ultimate end and consummation (*CWL* 4:34). The contingency element touched upon earlier is fully present so that, negatively understood, the contemplation, expression, possession, or achievement of a motive good—the four ways in which active love looks back to the motive good—may be the actuation of a false self-love. Lonergan attributes this to loving a wrong motive that decreases the loveableness in the lover with the result that the union of friendship is debased. Thus, the intensity of the loveableness that would otherwise develop on the level of grace is thwarted. Of course the reverse is also possible. In fact, it the more desirable of the two scenarios, in which case the self actuating itself on the level of grace would be another self "most intensively apprehended, loved, realized" (*CWL* 4:37). Lonergan is clear that the movement from one level to the next, in its different aspects, represents "an intensification of the higher by the lower, a stability resulting not from mere absence of tension but from positive harmony between different levels, and, most dynamic, the integration by which the lower in its expansion involves a development in the higher" (*CWL* 4:36). We see from this, then, that horizontal and vertical ends are viewed as complementary and part of the same system, with the intensification of the levels being a bottom-up process.[29]

The article is on marriage, and Lonergan's primary purpose is to provide an explanation of (Christian) marriage in the context of the general hierarchy in nature, reason, and grace. He assigns letters to each of the components he outlines, which he later casts into structurally diagrammatic forms. I have taken the liberty to collapse the two diagrams provided in the published article, filling out their structure with content (see fig. 3.1). I have also followed Lonergan's own hand drawn rendering photoreproduced by the editors of the *Collected Works* (*CWL* 3:xi). As it turns out, Lonergan's diagram far more adequately represents the three-dimensional object he had in mind than that which appears in the published article.

On the level of nature, then, he pinpoints fecundity and sex as spontaneous tendencies of nature. Their actuation is, looking at it in the context of marriage, in the organistic union of husband and wife. The horizontal end of this union is said to be adult offspring, which parallels the natural end of the emergence and maintenance of life. The vertical upthrust of this level, in other words, that which is nascent in nature but beyond purely natural spontaneity, is the desire for human friendship that is ratified by the marriage contract. These are described as secondary, not primary, elements on the level of reason because they are conditioned integrations of organistic union within the life of reason; they are not necessarily part of the life of knowledge and virtue (*CWL* 4:41). The same applies to the elements of the vertical upthrust from reason to grace. They too are secondary in that they are integrations of

Religious Experience, Reflection, and Philosophy of God 75

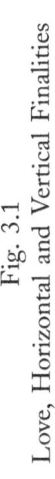

Fig. 3.1
Love, Horizontal and Vertical Finalities

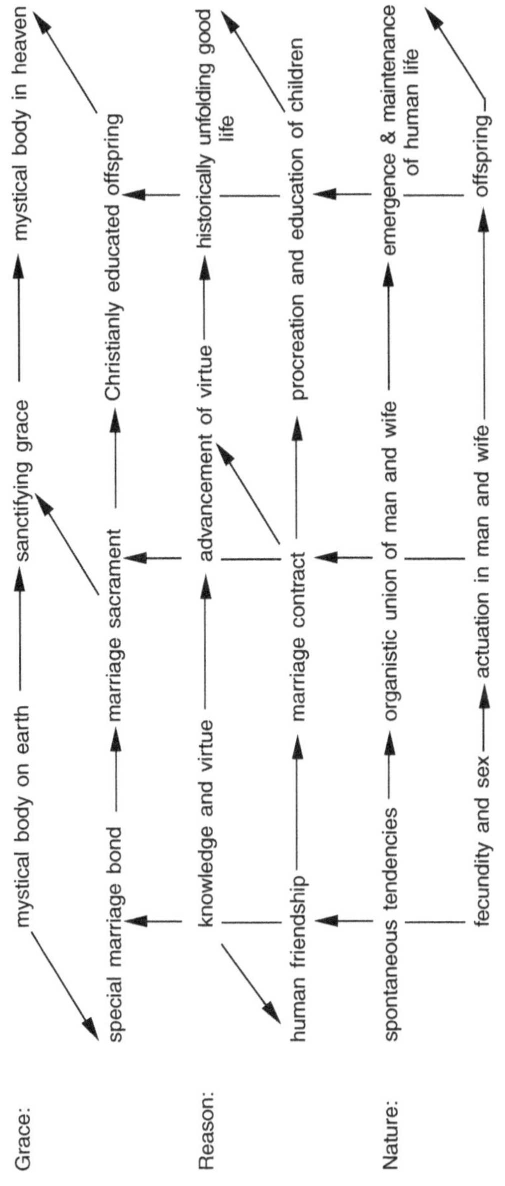

a rational spontaneity on the level of grace, not constituent parts of that level. "[A]s reason redirects the finality of fecundity to offspring into a finality to educated offspring for the sake of the historical process, so grace effects a further redirection to Christianly educated offspring that the mystical body of Christ may grow to full stature" (*CWL* 4:42). The sacramental marriage bond is an element of sanctifying grace through which a couple cooperates with God in working out, interpersonally, their salvation in fear and trembling (Phil 2:12b). The concrete realization of the good on the level of reason consists in bringing into and leaving behind in the world others like the presumably well-to-do couple. On the level of grace it consists, of course, in that and more. As representatives and instruments of Christ and his church, Christian couples are said to generate children "to have them regenerated in Christ, and they educate them for their eternal role in the triumphant mystical body in heaven" (*CWL* 4:47). Thus, the levels and aspects are distinct (not isolated) parts of a composite whole, integral to one another in the movement from one good or end to the next.

Immediately we perceive the problems such a model poses to the post-nuclear family, even one in good standing with the church. Take the least "scandalous" case of a heterosexual couple deciding to refrain from having children for medical, economic, or complicated personal reasons. Obviously, though they feel unflinchingly committed to the mission of their church—even if it happens to be "the" church—they will be said to be impeding the intrinsic natural, rational, and supernatural intention of their union. For the couple unable to have offspring, for the couple who have no choice in the matter, their union will be deemed valuable and indissoluble. It is a union judged to be potentially full of meaning.[30] For the couple deciding not to have children, exerting something of a closedness to fertility, the ruling does not seem as agreeable.[31] Problems are compounded, of course, depending on where one's convictions lie, as the cases become allegedly more scandalous. Understandings of the nature of the sexual act are further scrutinized, repeated more elaborately, as the issues of divorce and sexual orientation elicit the responses of a church as diverse and complex as the different responses it offers.

Lonergan is forthright about the "assimilative capacity" of his explanation of vertical finality with traditional doctrine. He is equally forthright about the fact that his account lacks the detail one normally finds in a treatise. To what extent the content of his view would change had he prepared a treatise is an open question. It is a fairly conservative assumption to doubt that it would change much. One should not expect too much in the way of radical change, especially as regards church doctrine, from one whose motto is to augment and perfect the old by means of the new (*vetera novis augere et perficere*).[32] The change offered, in other words, is less an issue of replacement through disputation than expansion through understanding. I am tempted to compare Lonergan to Erasmus of Rotterdam (1469–1536) whose stance against the revolutionary theological reforms of Luther was decisive if mixed at times. Given the different contexts and concerns, comparing the two is like comparing apples and oranges. Erasmus is far more critical of ecclesiastical hierarchy than Lonergan tends to be, which we may attribute to different visions of theology. Hence, one will find Erasmus agreeing with Luther on certain biblically based practices more than Lonergan would care to. But similarities do obtain in the same broad sense that apples and oranges are parts of the same genus. There is the obvious similarity of coolheadedness in the intellectual pursuit of truth. This doubtless underlies the more significant element of their attitude toward reform. Thus, when it comes down to deciding between the pope and revolutionary teachings about the way things ostensibly should be Erasmus and Lonergan prefer, in the end, to stick to the pope.[33] Here, at least with regard to my reference to Lonergan, "pope" represents authoritative teaching, which if disputable is to be disputed not for its essence but for the manner in which that essence is held. In "Finality, Love, Marriage" that essence is marriage and the manner in which Lonergan explains it is intended to agree with traditional doctrine. What is aimed at, to put it in the terms that appear at the end of *Insight*, is the significance of the old, what it really is or is about, opening "challenging vistas on what the [new] could be" (*CWL* 3:769). Ambiguity abides, however, about the extent to which these "challenging vistas" are permitted to encroach upon what is old, especially when what is old pertains to sensitive issues such as marriage and sexuality. This touches on issues of theological conviction, a scrutiny of which exceeds the scope of this study.

What connection is there, then, between what Lonergan is doing in this article and religious experience? In what way is the object of his concern properly described as religious? Obviously what Lonergan is doing is not particularly religious, although what motivates him may be of a religious nature. The distinction is one we have come across before, except this time it pertains to being in a religious pattern and reflecting on it in the rhythms of another pattern. Although the reflecting is equally a "being in," it is of a different sort. Andrew Louth, for instance, has drawn our attention to the fact that prayer is not simply a movement of the heart, but the response of the heart to some revelatory content. "We do not just feel something in prayer, we know something."[34] He has no argument from Lonergan there. Lonergan would, however, doubtless want to qualify the statement. The type of knowing that goes on in prayer is qualitatively distinct from that which goes on in a thinking about prayer. When one does the latter one is not absorbed in prayer; when one does the former one is not concerned with grasping the inner principles of prayer or what one is doing while praying. The distinction is not simply between emotive prayer and intelligently reflective prayer. Both are found in wondrously lavish form in Augustine's *Confessions* and Saint Anselm's *Proslogion*. It is a distinction grounded in the emergence of systematic understanding, the rules of whose language differs considerably from that assumed, say, in the *Confessions* or in any other writings of Augustine.[35] The form of language differs for one, triggering in us the spontaneous awareness of what we are encountering, a prayer or a discourse on prayer. The usage of terms differs as well, even if an overlap in terminology exists. More will be said about this in the next section.

But marriage is not prayer. Its connection to religious experience is not as obvious and so the inclusion of an article here in which marriage is the central feature may be viewed as questionable. What Lonergan understands as marriage on the level of grace may be cautiously identified with religious experience. However, it more closely corresponds to what Abraham Maslow takes to be "the high-plateau experience." David M. Wulff describes it as "a kind of precipitate of a life of insight and deep experience," consisting of "a continuing sense of illumination, of perceiving the miraculous in ordinary things. It is far more serene than the peak experience, though perhaps no less deep or touching."[36] Marriage is such an experience. In "Finality, Love, Marriage" Lonergan assumes that marriage is revelational. Elsewhere, in reference to interpersonal reality, he explicitly states that it can be religious.[37] Arguments to substantiate the claim are not really necessary here. Suffice it to say that it is the religious who experience marriage as religious. Some peak experience (though this is rare) or high-plateau experience, inspired or informed through religious teaching or whatnot, usually supports the judgment. More important for us is how this contributes to an understanding of the distinction between the philosophy of God in *Insight* and Lonergan's revamping of it in *Philosophy of God, and Theology*.

My assumption has been that Lonergan's early treatment of religious experience is pivotal for determining this. For instance, there is nothing in "Theology and Understanding" or "Finality, Love, Marriage" to suggest that prior to *Philosophy of God, and Theology* Lonergan thought religious experience contributed to the sort of thinking that philosophizes about God. Nor is this the case in the significant article "The Natural Desire to See God" (1949). Elements from this article were mentioned earlier in connection with the nature-grace distinction. "Finality, Love, Marriage" took precedence because of obvious parallels in it with religious experience as Lonergan conceives it. "The Natural Desire to See God" is basically an affirmation of what is said in chapter 1 about general and special transcendent knowledge in *Insight*, of which the former is a precursor. Knowing the existence of God (*an Deus sit*) is proportionate to the questioning that arises naturally. Proper knowledge of God (*quid sit Deus*), although arising naturally, exceeds the proportions natural to knowing that God is. Attaining proper knowledge of

God, then, is not simply natural but supernatural relative to the knowing whose attainment is acquired naturally. Unlike the knowing natural to knowing that God is, the knowing that knows what God is (not) presupposes revelation and faith. Also, its questioning subjects require grace to know what they know, although what they know is known by analogy and not directly, not "properly," as in the beatific vision. Both knowings, then, are not completely satisfying, although one is "higher" than the other (in the above sense). For knowledge of the object attained is proportionate to the finite intellect and not to the infinite object forever anticipated and hence not properly attained in the inquiry. Still, Lonergan writes, "we cannot do better" (*CWL* 4:83). Theologians may, on the basis of a systematization of what is given in faith, affirm an incomplete yet adequate, analogical knowledge whose proper fulfilment is as yet unattainable. Philosophers, on the other hand, must rest content with "the paradox that the desire to understand arises naturally, that its object is the transcendental, *ens*, and that the proper fulfilment that naturally is attainable is restricted to the proportionate object of finite intellect" (4:84). Of course, this is the theologian's conclusion, but it is one that includes what the philosopher may know.

As in "Finality, Love, Marriage" religious experience in "The Natural Desire to See God" is taken for granted as an aspect of consciousness proper to the level of grace and thinking that is theological. Lonergan is all but silent at this early stage as to its correlation with the level of reason and what it can attain about knowledge of God. This is brought out even more clearly in a segment of *Verbum* that appears to contradict our thesis. Lonergan is discussing mystical experience in the thought of Aquinas. He has just finished demonstrating how one can detect in Aquinas, in spite of heavy metaphysical terminology, an acute sense of presence to self in rational consciousness. He then goes on to add that "from that presence to oneself it is not too easy a step to the presence of God to oneself. Philosophic thought can achieve it through the theorem . . . of divine ubiquity. But it takes a rather marvelous grasp of that metaphysical theorem for constant actual knowledge and love of God to result" (*CWL* 2:102). A tenuous but feasible case could be made that the presence of cryptic terms here (i.e., "can" and "rather marvelous grasp") suggests that attaining such knowledge solely philosophically is, in Lonergan's estimation of Aquinas's meaning, rather unlikely, even if possible. One could also make the case that by "constant actual knowledge" of God Lonergan understands Aquinas to mean knowledge of the "whatness" of God, which transcends knowledge attainable on the level of reason, namely, God's "thatness." True, by "constant actual knowledge" Aquinas intends a "simple and continuous intuition" attained indeterminately. This suggests that such knowledge is dissimilar from knowledge on the levels of reason (thatness) and grace (whatness). But the beatific vision also is regarded as intuitive *knowledge* anticipated, held in and by faith, on the level of grace, not reason.

In any case, all this is circumstantial. The direct response of Lonergan to the question whether one must enter into the domain of religious experience to attain an awareness of one's spiritual self prolonged, he adds, into an awareness of God is more convincing. "That prolongation," he states, "does not seem to be a datum within the range of ordinary introspection" (*CWL* 2:103). Put in terms relevant to our discussion, religious experience does not enter into the type of reflection that treats of the thatness of God, which occurs on the level of reason. If it is present on the level of reason, it is not to make clearer the insight necessary to grasp God's existence. Nor is such experience of a degree that can know, in faith or explanatory reflection, what God is. We glean this from what Lonergan says about Aquinas in connection with the concept of *imago Dei*. The issue is to what extent mystical experience is relevant to this concept. The long and short of it is basically that it is not terribly relevant. He does acknowledge a "possible relevance," even that Aquinas was deeply influenced by mysticism. But he also mentions that "indubitable references to mystical experience in [Aquinas's] discussions of the *imago* at best are few and, at least by later Theresan standards, anything but explicit" (2:104). He emphasizes Aquinas's interest as a theologian in nature, not mysticism, pointing out as well how his theory of Trinitarian processions in its basic analogy is psychological, not mystical. As, in Lonergan's opinion, religious experience is, for the most part, inconsequential to the concept of the *imago* in Aquinas, so too we may infer religious experience in the early Lonergan is immaterial to knowledge of God's thatness. The point is that mystical or religious experience is relevant to knowledge proportionate to the level on which or pattern according to which it operates. For Lonergan that level is grace. If actual knowledge of God, supported by something like religious experience (whether of the peak or high-plateau variety) appears to be present on the level of reason, it is not knowledge attained solely through or on the level of reason. Rather, such knowledge is attained on the level of grace augmenting or sublating reason.

RELIGIOUS EXPERIENCE IN PRE-*METHOD* LITERATURE

We have taken a fairly long route to demonstrate what is merely asserted in chapter 1. In Lonergan's pre-*Insight* works and, as we are about to see, in *Insight* itself religious experience is regarded as an important item in the movement of life. Its relevance for reflection, however, is hardly dwelt on, if not minimized. When it is referred to as relevant for reflection it is seen to be so, to take up the distinctions of "Finality, Love, Marriage," on the level of grace. Religious experience is pertinent perhaps to theology. And even then Lonergan feels it necessary to distinguish between theology and the content it receives via religious consciousness. "Theology is not all the more theological the more assiduously it ponders revelation—that is rather the role of faith—but the more clearly it evinces an understanding of what has been revealed" (*UM*:10). As the date of this quotation suggests (1959), Lonergan thought this way well after *Insight* and arguably well after *Method* as well. What changes in his thinking about religious experience is not its distinction from theology or philosophical theology, but its bearing on these endeavors.

Looking further now into the data of *Insight*, we notice that the issue of religious experience is more or less grappled with in connection with myth and mystery. Mythic consciousness can be seen as a reference to religiously patterned experience, which hasn't made its way to a properly reflective, explanatory understanding of itself and its content. As such it lacks the self-knowledge explicit metaphysics brings to term. Obviously the meaning is pejorative, which Lonergan is quite frank about: "In deference to the commonly pejorative meaning attached to the name 'myth,' we have identified mythic consciousness with the counterpositions, with the inability or refusal to go beyond description to explanation" (*CWL* 3:567). Context is everything though, as he indicated once to one of the concept's critics (*BeLR*:309). If one turns, for instance, to his treatment of mythic consciousness under the rubric "symbolic mode of thinking" in "Understanding and Method"—only two years after the publication of *Insight* and before any substantial critique of the concept—one can discern a completely different feel in his handling of the concept. In *Insight* the ideal is to decisively transcend mythic consciousness through explicit metaphysics, which entails "a more conscious use of mystery purified of myth" (*CWL* 3:572). In "Understanding and Method" mythic consciousness qua symbolic mode of thinking consists in "all that is fundamental and true and proper to human knowing" (*UM*:44). But because such qualities are found in the symbolic mode implicitly, the risk of mixing truth with error is greater than is otherwise the case with self-critical explicit knowledge. I say this because of the common aversion to the self-critical mediation of that which is held, rightly or wrongly, to be true. In *Insight* the negative aspect comes to the fore on account of its aim to assist readers to attain an ever-greater knowledge of themselves. In "Understanding and Method" the aim is not nearly as personal and genetic and so the solemnity of judgment that comes with the call for decision is virtually absent in it. That the context is method in theology, not self-appropriation, is another contributing factor.[38]

Still, the context Lonergan advises his critics about is not about the difference between *Insight* and "Understanding and Method." That is just an observation regarding the fluidity of his treatment of topics from one work to another. As with most careful thinkers, caution needs to be exercised when trying to determine the opinion of Lonergan on a matter. What he asserts dogmatically in one context may be mitigated in another. The essence of what is said may suffer little change, which is usually the case. When compared to another context, however, the difference can strike one as a conversion of opinion, when really it is only a question of asserting the same thing differently. This tends to change the tone or the implication of his original assertion.

The context is *Insight*, which Lonergan believes, as he tells critics of his proof, makes room for what appears to be missing from it. What is missing from it, according to David M. Rasmussen, is a notion of myth as symbolic narrative. Lonergan's treatment of myth betrays vestiges of a now virtually obsolete scientism; it aims to eliminate the plurivocity of mythic meaning in favor of more acceptable, univocal ones. The model of meaning he presupposes has its origin in nineteenth- and early-twentieth-century distinctions between the primitive and scientific mentality. The latter is thought to be the ideal of intentional consciousness as it seeks to discard the false presumptions of prelogical mentality, superimposing its own, presumably superior, models of meaning. This approach has since fallen into disrepute, at least in religious studies, with the advent of eminent scholars such as Rudolf Otto (1869–1937), Mircea Eliade (1907–1986), and Claude Lévi-Strauss (1908–). Their discovery of the complexity of myth and symbol has come to mean "that mythic-symbolic language, for example, is as complex as any other type of language, as well as the discovery of the category of the sacred."[39] This has evolved a whole new set of presuppositions in the approach to mythic-symbolic phenomena that avoids the pitfalls of hermeneutic eliminativism in the scientism Lonergan ostensibly mirrors in his treatment of myth. Rasmussen looks to the phenomenology of Paul Ricoeur as a means of rectifying the "hermeneutic of demystification" implied in *Insight*. He is open to there being within Lonergan's system the possibility of a correlation of the hermeneutic of demystification with what he calls the "hermeneutic of recollection"; Ricoeur has contributed substantially to our understanding of the latter. However, as it now stands, *Insight* is implicitly reductionistic with regard to myth. The way in which it reduces myth to an explanatory scheme assumes the scientistic mentality, which has close to zero tolerance for the plurivocity of meanings mythic symbols invite. If Lonergan were less emphatic about the need to move from common sense (mythic consciousness) to theory (metaphysics), if his theory of cognition were less evolutionary, less hierarchically constructed, there would be a greater chance for what is described above to become an actuality.

> [W]hereas *evolutionary categories function well in the field of the natural sciences*, they *function rather poorly in aesthetic fields*. The *symbolic products of cultures*, myths, artistic creations, literature, etc. simply cannot be explained in evolutionary categories, instead they have an integrity of their own. Hence we are left with the question, is the theory of evolution essential to the theory of cognition? I think the

answer must be one which gives a greater status to non-scientific modes of cognition. Evolution should be essential only to those areas where it functions most usefully. The theory of cognition should be universalisable without associated theories of evolution.[40]

In his rejoinder, Lonergan does not seem the least bit disconcerted by the scientistic accusation. For him, what Rasmussen desires is adequately accounted for in his appreciation of symbolic narrative as mystery. "I did not contend that as metaphysics advances, mysteries recede, and so I see no difficulty in finding room in my position for symbolic consciousness or for a hermeneutic of recollection" (*BeLR*:309). Mythic consciousness is countered by Lonergan for reasons not unlike those predisposing him negatively toward the uncritical scientist who imagines his world of quarks and atomic particles to be what reality really looks like (*CWL* 3:278, 562). As to mythic consciousness in particular, the tendency, being overwhelmed by the power and beauty of what is experienced and described, is to attribute an explanatory significance to that which requires explanation. What more "explanation" does one need than that provided by the Bible, a religious leader, a political figure, or the witness of one's own heart? One may devise elaborate views that basically safeguard the underlying premise of such a question. But in doing so one moves beyond, perhaps leaving completely behind or expanding, the horizon in which great patronage is expressed toward these sources of meaning. Rasmussen accepts this point, as the word *re*collection in the phrase "hermeneutic of recollection" suggests. He is unpersuaded, however, that explicit metaphysics offers anything more than reduction. If reduction is how one prefers to see it, Lonergan would claim that what he intends in the desired shift from mythic consciousness to explicit metaphysics is the *diminution* of faulty assumptions, not what finally is unanswerable and hence multivalently expressible. He is not as concerned with the content or expressions of mythic consciousness as he is with its inadvertence to the boundaries of its particular pattern of experience and what he later calls the "realm of meaning" within which it moves and has its being. Thus, when confident about its ability to gauge particular matters correctly, mythic consciousness goes on to assert that its viewpoint is as universally applicable as it is theoretically viable. But it may also succumb to relativism bewildered by the unmanageable shifting tides of the particular. Whatever the case, in both, according to Lonergan, is the stifling of the horizonal movement that explicit metaphysics brings about. Epistemic overconfidence or despondency may be the source of the problem here. Also, it is not the case that *a* univocal, explanatory-seeking treatment of symbols has to or need be predisposed to eradicate the plurivocity of symbolic meanings. Explanation will be relative to the particular meaning focused on. Moreover, that concentration will only serve "to put more clearly and distinctly the question of transcendent being" inherent in and evoked by the symbol (*CWL* 3:570). As the answers explanation provides increase, so too will the questions.

All of this pertains primarily to the subject and is, finally, what is relevant for our analysis of the "invasion" of religious experience into Lonergan's philosophy of God. Yet a grasp of those elements he assigns to the sphere of variable content relevant to the primary field of mystery and myth is also beneficial to us. The sphere is that of "the ulterior unknown, of the unexplored and strange, of the undefined surplus of significance and momentousness," which Lonergan distinguishes from the sphere of reality "that is domesticated, familiar, common" (*CWL* 3:556). Part and parcel of this sphere is the "paradoxical category" of the known unknown: knowledge of an unknown revealed yet simultaneously concealed in our unanswered questions. Myth and mystery are different responses to, in the orientation of consciousness toward, this known unknown. What they consist in are affect-laden images and names that in their aspects as image, symbol, sign, and mystery are related to the known unknown in different ways.

> The image as image is the sensible content as operative on the sensitive level; it is the image inasmuch as it functions within the psychic syndrome of associations, affects, exclamations, and articulated speech and actions. The image as symbol or as sign is the image as standing in correspondence with the activities or elements on the intellectual level. But as symbol, the image is linked simply with the paradoxical "known unknown." As sign, the image is linked with some interpretation that offers to indicate the import of the image.[41]

Image as mystery captures the element of the image forever dodging our grasp. This is the case even though the field of mystery contracts with each advance in knowledge. Not even the totality of correct judgments, Lonergan concedes, can free human beings from "*the necessity*" of dynamic images that are partly symbols and signs (*CWL* 3:571). That is why he insists that the advance in knowledge represented by explicit metaphysics does not imply any rationalist sublation of mystery *or* myth, but "a displacement of the sensitive representation of spiritual issues" (*CWL* 3:572). Explicit metaphysics draws out of the image, whether in its aspect as image, symbol, or sign, that which is present in it already as mystery. Garrett Barden's observations about the interplay of mystery and myth are helpful:

> [J]ust as myth includes an interpretation that looks in fact to its own demise with the subject's growth, so mystery includes an interpretation that looks to its own completion on the purely theoretic level.

So the mysteries of Christ look to the fruitful understanding of theology and their ultimate completion in the supernatural vision of God. It follows that images which are descriptively similar are, from an explanatory viewpoint, now mysteries and now myths.[42]

We gather a number of things from Barden's comment. First, myth has a purpose that is defeated once exaggerated. As symbolic, it invites thought, as Ricoeur would say. Once that invitation is interpreted as supplying thought or the categories with which to think, then myth includes an interpretation that only seems to look to its own completion with, from the standpoint of intentionality, the subject's decline. Thus, what is "complete" when thought to look to its own demise with the subject's growth becomes something incomplete when thought to look at its own completion as if on the theoretic level. Supposing literary symbolic images like Yahweh, sitting on the circle of the earth, judging the nations to be an explanation of divine providence, or transcendence is not only confused, but it also renders inefficacious the power of such imagery, assuming it is still a carrier of meaning.

A second point gleaned from Barden's comment adds to what was said earlier about mystery being present in myth. Mystery is not appended to myth as though it were something extraneous, as though it came from the superior vantage point of explanation. Imagistically mystery and myth can, as Barden states, be descriptively similar. That it is detected as such *from an explanatory viewpoint* commends my suggestion. What is it, then, that an explanation contributes? Explanation is an explicitation of what is merely present in myth and is in danger of being reduced to mere myth when thought strictly descriptively. Let us think of this along the lines of Mystery^1 and Mystery^2. Mystery^1 is the known unknown felt in the image as image and grasped descriptively through the image as symbol and sign. Few would concede that the former example of a symbolic expression is bereft of mystery. But if one cannot "distinguish accurately between what one knows by experience and what [one] knows inasmuch as [one] understands" (*CWL* 3:565), the lines between mystery and myth become easily blurred. What often happens, evidenced, for example, in fundamentalist groups, is that the vehicle by which understandings of the unknown are expressed—and in that sense known—shrouds the unknown as unknown, which is present in, yet ever-drawing one beyond, the known. This pertains to what is negative in mythic consciousness or symbolic thinking. But it is not a tendency found solely among fundamentalists. So-called critical consciousness shows signs of it, albeit on a more critically conscious level. Jacques Derrida's "messianic" version of thinking religion "within the limits of reason alone" may be seen as a corrective, although many, both philosophers and theologians, have problems with his near-exclusive emphasis on the unknown.[43]

Mystery² is also the known unknown but integrated at a higher level of intellectual activity. Its "apprehension" is based on a self-critical knowledge. For that reason Mystery² is clearly distinguished from the myth that brings it to expression according to the dictates of a knowledge not critically conscious. Two things are involved here: (1) the move to an explanatory viewpoint, and (2) the return to a descriptive one. As with description, explanation contracts the field of mystery. But the field contracted through the symbols and terms of explanation involves a firmer grasp of what myth makes known descriptively. It also involves a more discriminating grasp of what is yet to be known or will forever remain unknown. Guarded against, as an added bonus, as it were, is the unwitting reduction of the field of mystery to that which myth describes. Explanation has limits of its own though. It "does not give man a home" (*CWL* 3:570). By itself, with its set of complex symbols, "cumbrous technical terms," and "bloodless ballet" of categories, explanation is incomplete. Thus, Longeran advises that explanation "must be applied concretely by turning from explanation back to the descriptive world of things for us." This consists in something of a reinvention of images "that release feeling and emotion and flow spontaneously into deeds no less than words." To these images Lonergan appends the term "mysteries," our Mystery², which is a higher integration of mystery, Mystery¹, which is present in but not critically self-consciously utilized in myth.[44] This is what Lonergan means by a *displacement* of the sensitive representation of spiritual issues introduced by the genetically based distinction between myth and mystery.

With *Insight* we begin to see a deeper recognition of the relevance of what can be deemed religious experience for or in systematic reflection. The sentiment still is that explanation is nothing religious or spiritual. However, Lonergan concedes that explanation can deepen the spiritual life of an individual or society as a whole through a more critically conscious utilization of images than afforded by myth. In "Finality, Love, Marriage" we are left with explanation. In *Insight* greater emphasis is placed on the need to return from explanation to the imagistic and the descriptive. The role of "religious experience" also becomes more overt. Still, the contribution of religious experience is thought to be primarily about images and descriptions, not about the concepts understanding thinks. We see this most clearly in chapter 19 of *Insight*. There religious experience, by being ignored, is virtually dismissed as relevant to the proposition: God exists. We already noted the historical accidents prolonging the emphasis announced in and inaugurated by *Philosophy of God, and Theology*. A little more needs to be said about the consciousness aiding and abetting Lonergan's tardy appreciation of religious experience for philosophy of God. But first one more stop needs to be made in the early corpus of Lonergan. The categories of the paper in question will be important for distinctions introduced in chapter 4.

The paper, "Openness and Religious Experience" (1961), is a short one. Lonergan submitted it in absentia to a congress in Italy. The theme for the year (1960) was religious experience. The invitation extended to Lonergan to participate in the congress provided him with another opportunity to develop his thought further on religious consciousness. In "Openness and Religious Experience," Lonergan makes explicit concessions not simply about the fundamental place of religious experience in consciousness. Enough has been made about how one can detect this in even earlier writings. Nor is it simply a concession of what he and many of his contemporaries were exploiting as the fundamentally religious nature of existentialist-type philosophy. He had done this more than a decade earlier in his "Lectures on Existentialism." The relevant concession in the light of what has been discussed is to the fundamental place of religious experience in the reflection that produces explanatory proofs for the existence of God; "explanatory," because that is what the philosophy of God in *Insight* is, a meta-proof. As Quentin Quesnell observes, one of the main purposes of Lonergan's philosophy of God in *Insight* is to spell out the pre-premisses that lie behind all other formally valid proofs.[45] The concession about the fundamental place of religious experience in philosophy of God is simply missing from *Insight*. The placement of chapter 19 in *Insight* is only one indication of this.[46]

This new development is discussed in the paper in terms of the aspect of "openness as gift," which is an effect of divine grace. This aspect is one of three integral to the "philosophy of" proposed in *Insight*, openness as fact and openness as achievement. Openness as fact refers to the pure desire to know, which is the basic orientation delimited in *Insight*'s "philosophy of" in terms of the basic terms and correlations of rational self-consciousness. Openness as achievement has two aspects of its own commonly earmarked by Lonergan with the terms Edmund Husserl introduced into philosophy, *noēsis* or the noetic and *noēma* or the noematic. The former, perceived as the more fundamental of the two, regards the acts of consciousness outlined in chapter 2. It pertains to the subject as subject. The noematic refers to the content of consciousness, its objects, whether subjective or objective. Achievement as regards the subject, the noetic, arises when the stages of one's self-acquisition coincides with the exigencies of the pure desire to know (*CWL* 4:186). This is communicated or objectified in precepts, methods, and criticism. For instance, an otherwise intelligent grasp of who one is according to the unformulated standards of commonsense knowledge is, on this reading, only a partial achievement. For common sense is predisposed to block the questions precipitating insights common sense cannot help but view as irrelevant for life. Achievement as regards the object, the noematic, arises when one is able to formulate a view of one's knowledge and the reality such knowledge attains. Lonergan feels that the lack of openness to revealed truths in philosophies since the Enlightenment is due to inadequate understandings of what is sought in this aspect of openness. What is sought is a fuller understanding of, and hence greater openness toward reality, truth. The real or true is what is given and we do our best to achieve contact with the given through our concepts. Because revelation is not an item of the given in this "choice" sense of the term (the already-out-there-now-real), it is excluded as something less than certain, as unworthy of the worthwhileness of objective knowledge. *Insight* stands in that class of literature in the 1950s written to undermine this widespread overconfidence of philosophical and scientific positivism.

Openness as gift, of course, pertains to a disposition of consciousness open to revealed truths, maintaining, ideally, a continuity with these other aspects of openness. It is different from them in that the horizontal enlargement achieved through its openness builds on and yet transcends that which is naturally achievable, though not always achieved, through the other aspects of openness. It transcends them in both a "limited" and "ultimate" sense. In the limited sense, it transcends them in the horizon where both types of openness are operative and yet lie under what Lonergan calls the "law of decreasing returns": "No one ever believed that the world would be converted by philosophy. In the language at once of scripture and of current philosophy [presumably existentialism], man is fallen" (*CWL* 4:187). There is a need for an openness as gift for there to be an openness to revealed truths, namely, that which is supernaturally given in the actual world. Humans are engaged not only with the enlargement of what is naturally possible to them. Openness as gift also transcends the other types of openness in an ultimate sense, in the sense that there is an ultimate enlargement "beyond the resources of every finite consciousness, where there enters into clear view God as unknown, when the subject knows God face-to-face, knows as he is known. This ultimate enlargement alone approximates to the possibility of openness defined by the pure desire."[47]

"Openness and Religious Experience" documents the first recorded instance of the term "philosophy of religious experience" in Lonergan. Religious experience, openness as gift, is the material component of this form of philosophizing. The event it signals is that of the self entering into a personal relationship with God. The philosophizing itself is the theory of cognition offered in *Insight*, which is the formal component. As we have seen, openness as gift was never excluded from its purview so that it can be said that Lonergan always held it to be fundamental in "man's making of man" (*CWL* 4:187). But that it is no less fundamental "in the reflection on that making that is philosophy *or, indeed, 'philosophy of...*'" (emphasis added) heralds a new development, if not in his belief system, then certainly in his explicit thought.

RELIGIOUS EXPERIENCE: EMERGENCE OF THE EXPANDED VIEWPOINT

Only five years after the Italian conference on religious experience, in February 1965, Lonergan would have his breakthrough to the eight functional specialties of theology. A central place is thus accorded to religious experience in intellectual inquiry. A number of factors contributed to this breakthrough. The years of preparatory work on the question of method in theology following his departure to Rome in 1953—a question to which he would devote an entire course at the Gregorian University in 1961, the year following the conference—was doubtless a contributing factor. His bout with cancer in 1965 should also not be underestimated. It drove the point home in a way that intellectual discovery alone never can. This traumatic episode and the care he would receive because of it—William Mathews names one Sister Florian in particular[48]—lent greater immediacy to what he was starting to see intellectually. Religious experience is more than a conduit yielding the matter upon which intellect reflects. It informs the intellect doing the reflecting whether the issues are of a revelational nature or are proximate to revelation as in philosophy of God. Was all that is implied in the expansion of consciousness that Lonergan saw as accommodating his new-found appreciation of religious experience in natural knowledge of God immediate? I don't wish to give the impression that it was. The fluidity of his terms alone suggests that what he apprehended clearly was taking time to clearly express. Nonetheless, the apprehension was clear enough for him to persistently comment on the level of decision, the level integral to religious experience, while students were rallying to talk with him about the three knowledge-generating levels.[49]

So in what sense, then, does religious experience as a fourth-level reality contribute to naturally attained knowledge of God? Indeed, what is a fourth-level reality? Answering the latter first seems only logical. The little collage of terms provided by Fred E. Crowe from *Method in Theology* on the fourth level merits full quotation (the page references in parenthesis are to *Method*):

> The first listing of the four levels refers to the fourth as the "responsible" level [9]. Later it is called "existential" [35]. Later still, it is the level "of freedom and responsibility, of moral self-transcendence and in that sense of existence, of self-direction and self-control" [121]. It is also the level for the exercise of vertical liberty [40]. Again, it is the level of "authenticity" (or unauthenticity) [35], and "the level on which consciousness becomes conscience" [268]. We are likewise told that "as we mount from level to level, it is a fuller self of which we are aware" [9], that on the fourth level "we emerge as person"

[10], that "a man is his true self inasmuch as he is self-transcending" [357], but there is a self-transcendence that is "only cognitive" [104], and "knowledge alone is not enough" [38] to determine values on the fourth level.[50]

The fourth level is the subject involved, morally, religiously, existentially, in that which is colored by his or her experience, understanding, and judgment. With regard to philosophy of God, which is the first question posed above, it is what lends momentum to questions about this universe possessing an intelligent ground, whether there is evidence for such a ground, and so on. The questions come in a variety of forms but, as far as Lonergan is concerned, they all meet in the question of God. Answering such a question, making explicit its particular *known* unknown, is important primarily to those who find the question meaningful. And those approaching the question solely from the standpoint of what the knowledge-generating levels can give, what about them? Are they not privy to the same conclusion existentially involved subjects are? The question is basically whether natural knowledge of God is attained without moral judgments and existential decisions, the Weltanschauung in which what argument tries to settle is already settled existentially. The question is raised and answered head on by Lonergan in a paper titled "Natural Knowledge of God" (1968). It is the only paper before *Philosophy of God, and Theology* that treats this question explicitly in connection with the level of decision.[51] Lonergan is not as blunt in it as he is in *Philosophy of God, and Theology* about *Insight*'s objectivist treatment of God's existence. The sentiment about the argument's validity, however, is mirrored exactly in it. In fact, one might say that in "Natural Knowledge of God" Lonergan is clearer than he is in his first Saint Michael's lecture about the symmetry of what is genuine in *Insight*'s argument and the experiential component rendering it meaningful.

He has just finished qualifying the sense in which God is understood as "object" in natural knowledge of God. He distinguishes it from an etymological or Kantian meaning where object connotes something sensible and localized over against the perceiving and thinking subject. This meaning has prompted a steady stream of criticisms from diverse philosophies of the nineteenth and twentieth centuries that posit "a not-to-be-objectified inner world of subjects striving for authenticity" against "the objectivist world of impersonal science" (*2C*:123). Lonergan's own meaning is one in which objects are what is intended in questioning. As the object in questioning is promoted through questioning from experience to understanding, understanding to judgment, it becomes more fully and hence more accurately known. However, the object is never completely known, "for our intending always goes beyond present achievement. The greatest achievement, so far from drying up the source of questioning, of intending, only provides a broader base whence ever more questions arise" (*2C*:123–4). This applies a fortiori to the question of God, a complete answer to which is the objective yet ever-elusive object of our questioning. Knowledge of this peculiar object, that it is, does not consist in its attainment, intellectual or existential. The former is impossible. Humans do not enjoy an unrestricted act of understanding, a knowledge of everything about everything. Humans know incrementally through a process of reasoning. An unrestricted act of understanding, for which the line between the known and the to-be-known is nonexistent, puts an end to questioning. Existential attainment of this object is ambiguous. It promotes a peculiar type of knowing, "life-relational" I call it. It excludes or frowns upon, for a number of reasons, treatment of this "object" as an object of knowledge rather than as the unidentifiable mystery toward which we are subjectively oriented. Lonergan believes his qualification accommodates this concern without capitulating to the often associated requirement of rejecting that which is available to us about God through so-called unaided reason as inauthentic, idolatrous even. The feeling, on Lonergan's part, seems to be that what is claimed about the object and the means to it are as important as the concerns leading people to reject what is established and how it is established.

The "what" is minimalist in intention. It is knowledge "from afar," so to speak. As the object of our interminable intending, God, the unrestricted act of understanding, remains interminably unattainable, forever outside, although glimpsed in, every act of understanding. It is not in knowing such an object that provides knowledge of it, that it is. That would be equivalent to knowing what the object knows, putting us on an equal footing with it. Lonergan stands in a tradition that rejects this option. Rather, knowledge that this object is—"is" being that which simultaneously underpins, permeates, and is the objective of the unrestricted desire to know—consists in intending, not this object per se but an understanding of everything about everything. The jump from this unrestricted intension to the existence of the wholly transcendent is not obvious. John O'Donnell's explanation is among the clearest available.

> I cannot describe the transcendent. But from limited acts of understanding I can grasp in a judgment that the condition of possibility for all limited understanding is the intelligible as such. In other words, every virtually unconditioned raises further questions, and the process of questioning would have to continue until the mind reaches an absolute intelligibility which is the ground of all limited intelligibility.... In finite acts of judgment we know finite being. But these acts are only fully intelligible if they are grounded in the infinite reality whom we call God. Our restricted acts of understanding lead us to affirm an unrestricted act of understanding.[52]

The argument's validation is said to be in the "how" of its attainment, that is, by catching oneself in the act of thinking and desiring to know what is thought, whatever the object of the thinking and desiring may be. "It is only by the actual use of our minds that any inquiry and any process of verification can be carried out. Hence, every appeal to verification as a source of validation presupposes a prior and more fundamental appeal to the human mind as a source of validation" (*2C*:126). The force of the argument lies in what subjects may know about themselves, that they are experiencing, understanding, judging, and decision-making beings. This, in turn, equips them to render explicit what Lonergan believes every human being is in possession of implicitly: knowledge of God.[53] The unrestricted act of understanding implied in our restricted acts of understanding is, to recall the phrase of Aquinas and all it implies, what is meant by God, what a naturally held or attainable knowledge of God is fundamentally.

As O'Donnell notes, the argument's definition of God and, I would add, the pattern in which it is reached, is strongly intellectualist.[54] One need not be in love religiously, to use Lonergan's language, to grasp the argument or the definition. His opinion on this does not change, even after *Insight*. What, then, is it that his post-*Insight* judgment contributes to this opinion? The best answer is that it supplies a more holistic understanding of the way in which human beings approach such matters. That is, it varies from person to person and "in the real" world the existential predisposition of people who raise such questions is somehow involved in the attainment of an answer. One may or may not hold that the unrestricted act of understanding is validly inferred from restricted acts of understanding. But who starts or finishes this kind of query without the world of meaning brought to it influencing one's regard or disregard for the conclusion and the particular means to it? Not only does Lonergan capitalize on the fourth level to account for this fact. He also forges the broader concept—and I think more fitting concept given the particular issue in hand—of the differentiations of consciousness, which comes into prominence in his work at this time. Thus, his thoughts in "Natural Knowledge of God" on whether natural knowledge of God is attained with or without moral judgments and existential decisions is immediately preceded by an exposition of the differentiations of consciousness. *Philosophy of God, and Theology* actually begins with a lengthy discussion of the differentiations of consciousness. A differentiation of consciousness is a specialization of some aspect of our experience (general, including now the level of decision) that is initially undifferentiated. "As intellectual, it becomes technical. As moral, it concentrates on moral development. As religious, it heads toward mysticism."[55] In undifferentiated consciousness these aspects are compacted, more global, and so undeveloped or underdeveloped and instinctively acted upon. In so far as some aspect of our experience remains undeveloped consciousness may be differentiated in one way but undifferentiated in another. If one is of a consciousness specializing in technical matters, whether of a moral, religious, or intellectual nature, and yet is not concentrating on moral development or heading toward a consciously explicit mysticism, then that consciousness is intellectually differentiated but morally or religiously undifferentiated. What is not at issue is the moral or religious integrity of the consciousness so defined. The issue is a specialization of consciousness in contrast with one that is unconcerned or dead set against such affairs.

Natural knowledge of God, according to Lonergan, is present in an undifferentiated way in human beings. Saint Paul or John Calvin would describe the universal sense of divinity as an undifferentiated perception that revelation alone properly differentiates. Lonergan does not mean it in this way. For him, the language of revelation issues from undifferentiated consciousness. The form is clearly intelligent. Indeed, if we accept snapshots like Harold Bloom's "J," for instance, an unprecedented sophistication can be discerned in what appears at first crass or childish.[56] But it is still a language "for us" (*quoad nos*). It addresses at once the whole being of the reader or hearer, not demanding a specialized attention to one aspect of what is being addressed in the subject or about the object. The image of God reconciling the world to Godself in a moribund, cross-bound Savior is a powerful symbol. It assails the heart and mind in a way and at a level at which an understanding of it does not. A change ensues once the move to a differentiated apprehension is effected. Not only does the disposition appropriate to an undifferentiated understanding change but the terms by which it is expressed change as well. "[I]f we are not only going to speak about God's grace and man's sinfulness but also we are going to say what precisely we mean by such speaking, then we are going to have to find some third term over and above grace and sin" (*2C*:131).

Natural knowledge of God is like that. It is experiential knowledge at first, acquired from diverse sources, from societal conditioning all the way to, if we are to believe psychoanalysts, the unconscious. Undifferentiated consciousness expresses this knowledge in numerous ways, sometimes clearly and creatively, sometimes incoherently and inconsistently, paying little heed to the technical terms it uses and their systematically acquired meanings. This is not proof for what is held, of course, but a simple observation. What the form of the knowledge is Lonergan does not seem too troubled by. As a theologian and philosopher of God he concentrates on God as understood in Western religious traditions. But as his philosophy of God develops he comes to include knowledge in other traditions as signaling the same deep-seated disposition possessing innumerably different forms. Proof for God in this context functions as a means of (1) understanding at a differentiated level what exists already as undifferentiated, and (2) securing the intellectual integrity of what is held, albeit compactly, at this level as well as a differentiated understanding of it.

The question of whether natural knowledge of God is attained without moral judgments and existential decisions may be seen in this light. As an undifferentiated fact, natural knowledge of God is tied to our moral judgments and existential decisions. As a differentiated explanation, in the form of "proof," it is also tied to our judgments and decisions but remotely. When one asks whether natural knowledge of God corresponds to something independent of us, one invokes a language game whose rules and meaning are considerably different from those one functions with day-to-day. Becoming familiar with the language does involve moral and existential choices, whether one ought to bother with such questions and acquire the know-how to approach them; but actually being involved in the language, comprehending it and that which is claimed via its rules, is a question of understanding and differentiated apprehension. Knowledge of God and a differentiated grasp of it are a natural acquirement. However, Lonergan does see a supernatural hand at work in the naturally attained, intellectually differentiated knowledge of God. Now we come to the part to which all the preceding, in the absence of this element, has been leading.

There are about two senses in which Lonergan in his post-*Insight* work recognizes experience to contribute to arguments for God's existence, his own included. The first is the more overt in relation to religious experience. The second is more generally an experience-related issue, although connotations of what the religious hold are clearly to be seen there as well. Both senses are in "Natural Knowledge of God." The first sense is the one that dominates in Lonergan's later writings. Nonetheless the second is a part of his overall view. It is significant because it, of the two senses, is the one that touches directly upon the proof itself, the product of differentiated consciousness and not just natural knowledge of God.

The first sense, as it is played up in "Natural Knowledge of God," is the way in which proof and natural knowledge of God are contiguous. Relevant for us are the points mentioned earlier about proof being a means of grasping at a differentiated level what exists already at an undifferentiated level. It gives philosophic form to the doctrine of natural knowledge of God, that is, "that God lies within the horizon of man's knowing and doing, that religion represents a fundamental dimension in human living" (*2C*:130). This is what Wolfhart Pannenberg means when he writes of anthropological arguments—among which Lonergan's may be classed (though as a meta-proof)—that "[a]ll that is maintained is that we are referred to an unfathomable reality that transcends us and the world, so that the God of religious tradition is given a secure place in the reality of human self-experience."[57] What is at stake, in other words, is the philosophical respectability of the question that these arguments attempt to answer, however tentatively. Lonergan and like-minded theologians want to ensure that the question of God's existence is not written off as meaningless for secularist society. As Aquinas enlists Aristotle to render systematically explicit what his contemporaries held implicitly, Lonergan does the same with methods of thinking that are part of the common sense of the twentieth century. Sensitivity to context is what this implies, and the context, if polls are at all reliable, continues to be constituted by subjects who find belief in God or the divine valuable and hence worthy of intelligent consideration, even if it is not always held intelligently.

It is not that Lonergan is averse to this understanding of proof in *Insight*. He is silent about it, which he attributes, in *Philosophy of God, and Theology*, more to a limitation in philosophical vision than to anything in the argument itself.[58] The culprit seems to be the scholasticism upon which he was reared and with which he had always had an ambiguous relationship. All that he condemns in chapter 19 of *Insight* is easily identifiable with its particular form of objectivism or logicism. The assumption that appears to capture all of its other assumptions Lonergan puts as follows: "that there is one right culture so that differences in subjectivity are irrelevant."[59] Context is as irrelevant as the horizon, religious or otherwise, that individuals bring to an argument. This is an approach to objectivity that approaches the object "from the outside," where all that is needed to make a case as non-subjective as possible are definitions based on first principles. True, one wants to avoid subjectivity, if by "subjective" one understands the tendency to accept only that which seems true to oneself. But in rightly avoiding this stance, objectivist or logicist thinking complicates the situation by functioning as if demonstrative knowledge were fundamental.

> Proof is never the fundamental thing. Proof always presupposes premises, and it presupposes premises accurately formulated within a horizon. You can never prove a horizon. You arrive at it from a different horizon, by going beyond the previous one, because you have found something that makes the previous horizon illegitimate. (*PGT*:41)

Whether Lonergan ever considered proof to be fundamental I am in no position to answer. Nor do I wish to argue that his practice in the pre-*Method* years, in *Insight* itself, suggests that he did. What alone is clear is that there is an unprecedented *theoretical* sensitivity on Lonergan's part to the religious horizonal aspect of proof, which is left undeveloped in writings before and a little after *Insight*. Proof is only as convincing as the horizon that permits one to grasp what is argued, what is proportionate to an argument's fundamental horizon. Few will be convinced by conclusions such as those found in chapter

19 of *Insight* without shifting from a horizon that is closed to religion to one that is relatively open. This is the "religious" aspect of the argument, if we can call it that. It goes beyond anything that might be intellectually compelling or uncompelling about the argument. Nor will they be "convinced" without shifting, ironically, from a religious horizon, one closed to such pursuits, to one that is more properly intellectual. Different things are being claimed and attained at different levels and in different ways. Collapsing them as though they were about or after the same thing is an oversight symptomatic of undifferentiated consciousness. Hence, Lonergan is dissatisfied with Pascal's distinction between the genuine God of Abraham, Isaac, and Jacob and the false God of the philosophers. Its poignancy lies in the prophetic call to unite both heart and mind, to advise philosophers that the reasoning heart that holds fast to the claims of revelation exceeds in excellence the reasoning mind dominated by first principles. But as a theoretical expression of cognitional reality (natural knowledge of God argued philosophically) it has its limitations. Moreover, few will be convinced by the conclusion if self-appropriation is taken to be a mere concept, as something to be understood rather than experienced.[60] What this requires is a revamping of one's philosophical presuppositions. Indeed, Lonergan sees our philosophical presuppositions as a notable hindrance to what self-appropriation reveals about oneself through a relatively unbiased thinking about thinking. Dispense with assumptions about what it means to perceive, think, and judge, the feeling is, and one will be a lot closer to understanding the notion fundamental to human existence, namely, God and that God is.[61] This is where we see the relevance of the second sense religious understanding and experience contribute to arguments for God's existence in Lonergan.

Concomitant with his philosophical ideas is Lonergan's stance as a theologian. David Burrell capitalizes on this as the reason for Lonergan's disinterest in philosophy of religion as a subject.

> Vocationally, he always saw himself as a theologian: everything he did, including and especially *Insight*, is ordered to understanding the faith we have received. Contextually, that faith is one in whose development reason has long been intimately engaged, and we are part of that development. Philosophy of religion as a distinct discipline, however, seems to flourish in a setting where faith is considered to be given, and philosophy has the role either of preparing people for it (as in a post-Tridentine understanding of *preambula fidei*) or of defending it (as in some conservative Christian milieux).[62]

Burrell makes an interesting point without really making it. Lonergan does not see his proof either as preparatory for or as a defense of faith. It is an explanation of what most people know about, what, as Aquinas would say, everyone means by God (*PGT*:41). This goes hand in hand with what he always held as a Catholic and sympathizer of the views of Aquinas on the symbiosis of the principles of faith and reason. He puts it in provocative terms in the Epilogue of *Insight* as follows:

> The Catholic admits neither the exclusive rationalism of the Enlightenment nor, on the other hand, the various irrationalist tendencies that can be traced from the medieval period through the Reformation to their sharp manifestation in Kierkegaard's reaction to Hegelianism and in contemporary dialectical and existentialist trends. But this twofold negation involves a positive commitment. If one is not to affirm reason at the expense of faith or faith at the expense of reason, one is called upon both to produce a synthesis that unites two orders of truth and to give evidence of a successful symbiosis of two principles of knowledge. Clearly, this positive commitment goes beyond the assertion that irreligious rationalism and irrationalist religiosity are not the contradictories that exclude a third possibility.[63]

Besides affirming that proofs do not establish the view from nowhere, that in order to get somewhere truly, objectively, one must begin from a so-called unprejudiced standpoint, this allows Lonergan to attribute the good fortune of developing such proofs, not to nature but to grace. Grasping that the conditions for the argument of God's existence are fulfilled in the intending of complete intelligibility; seeing this as an explanation of what presumably everyone knows or has a notion of (i.e., God, that God is) is completely natural, proportionate to the knowing of which humans are capable. What, evidently, is not completely natural is that which yields the conditions for such naturally attained knowledge.

> In the present instance men must exist. They must be healthy and enjoy considerable leisure. They must have attained a sufficient differentiation of consciousness to think philosophically. They must have succeeded in avoiding all the pitfalls in which so many great philosophers have become entrapped. They must resist their personal evil tendencies and not be seduced by the bad example of others. Such are just a few very general conditions of someone actually grasping a valid argument for God's existence.

Thus, in a statement containing what some might consider contrary claims he says:

> I do not think that in this life people arrive at natural knowledge of God without God's grace, but what I do not doubt is that the knowledge they so attain is natural. (*2C*:133)

The knowledge, the means for grasping it, at both undifferentiated and differentiated levels, is naturally acquired. The conditions yielding it, allowing it to be naturally acquired, are grounded in grace. Only one who affirms that the cosmic order is a unity of intrinsically related parts, natural and supernatural, can make this claim. As noted earlier, Lonergan held this view early in his career. His later appreciation for decision as a distinct level of consciousness and the concept of the differentiations of consciousness is what contributed to the bringing of general transcendent knowledge in its purview.

A couple of things have been established in this chapter. First, that religious experience or feeling is, from his earliest relevant writings, acknowledged by Lonergan as basic to consciousness and reflection. However, because it is distinct from the differentiation of consciousness that thinks it (its content) religious experience should not be confused with the differentiation that theology and philosophy have come to represent. This sounds simple enough, especially today when one hears a great deal about "language games" and the need for adjusting expectations of what they establish according to the different rules by which they function. However, Lonergan was convinced that the growing popularity of existentialism in Catholic circles—doubtless due to the ubiquitous presence of pallid, existentially alienating scholasticism—was causing many to lose sight of this in the fight against systematic reflection. His concentrated effort in his early writings to restore systematic reflection to its rightful place in theology doubtless explains why Lonergan brackets the influence of religious experience *in* explanation in his early writings. The political reasons outlined in chapter 1 comprise another factor.

The second thing we have established is how Lonergan, in some of his later writings, understands religious experience to influence philosophy of God. Attention to the level of decision played a great role in this development of his thinking. The concept of the differentiations of consciousness was the means by which he would explain the way the two are related. Knowledge of God exists naturally and "religious experience" is the term usually used to describe its manifestation. As undifferentiated, it addresses the whole person, without distinctions. As intellectually differentiated, namely, as explicative and demonstrative knowledge, it is equally natural, although it is a transformed knowledge, addressing specific questions as to the reasonability of that which is given in experience (the desire to know God). I might restate this in terms of the desire to know that which lures us beyond our present horizon. More often than not the differentiated transformation of this knowledge into "proof" is based on religious experience. "One cannot claim that their religion has been based on some philosophy of God. One can easily argue that their religious concern arose out of their religious experience" (*PGT*:55). Whether philosophy of God is driven by religious concern is another question. Lonergan's desire to reclaim it as a genuine practice of systematic theology seems to suggest that he thought it was. Nevertheless, although he always held God to be the condition of possibility and the end of knowledge, he only later came to see how basic religious experience is in that which he thought could be established solely philosophically. There is considerably more overlap between faith and reason in grasping the "whether" of the formally unconditioned than philosophical argumentation alone indicates.

Chapter Four

From Philosophy of God to Philosophy of Religion

The verdict about Lonergan's attitude toward his early philosophy of God has to be mixed. The situation is yet again complex. Whatever may be said about it, it is relatively clear that he never thought his 1970s reorientation rendered superfluous the engaging of the argument and the mind-set in chapter 19 of *Insight*, as suggested by Louis Dupré.[1] It is still valid, in Lonergan's opinion, despite vestiges of a jaded objectivism that does not really affect the argument anyway. If one can dispense with out-there- and in-here-now-real conceptions of what it means to experience, understand, and judge; if one can lay aside abstractions of disparate world orders, a natural and a supernatural one—assuming one is open to there even being a supernatural world order—the argument remains powerful in its suggestion. What it argues, however, is often perceived as effective only to those who accept already what the argument concludes. Describing this as the "push" making the argument more than a mere argument would not be too far-fetched. Besides, theologians and philosophers do not share the same standards of proof. There are the various philosophical presuppositions that Lonergan tallies as hindering an affirmation of the argument's conclusion. There are also the deeper, and for that reason, more effective existential obstacles that predispose one in a certain way toward not only such arguments, but also the whole psychic impulse to accept as meaningful the practice of raising and attempting to answer such questions. "Proof is never the fundamental thing" (*PGT*:41). Is this why Lonergan turns more explicitly to religious experience in his philosophy of religion, loosely so called? It could be, as long as we understand that he turned to it in the knowledge that he could not make any more meaningful adjustments to what he turned from. He doubtless felt that enough ink had been spilled on the topic.

In this chapter, I look at the eventualities that incite the raising of this question, that is, the fact that Lonergan began to address other issues in his philosophy of God. We can say that his philosophy of religion, technically so called, was a direct result of this eventuality, although we must not understand this too linearly. His philosophy of religion grew out of a concern with a history-of-religions approach to the phenomenon of religion. Its modus operandi is considerably different from his philosophy of God. Accommodating this shift was his appreciation for the extent to which religious experience affects what we think. Notwithstanding, his philosophy of God and his philosophy of religion appear to have arisen concurrently. Thus, it is more reasonable to conclude that their emergence is due to a vibrant mind turning in several different directions at once than to any linear explanation of their origin.[2]

THE MODEL OF RELIGION: THE POINT OF DEPARTURE

The basis for any discussion of the distinction between Lonergan's philosophy of God and of religion is found in his expressed desire to merge philosophy of God and the functional speciality systematics. Systematics is the "seventh" functional specialty of method in theology. Its function is to promote an understanding of what is affirmed in the sixth functional speciality doctrines (*MIT*:335). Lonergan lists eight functional specialties in the execution of an attentive, intelligent, reasonable, and responsible theology: research, interpretation, history, dialectic, foundations, doctrines, systematics, and communications. The position of systematics, and now as a consequence philosophy of God, is very significant. Lonergan places it in what he calls the "mediated phase" of method in theology. The "mediating phase," in which one encounters the past through research, interpretation, history, and dialectics, does not require a personal interaction with one's moral, religious, and intellectual foundations. That is, adequate mediation of the past does not require that one be so involved. One need not be religiously concerned, religiously "converted" to use Lonergan's language, to determine whether, say, Exodus 3 comprises diverse sources; whether 3:1, 4b, 6, 9–15 come from the hand of an anonymous author or compiler identified as "Elohist" on account of, among other things, his characteristic use of the term Elohim (God); whether 3:14 is a gloss shrouded in yet another narrative (i.e., 3:2–4a, 5, 7–8, 16–22) attributed to a hypothetical figure named "Yahwist" due to his (or her) reliance on the revelational name for God, "Yahweh"; whether, in fact, this is simply unsubstantiated theorizing coming from the heads of scholars rather than anything internally or externally evidential. What will determine this for one is an attentive gathering of all the relevant texts, primary and secondary, a familiarity with the language and the history of the people who gave us this text; comprehension of the arguments brought forward for and against hypotheses, and a sensitive eye for what is in texts. These are things all exegetes know about and conduct themselves in through force of habit.

On the other hand, reflection on the foundational stances of those texts, the specific domain of meaning to which they are thought to apply, and the doctrines resulting from them, does require that one addresses one's own foundational reaction to the stances having been supposedly responsibly mediated.[3] In this way, the mediated theology that confronts the future, through systematic reflection and culturally sensitive communication, will better approximate an authentic gesture toward what is contemporaneous and true in mediating meanings. Knowledge of the meaning of Exodus 3 or any other passage does not require engaging foundationally that which is affirmed. Authentic mediation of it, that is, in line with what is affirmed, if one can affirm it, does.

Foundations regards a consciously deliberate decision about one's stance toward things, how one is oneself morally, intellectually, religiously, socially conscious. Mediating knowledge, particularly as regards ancient texts, won't give one that. What it delivers, if one is lucky, are the implicit and, as is sometimes the case, explicit stances of mediating meanings. However, and if one can find any relevance in the particular concerns of those stances, the honest, self-critical individual will have difficulties claiming them as one's own. The distance between the world of meaning being scrutinized and the one in which the scrutinizing is carried out are often just too wide. Let us hear from biblical exegete Sean McEvenue:

> Most of the meanings [...] discovered are not directly relevant to us today. For example, that God intervened in the life of Moses, or that God was free in liberating ancient Israel from the Pharaohs, or that "Yahweh" is the right name for liturgical use, or that Israel is more powerful than Egypt, all these teachings are historically intriguing, but spiritually irrelevant to a modern reader. All that happened three thousand years ago. And one cannot easily see a justification for applying, for example, to Canadian politics the "messages" given to Solomon or later Northern kings in ancient Israel. And as for the obligation to use the name "Yahweh" ... who could agree to that? The original meanings of the biblical text, even if they were to be securely established, do not seem to be very useful in a contemporary religious context.[4]

The stance of faith is presupposed here. What is matter-of-fact to the person of faith is to the philosopher a question requiring examination. For the person of faith questions about divine intervention do not require argument and hence are inconsequential. It is the business of the philosopher not to be as accommodating and so such questions are highly significant. The sociologist might also take issue with McEvenue. The fact that groups exist that do agonize over such things as getting God's name right seems to suggest that for many this is a useful and meaningful issue. Still, McEvenue's point is valuable. There is a gap between contexts, and foundational examination is requisite if mediated meaning is to be done rationally self-consciously.

In terms of the relevance of all this for Lonergan's merger of philosophy of God and systematics, proof for God, qua knowledge of that which grounds complete intelligibility, becomes fundamentally a question of one's religious foundations. It's not that the knowledge secured through intellectual conversion and the knowledge secured through religious experience are equivalent. Intellectual conversion vis-à-vis proof of God grounds a grasp of the nature of reality as itself grounded in an unrestricted act of understanding. Religious experience identifies that ground analogously with the one with whom one is in love in an unrestricted fashion, to use the language of *Method*. Systematics takes care of the linking of the conditioned to the conditions of the proof. Foundations articulates the "categories" rooted in conversion providing for the worthwhileness of this linking. Affirming an unrestricted act of understanding is expressive not only of an intellectually converted consciousness, but more fundamentally of a religiously converted one or one on the brink of conversion.[5] Indeed, as regards proof for God both types of consciousness are so integral to one another that separating them is like trying to separate thought from language. The argument is thoroughly intellectual but it is wedded to a disposition of consciousness in a certain relationship with "religion," however amorphous or fragile that relationship might be. Lonergan sees this as philosophy of God and systematics having a common origin in religious experience and sharing in the objective of discovering and estimating the significance of religious experience (*PGT*:58).

Proof in this light seems to have taken on a minimalist function while retaining its significance as a relevant pursuit. It aids in the refutation to eliminate talk of God from the so-called intellectual sphere of human experience, as something unavailable to unbridled inquiry. It is not difficult to imagine the logical consequence of this, which may be put as follows. Pursuits of this kind, while retaining a modicum of respectability among the generously minded, are of a lesser caliber than those pursuits that help us get our hands around things, to borrow an appropriate colloquial metaphor. In this respect, Lonergan's proof shares a similar trait with that of Anselm in recognizing that God is integral to human thinking.[6] As said earlier, the force of Lonergan's argument, as in Anselm's, lies in what subjects may know about themselves, in Lonergan's terms that they are experiencing, understanding, and judging beings. Part and parcel of this knowledge is the realization that limited acts of understanding are grounded in an unlimited act evidenced by our endless stream of questions. This unrestricted desire to know is what points to an unrestricted act of knowing which everyone calls God. Intending this end is what indicates *that* it is, not knowing *what* it is since that is impossible. Knowing such an end would be equivalent to saying that no further questions can arise and that we are in possession of a knowledge of everything about everything, which is obviously false. The parallels of this part of Lonergan's argument with the implications of Anselm's rule of thought are apparent.

Belief, faith, and religion—these come to the fore in Lonergan's philosophy of God as questions about proof and the existence of God are answered to his satisfaction. Besides, with the expansion of consciousness from three to four levels he was in a better position to comment on these more fundamental issues. Not only could he situate the discussion of these issues more clearly than previously, he could also nuance, relax his earlier treatment of them overshadowed as they were by intellectualist concerns and the strictly cognitional levels.[7] These issues and levels were now to be considered in the larger framework of the level of decision sublated by it in an unmitigated process of self-transcendence. This means that the issues have a different texture. We might put this differently in terms of issues being "textured" by concerns of a different operation of consciousness.

The relevant literature in this period of reorientation are, primarily, a paper prepared for the Pax Romana Symposium on Faith in Pittsburgh, "Belief: Today's Issue" (1968), a paper read before the American Academy of Religion, "Faith and Beliefs" (1969), another paper delivered as a lecture in Toronto, "Religious Commitment" (1969), and of course *Method in Theology* (1972).[8] Because "Religious Commitment" includes many of Lonergan's generalist observations in the first paper mentioned in the specific context of religious beliefs and is basically an early draft of the relevant chapter "Religion" in *Method*, incorporating as well large chunks of the paper "Faith and Beliefs," I will focus on it. However, since "Faith and Beliefs" contains parts that are not in "Religious Commitment" and includes fragments of a public response by Wilfred Cantwell Smith to Lonergan's paper, some attention will also be given to it.

The big issue is religious involvement or human beings' capacity for it. At least this is how Lonergan puts it, summarizing Cantwell Smith's position. The relationship between faith and religious beliefs is acknowledged as playing an important part in this capacity for religious involvement.[9] Lonergan's entry into the discussion is via the topic of self-transcendence, which acquires considerable import in his thinking at this time. A literal meaning is attached to the term. Self-transcendence is all about dynamic transitions within the unity of consciousness. It "begins" in the fragmentary consciousness of one's dreams of the night and morning, particularly in the latter as the waking state is anticipated.[10] The transition, then, is into the familiar states of our sensations, feelings, and movements, as well as our more outwardly directed states of a tactual, olfactive, and auditory nature. By means of these states, and the different rules of being they communicate, we have transcended the dream world and our fragmentary awareness of self in it. The world more consciously immediate to us has been entered as the dream world is put to an end. Yet ideas such as the "world" of immediacy "communicating" different "rules" show just how abstract it is to talk about this immediate experience.

> Imagination wants to fill out and round off the picture. Language makes questions possible and intelligence makes them fascinating. So we ask what and why and how and what for. Our answers extrapolate and construct and serialize and generalize. Memory and tradition and belief put at our disposal the tales of travellers, the stories of nations, the exploits of heroes, the meditations of holy men, the treasures of literature, the discoveries of science, the reflections of philosophers. Each of us has his own little world of immediacy, but all such worlds are just minute strips within a far larger world, a world constructed by imagination and intelligence, mediated by words and meaning, and largely based upon belief. (*RCo*:50)

Responsible for all of this are the second-level operations discussed in chapter 2, inquiring, imagining, understanding, conceiving, formulating. Through them our "minute strips" of immediate experience are transcended in and by the subject operating in this capacity. However, as sublated experience—to use our earlier terms, specific experience—what is "communicated" immediately through its states is preserved mediately in the worlds of meaning like those Lonergan outlines in the quotation above. He considers this to be an enriching process rather than one that impedes our attainment of reality as it presents itself immediately in our sensations and perceptions. In fact, what we mean by "reality" is indistinguishable from the worlds of mediated meaning we inhabit.

But one person's reality can be another's nightmare, indeed that of a whole society. Insights, Lonergan used to say, are a dime a dozen. If there is a sublational value to them, it is in their potency for being true, not in their actuality as expressions of a keen, even if brilliant, mind. I have outlined Lonergan's position on how we determine whether this potency is in fact one for what is true. For a more definitive word on this the reader is encouraged to turn to chapters 9 and 10 of *Insight*. What concerns us here is Lonergan's point that "the greater statement," whether something is true or probably true, "is not reducible to the lesser" (e.g., that the nature of *x* is such and such). In the reflex of confirming a formulated insight by a reflective "yes" or "no" or "maybe" the former is transcended by the latter, not vice versa. The intelligent becomes the reasonable. "When we affirm that something really and truly is so, we mean that we have somehow got beyond ourselves, somehow transcended ourselves, somehow got hold of something that is independent of ourselves" (*RCo*:51). We have transcended ourselves as merely intelligently conscious and we have transcended our cognitional selves through reasonable consciousness to what is other than ourselves.

This pertains to the cognitional aspect of self-transcendence and its sublational quality. Nothing is disjointed in this movement; it is a unity of operational functions and intentional states. Whether operations are followed through adequately or one is on target with regard to that which is operated on is another question. Integral to consciousness as well, then, are its deliberative, evaluative, and decisional moments of operation. They are constitutive of our being-in-the-world. Practical and existential in orientation they are the means by which we choose whom we are to be and how we are to be in symphony, ideally, with our self- and communally corroborated understanding.[11] Religious consciousness is taken to be simultaneously the "ground and root" and "apex" of this topmost operational level; it is the achievement of our capacity for self-transcendence. This is how he puts it in "Faith and Beliefs." "Realized" seems to be the preferred term in "Religious Commitment." The possibility of human self-transcendence is realized when one's being becomes being-in-love (with God).

This concept of sublation is key to understanding Lonergan's later appreciation of the influence of religious experience in arguments for God's existence. Put otherwise, philosophy of God has an origin in religious experience. Grasping traces of a formally unconditioned in our limited acts of understanding is a cognitional, intellectual achievement, but as it stems from fourth-level concerns, as sublated by decision. On the surface the question of God, which arguments for and against God's existence attempt to pose as answers, appears strictly as "brainteasers." Were we to answer this question, it is often thought, life's most puzzling riddle would be solved. Is it any wonder how much intellectual energy is poured into answering this question? A deeper look, however, will reveal that driving the question are concerns of a far more practical and existential nature. The process of attaining an answer is thoroughly intellectual but as wedded to or sublated by decisional consciousness. The response is that of the questioner who views the question as worthwhile. Whether Lonergan would have framed it this way must await the judgment of the Lonergan community. The data suggests that he himself at this time was interested in a model of religion and not in further situating his argument on the level of decision. That model would overtake his concerns apropos to the cognitional levels in philosophy of God. In relation to the model he would restructure his basic contribution to these fields (i.e., cognitional theory) to accommodate the expansion of consciousness by another level, decision, in which we respond to values and, in another moment of it, in which believers perceive God to transvalue our values. Not that philosophy of God would be substituted by philosophy of religion as a result, as though the latter were a superior endeavor. As I have stated several times, Lonergan never renounced his philosophy of God, in whatever form. Adjustments were made to it but that's about it. In any case, philosophy of religion did become the means by which Lonergan would hone his contribution to this issue of religious experience.

It is useful to pause for a moment and track our development. I might situate Lonergan's different "philosophies of" in relation to the levels of consciousness, with which they are thought to be largely preoccupied, as in fig. 4.1. Again, it is important to remember that the components "cognitional" and "existential" are, in Lonergan's thought, distinctions within the unity of consciousness. The arrow, which represents the sublational movement of consciousness, is an indication of this. The placing of these "philosophies of" in proximity to the levels of consciousness pertains to the operational function of their material component. It is not a comment on the nature of the "philosophies of" in question, what levels of consciousness they are products of. When we come to discuss Lonergan's philosophy of religion more will be said about these delicate distinctions. With this in mind we can make some general observations. Worth noting is where Lonergan's later philosophy of God is located. I will suspend discussion of the secure placement of his philosophy

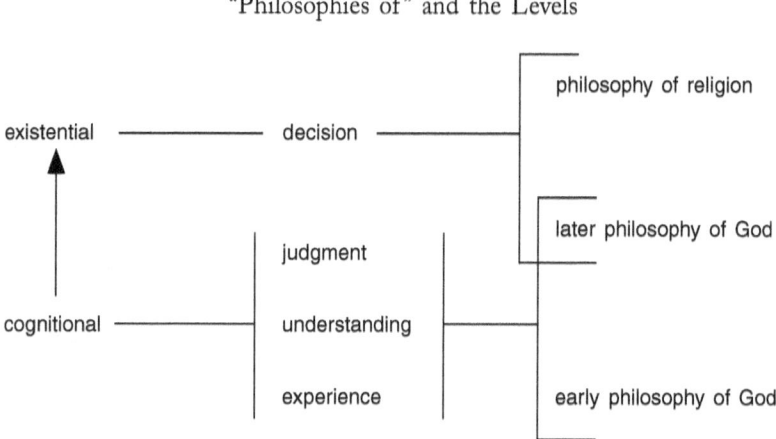

Fig. 4.1
"Philosophies of" and the Levels

of religion proximate to the level of decision for the appropriate time. The reason for placing his later philosophy of God between the cognitional and existential is due to its connections with proof refurbished with the level of decision in mind. There is a point, too, when the function of Lonergan's later philosophy of God is indistinguishable from his philosophy of religion. However, because all references to the former and its refurbished understanding of the role of proof is dropped when philosophy of religion is addressed, I prefer to see them as distinct in the development of his thought on God and religion. This explains my inclusion of the two "philosophies of" proximate to the level of decision as distinct. For more on this we will have to wait until we get to Lonergan's philosophy of religion. Required now is a more detailed discussion of this *model* of religion.

"Model" is Lonergan's term mentioned casually at the end of "Faith and Beliefs." By it he intends both individual and corporate dimensions of religious life. Basic to religious life is religious experience and what he also deems "knowledge born of love." Model is used to convey a sense of "a construct" or "ideal type," which for Lonergan contains a systematic distinction between faith and belief (*FBe*:20). One doesn't come across the term in *Method* as a description of the same reality. Nonetheless it is useful given the sense it imparts about the skeletal nature of the model. Lonergan states this expressly in "Faith and Belief" (see note 40 below)—the sentiment is practically absent from *Method*. The suggestion is that the model is tentative which, as we will soon see, is quite significant in determining its role in Lonergan's philosophy of religion. When speaking of Lonergan's model, then, I include the components of individual and communal acts of religious meaning and praxis "born of" religious experience. The focus, however, is on religious experience, with which we have been largely preoccupied in this book. The reason for this is plain: no other element in Lonergan's model of religion is as crucial for an understanding of the development of his philosophy of religion. Be that as it may, these other components will receive mention given that we are discussing Lonergan's model.

The first thing to note is that Lonergan expresses the basic component of his model, religious experience, in very Judeo-Christianly terms. The Judeo-Christian tradition, of course, has its own surplus of models to describe the encounter with the divine. In grafting his own explanatory model Lonergan borrows selectively from the descriptive language most familiar to him to express what he takes to be culturally invariant. This could also be said of the more explanatory models he relies on, which I will get to shortly. Thus, the terms he uses are "being in love with God" as religious faith ("knowledge born of love") and religious belief, knowledge common to particular religious traditions. The following references to being-in-love are to this particular form, since, as we caught glimpses of earlier, Lonergan does recognize love to come in a variety of forms. Unlike the knowledge born of general experience (i.e., experience, understanding, and judgment) knowledge born of love is of another kind "reached through the discernment of value and the judgments of value of a person in love" (*RCo*:65).

Lonergan's understanding of "value" presupposes the moral connotations commonly lent to the term. He does give it a rather elaborate structural meaning though. The short of it is that value is "a transcendental notion . . . intended in questions for deliberation" (*MIT*:34), whether this or that is truly good or not, worthwhile or not. As notional it is the drive toward the good and worthwhile, and is rewarded in self-transcendence with a happy conscience, saddening failures with an unhappy one (*MIT*:35). Just as there are judgments of fact on the cognitional levels, there are judgments of value on the level of decision. By them "the subject moves beyond pure and simple knowing." By them "the subject is constituting himself as proximately capable of moral self-transcendence, of benevolence and beneficence, of true loving" (*MIT*:37). Lonergan further distinguishes between an "apprehension of value" and a judgment of value, in that the former is something of a go-between judgments of fact and of value. The difference seems to lie in the potency of what is so apprehended for being good. In a judgment of value what is apprehended as good is truly known to be so or only apparently so. Like judgment confirming whether our concepts are true or merely intelligent, judgments of value confirm whether our apprehensions of value are of the truly good or that merely perceived as such.

Religious values, which Lonergan places on the top rung of his integral scale of values (vital, social, cultural, and personal) are "at the heart of the meaning and value of man's living and man's world."[12] Vital values are basic to our being and consist of such things as health, strength, grace, and vigor. Social values, such as the good of order, are a means of insuring vital values to the whole community. Cultural values outrank vital and social ones, although they are underpinned by vital and social values. It is through cultural values that being healthy and having a society to insure this has a meaning. Lonergan views as apt here the words of Jesus in Matthew 4:4: "One does not live by bread alone." Personal value is a reference to self-transcending subjects as loving and being loved, originating values in the community and inviting others to do likewise. Religious values are a heightening of personal value as a response to grace. The attainment and continual intending of religious values transvalues all other values (vital, social, cultural, and personal) through faith. It is through this achievement that all other values are seen as expressions of God's love in the world. As a result the focus shifts from human beings as principal agents of self-transcendence and originators of value to God. Through this achievement a whole new horizon is instituted.

Without faith the originating value is man and the terminal value is the good man brings about. But in the light of faith originating value is divine light and love, while terminal value is the whole universe. So the human good becomes absorbed in an all-encompassing good. Where before an account of the human good related men to one another and to nature, now human concern reaches beyond man's world to God and God's world.... To conceive God as originating value and the world as terminal value implies that God too is self-transcending and that the world is the fruit of his self-transcendence, the expression and the manifestation of his benevolence and beneficence, his glory.[13]

No critique of "faithless" values is suggested here. They regard, in Lonergan's later terms, a crucial aspect of a *creative* development from below upwards in which consciousness attains and implements terminal values, resulting in fruitful courses of action (*3C*:106). The transvaluing of these creatively attained values pertains to a development from above downwards, what he calls a *"healing"* development. The healing development is, to put it in Kantian terms, the condition of possibility of creative development. It animates the whole process from below upwards, supplying the means of reorientation to a development that may be undergoing a breakdown in values. Theologically this is significant as well, for as transvaluative our valuing is kept in check, whether it is idolatrous or not.

Lonergan relies on the model of Friedrich Heiler (1892–1967) in postulating that the originating value of this development is common to world religions like Christianity, Judaism, Islam, Hinduism, Buddhism, and Taoism. The bare essentials of this commonality Lonergan outlines are "that there is a transcendent reality; that he is immanent in human hearts; that he is supreme beauty, truth, righteousness, goodness; that he is love, mercy, compassion; that the way to him is repentance, self-denial, prayer; that the way is love of one's neighbor, even of one's enemies; that the way is love of God, union with him, or dissolution into him."[14] The use of Heiler by Lonergan has sparked some controversy in theological circles. We gather from George A. Lindbeck's critique of Lonergan that it is key in linking Lonergan to the theological liberalism that has its roots in the "experiential-expressivism" of Friedrich Schleiermacher (1768–1834). Heiler represents an early species of religion scholars who take the kernel of Schleiermacher's position on religion and apply it, under a theological burden, to the scientific study of religion. Schleiermacher's position is that there is a unitary essence of religion of which various world religions, their teachings, are mere expressions. While Lindbeck accepts this move as well-intentioned, he is hard-pressed to see it as defensible.

Indeed, he thinks that the assertion of commonality is logically and empirically vacuous, especially when that which makes religions distinctive is skirted on the grounds that it would be difficult or impossible to specify this.[15]

The response from Lonergan scholars has been varied though harmonious in rejecting this reading of Lonergan, his connection to Heiler and, indirectly, to Schleiermacher. In a review of Lindbeck's *The Nature of Doctrine* Charles C. Hefling, Jr., takes issue not only with Lindbeck's understanding of Lonergan, but with his model of doctrine as well. This is supported by extensive research into the nature of doctrinal development according to Lonergan.[16] In the review itself, Hefling focuses on the centrality of judgment, framing his assessment of Lindbeck mostly with the functional speciality doctrines in view.[17] He follows this up with a detailed study of Schleiermacher and Lonergan in which their hermeneutics, cognitional theory, and Christology are contrasted and compared. Hefling shows, convincingly in my view, that Lonergan "cannot be dubbed 'a Schleiermacher for our time,'" whether one intends this as an accolade or reproach. Despite seeming similarities, Schleiermacher's line of thought, "extended and applied to particular expressions of Christian meaning, diverges so far from Lonergan's as to delineate a completely different horizon."[18]

More relevant for our present concerns is an article by Philip Boo Riley. He contends that Lindbeck forces Lonergan unfairly into a theory of religion "that is derivative of Heiler and other theologically oriented historians of religion."[19] Moreover, Lindbeck's description of Lonergan as an experiential-expressivist neglects Lonergan's differentiation of the world of immediacy and the world mediated and constituted by meaning. Contrary to what experiential-expressivism is about, Lonergan's concept is a clarification, not a separation, of the two worlds of meaning. Riley admits that Lonergan may have been ill-advised to use Heiler's model in his generalized theory of religion, but in doing so he was most certainly "not arguing for the unitary essence of religions, nor was he promoting the religious harmony and interreligious cooperation that Heiler predicted would follow from the scientific study of religion."[20] Lindbeck's model is in need of some serious fine tuning. Riley makes the important suggestion, beyond that which he has said about Lindbeck's relation to Lonergan, that one misses Lonergan's contribution to this area of study if one limits it, presumably like Lindbeck and others have, to his theory of religion. The real import of his thinking on the question is in his theory about how theologians and religion scholars no less may approach the phenomenon of religion critically self-consciously. It is at this level of his discourse that a religion scholar may profit from Lonergan. Still, we are getting ahead of ourselves again. A methodological observation needs to be made about Lonergan's treatment of religious experience, after which his treatment of faith and belief will be dealt with. I will return to what I think is Riley's valid suggestion when consideration is given to Lonergan's philosophy of religion proper.

From the perspective of being-in-love, then, the development we have been discussing is cooperative, even though grounded in wholly transcendent love. Christians speak of this in terms of operative and cooperative grace, prevenient and sanctifying grace. Lonergan does, too, of course. However, in his model of religion, in which religious experience is distinguished from Christian experience, he is at pains to use less Christianly loaded terms as best as a Christian theologian may be expected to.[21] Thus, when discussing philosophy of God, particularly in the later stage of its development and especially in his philosophy of religion, one hears Lonergan talk less of sanctifying grace and more of broader categories such as intrinsic and extrinsic requirements of the creative and healing process (*2C*:107). He is being consistent with his principle of explanatory consciousness as applied in philosophy of God and religion, that some third term is required over and above grace and sin (*2C*:107) and strictly theological third terms such as cooperative and operative grace. The methodological means to this end, in Lonergan's sense of method, may be similar, but the terms under which it operates vary in accordance with the nature of that upon which it operates. The observation is general. One detects theological overtones in his generalist pronouncements about religion. He never attempted to conceal this. He spoke as a theologian to philosophers and students of religion as he conceived their essential task. With a little bit of caution we might view this as something of a "middle" ground where the concerns of generalized empirical method and method in theology converge.[22] Still, Lonergan is mindful of the distinctions as he outlines his model in the most general of (Christian) terms. The method is not particularly Christian; the model of religion arguably is.

Faith is identified by Lonergan as distinct from being-in-love. It is *knowledge* born of love whereas love is not typically objectified. In his response to Lonergan Wilfred Cantwell Smith expresses some confusion over the notion. I don't think his confusion is unwarranted, nor, incidentally, did Lonergan, tracing it to Smith's Protestant background. As a Catholic, Lonergan says of himself, he is prone to see faith as connected to judgment.[23] Smith, influenced by the Reformers' notion (Lonergan presumes Luther's most of all), is bound to see it differently. Still, Lonergan is reassured that Smith's notion of faith as involvement is well-represented by being-in-love. Indeed, Tad Dunne believes that Lonergan's definition of faith is closer to the old Protestant emphasis on trust in God than, presumably, the Catholic tendency to unite faith with beliefs.[24]

Faith is one with being-in-love as objectified response to God's gift of love. It involves decision based on knowledge of God's love, whether one accepts or rejects it, whether one lives it out or withdraws from it. We see here Lonergan's connection of faith with judgment, its expansion of decision in compliance with some sort of judgment. That judgment, in turn, is related to a knowledge that transcends regular experience, what I have frequently referred to as specific experience, and yet is present in the experience of being-in-love. Interesting, too, in line with our earlier discussion of proof, is Lonergan's statement in "Religious Commitment": "Only secondarily do there arise questions of God's existence and nature, and they take the form either of the lover seeking to know him or of the unbeliever seeking to escape him. Such is the basic option of the existential subject once he has been called by God" (*RCo*:65). Issues of faith, for Lonergan, are more basic than issues of proof. Existential consciousness may be labeled "fourth" in the spectrum of consciousness but it often underpins what the other levels do or how they function. Perhaps it might be better to say that decision colors our general experience, whether the data is of a natural or supernatural origin.

Faith, then, is the horizon, for Lonergan, within which our vital, social, cultural, and personal values are transvalued by otherworldly love. Such love is claimed to be wholly concerned with this world. The claim is verified in the experience of being-in-love (religiously converted consciousness). What might be dubbed "being-not-in-love" cannot accept the claim as verifiable since it adheres to one order of criteria, one aspect of development, contained in the general experience of human beings and conforming to their plans and aspirations alone. To give a different twist to Pascal's famous insight, it abides by those reasons of the heart that it may know. Being-not-in-love, after all, is not without intentional responses to values, vital, social, cultural, and personal. However, when it comes to reasons of the heart that being-not-in-love cannot know, it is hardly as accommodating. Still, however successful being-not-in-love has been in marginalizing religion, Lonergan writes several years later of secularism, "it has not succeeded in inventing a vaccine or providing some other antidote for hatred" (*3C*:106–7). Being-in-love is, with its reasons of which reason does not know, the more likely candidate for that. Nonetheless, being-in-love, too, as history and the daily news show in abundance, is not immune to the hatred endemic to human being.

Belief is classed among the values of faith. It pertains to the word of religion, which is the very stuff of faith. There is not just the faith of an individual; there is the faith of the community, past and present. In many respects the faith of the community is the condition of possibility of an individual's faith. Consider the element that is part and parcel of this aspect of the model alone, expression, which Lonergan says community invites. A community's narrative or its story shapes what one takes to be one's faith by preparing the way for it, historically and in some form of catechesis. Its stock of meanings serve as a touchstone for identifying one's faith once one is aware of it. The fabric of one's faith, one's working out of it, is greatly influenced by the expressions of a community. Immediate examples are Lonergan's general theory of religion, which we saw contains a definite Christian tone, and Lonergan's own admission about the largely Catholic character of his concept of faith. Besides narrative, expression may be aesthetic, mystical, or theoretical, or some combination of these.

The structure of belief in religion functions in much the same way as it does in other realms of meaning. Only a small fraction of our knowledge is immanently generated. "Science is often contrasted with belief," Lonergan says about the endeavor many regard as the religion of our times, "but the fact of the matter is that belief plays as large a role in science as in most other areas of human activity" (*MIT*:42). This is especially true of science whose desired advancement depends on belief in the observations and experiments of fellow researchers. Think of where science would be if it operated on a principle of doubt: that theory alone is true whose basic presuppositions, the immanently generated knowledge of theorist x, has been verified or falsified by theorist y or z. Belief seems the reasonable response, unless one's findings contradict or bring into question some tenet of that relied upon in one's own observations and experiments.[25] Although the nature of that which is believed in religion is of a different constitution, although the means by which it is acquired is different, the structure and centrality of belief in endeavors as far removed from one another methodologically as science and religion are virtually indistinguishable.[26] Lonergan emphasizes the analogy in relation to intellectually patterned pursuits on account of the widespread assumption that it is at this juncture of intelligence where belief is least operative. Belief is as valuable and pervasive a phenomenon in the affairs of trained individuals as it is in the affairs of lay persons. Often we believe what these trained individuals say, consoling ourselves in the knowledge that they "possess a high reputation for intellectual integrity" (*CWL* 3:734). How many of us are able to recount, let alone comprehend, all the fine points of relativity theory or differential calculus? Innumerable books, especially "popular" ones, exist to bridge this gap. These are proposed for our belief. Learned journals and articles function in much the same way in academic circles. They lessen the workload and place fewer harsh demands on the scope of one's immanently generated knowledge.

In Lonergan's model of religion belief also functions at various levels. At a fundamental level, persons in love religiously believe certain things about what their experience of transcendent love reveals to them. Just as scientists believe in things that are foundational to what they do, such as the intelligibility of the universe; just as philosophers believe or trust in the powers of reason, even when rallying all their energy against it, so, too, religious believers believe things foundational to their faith such as what Lonergan outlines from Heiler.[27] I use the term "foundational" with discretion. Beliefs like these are not or do not begin as propositionally basic to pronouncements inside or outside their field of concern. They are basic or foundational in that they are reflex beliefs that proceed *from* the experience of love, hence their universal presence. As to the centrality of beliefs at more reflective levels, the examples are plentiful. Think of professors when pressed by their students with regard to the finer points of their argument. A number of studies may be invoked for the students' belief. Students may also be encouraged to believe what they are receiving has the backing of weighty studies one cannot expect to verify in a course or two. More often than not this requires a lifetime of research in which, incidentally, one relies on the conclusions of others as one acquires one's own immanently generated knowledge. Thus, scholars of religion have to rely on the work of historians and textual critics, as historians and textual critics have to rely on each other. Theologians, too, must rely on the work of historically oriented colleagues if their work is to have a basis in fact, as scholars of religion are to rely on the work of theologians if they are to understand the mentality of that which they are mediating and how that knowledge ought to be mediated today. Our beliefs pervade every level of understanding. They are the rails along which knowledge travels.[28]

The model I have been tracing flows directly from Lonergan's realization that context is what is wrong with chapter 19 of *Insight* and necessarily its content. What is so strange is that it appears in a book that contains all the elements that, according to Lonergan, are necessary for a new philosophy of God, but ignores them precisely in this regard. And yet it is not so strange given the suggestions offered in chapters 1 and 3. To repeat an earlier point, time was needed to express clearly what was clearly apprehended. The experience, I trust, is a familiar one. What was clearly apprehended was that the dialogical ground for engaging being-not-in-love had shifted. As he states in the last of his Larkin-Stuart Lectures (1973), the old means of philosophizing about God began from the material universe and concluded to God. *Insight* chapter 19 is an unwitting prolongation of this. The new, by contrast, "advances from the existential subject to God by the claims of a full rejection of obscurantism" (*SRe*:100). Needless to say, the grounds for that rejection are the chapters preceding chapter 19. It concludes to God as did the old. "But it does so in a manner that begins from what the secularist can discover in his own reality," his (or her) own experience, "to overcome his own secularism" (100). The model we looked at constitutes Lonergan's expression of this apprehension for philosophy of God. The little he says about proof in connection with this apprehension indicates that the effects of this model on his philosophy of God were strictly of a structural nature. As we read immediately above, philosophy of God still concludes to God, although it begins from the self-appropriation of the existential (read: decisional) subject. At the end of the last chapter, I attempted to provide some suggestions as to the significance of this structural change for the function or purpose of proof in his philosophy of God. Presently I wish to make another suggestion.

Philosophy of God, and Theology and the Larkin-Stuart Lectures show that Lonergan intended philosophy of God to be included in the purview of his model of religion. In many ways, his early philosophy of God served as a catalyst in drafting his model. However, there is little that an endeavor, whose questions arise only secondarily (*RCo*:65), can contribute to an analysis of questions of a primary nature. To complete Lonergan's thoughts on the secularist, it is not philosophy of God that allows secularists to discover in their own experience the primary ingredient for overcoming their secularism. In so far as the existential subject is at issue, reflection on the "object" of this endeavor proper to philosophy of God will contribute little to this end. This is where the categories that Lonergan introduces in "Openness and Religious Experience," discussed in chapter 3, come in handy. The formal component of philosophy of God is apropos and remains a constant, that is, "philosophy of."[29] The material component, "God," shifts, however, as the proper subject matter becomes the existential subject. And although the advance from the existential subject is one that is to conclude to God, the advance itself involves issues that are beyond the scope of philosophy of God. Discovering what is in my own experience to transcend myself, to transcend that which I rightly or wrongly view as worthwhile, is not an event that happens in isolation. I do it in relation to what I perceive as my past, my present, and in relation to past and present communities, their expressions; these expressions have in many ways conditioned what I take to be worthwhile. Naturally, others have done similarly, evolving sophisticated means of understanding the past and present in relation to which one may think critically about one's own valuing. As itself a sophisticated means of arriving at self-knowledge, as a generalized empirical method that is at once generalizable, "philosophy of" must address itself to these sophisticated means of understanding. As a result, it must address itself to the one inquiring self-critically into the data of one's existential self. This is the unspoken assumption in Lonergan's later fixation on philosophy of *religion*. That fixation is not so much an indication that Lonergan viewed philosophy of religion as the more fundamental of the two philosophical endeavors. More fittingly, it is a question of focusing on something that is better suited to the concerns of historical consciousness and the methods by which it is analyzed. Philosophy of God may draw from these methods insights relevant to its own primary difficult task. However, as a pursuit caring "for the clarity of terms, the coherence of propositions, the rigor of inferences" (*3C*:139) *vis-à-vis* the existence and nature of God, scrutinizing the historical data of religious consciousness—to say nothing of scrutinizing the methods that do this—is beyond its scope and competency.[30] Whatever the case, we may be clear about the following: the basic element of self-appropriating analysis of one's existential self is common to both endeavors, conveyed in the phrase "philosophy of." But where philosophy of God branches off in bringing this to bear on what many consider *the* question of philosophy of religion today (namely, God's existence) philosophy of religion brings this element to bear on the methods intended to give us some critical understanding of the traditions in which the existential questions have been articulated. And it is in relation to these traditions that we live out and think through our own existential questions. The remainder of the chapter is given to developing this in greater detail.

LONERGAN'S PHILOSOPHY OF RELIGION

As far as I can tell, the term "philosophy of religion" makes its first technical appearance in Lonergan in 1970, two papers in particular: "The Example of Gibson Winter" (*2C*:189–92) and "Philosophy and Theology" (*2C*:193–208). We encountered a similar term, "philosophy of religious experience," in chapter 3 in discussing Lonergan's paper "Openness and Religious Experience" (1961). That term, however, bears early connotations of religious experience as influential in explanatory thinking about the nature and existence of God. The pinnacle of its formulation in relation to philosophy of God is reached in *Philosophy of God, and Theology, Method*, and the Larkin-Stuart Lectures. The term "philosophy of religion" in "The Example of Gibson Winter" and "Philosophy and Theology" signals a different elaboration in connection with a different subject-matter. It is put most succinctly in the fourth of Lonergan's five points in "Philosophy and Theology" about the core contribution of philosophy (read: his "philosophy of") to the then contemporary theological need.

> Philosophy of religion reveals how basic thinking relates itself to the various branches of religious studies. Thereby it offers theology an analogous model of the way it can relate itself to religious studies...." (*2C*:204)

Its relation to philosophy of God is, manifestly, remote. It leaves to philosophy of God, as basic thinking ("philosophy of"), the task of how it relates itself to philosophic questioning about God. Philosophy of religion is geared more toward the methodological questions of analyzing the religious phenomenon.

"The example of Gibson Winter" is about Winter's program of translating, via a social ethics, the work of social science to specific problems confronting society. Winter felt that the social sciences were becoming increasingly out of touch with the processes of society through a preoccupation with abstract models. For this reason he urged "the need for a critique of the social sciences by their partner in the theory of social practice, the discipline of social ethics." And yet if social ethics is to develop as a significant factor in the shaping of social policy, he continues, it must come to terms with the work of social science, collaborating in the scientific enterprise.[31] *Elements of a Social Ethic* is given to the development of this relation. Lonergan thinks that Winter's move is worth emulating in a philosophizing about religion. As Winter inserts social ethics between social science and social polity, a distinction grafted by Max Weber (1864–1920), Lonergan wants to insert philosophy of religion and its extension into theology between religious studies and the policies of religious groups (*2C*:191). The task is stated baldly in "The Example of Gibson Winter," identifying it with a notable historical precedent. In "Philosophy and Theology" it is taken up more elaborately with theological studies primarily in mind.

This evolution in Lonergan's thought owes itself to his study of history and hermeneutics.[32] When one is dealing with religion, one is dealing with history. When one is dealing with history, one is dealing with the German Historical School. "It was the German historical school which introduced historical thinking, defined it" (*CAMe*:25). When one is dealing with the German Historical School, one is also dealing in one way or another with hermeneutics. In so far as philosophy of religion reveals how basic thinking relates itself to religious studies, some thought must be given to these.[33] The tardy appearance of *Method* after *Insight* testifies to the gravity of these issues for his generalized empirical method in general and his philosophy of religion in particular. "I had to master interpretation and history and dialectic and get them in perspective" (*CAMe*: 59). Once he did that he could speak to the issues of method in theology, whose functional specialties, particularly in the mediating phase, are broad enough to be relevant to the methodological particularities of religion scholars. As he writes in *Method*, "the functional specialties of research, interpretation, and history can be applied to the data of any sphere of scholarly human studies" (*MIT*:364). Today, of course, the nervousness triggered by such universal claims has only intensified. To mention only one example few hesitate to see as a generally sensible interpretive rule of thumb, Lonergan understands a correct grasp of a text's meaning to be in an understanding of a word in its immediate context, sentences, paragraphs, chapters, and so on. This includes a precise grasp of the historical context, of authors, the state of the question in their day, their problems and concerns, those of their audience, and so on (*MIT*:163). One can almost hear the snickering coming from biblical quarters. If ascertaining the meaning of biblical texts were subject to these rules, we would be very much in the dark as to their meaning. Biblical scholars often despair over the possibility of establishing by and large the historical identity of biblical authors and editors in their historical sequence. In fact biblical authors and editors often disguise their identity, deliberately confusing historical contexts to exclude such genetic history.[34] What may work for interpreting texts like the *Summa* runs afoul for interpreting texts like the Bible. The criticism is valid and one that Lonergan would appreciate. However, I do not see him as particularly troubled by it since his concern is generalist. It can be adjusted to meet the particularities he, as a generalist relying on the specific and limited methods of his time, overlooked or was not privy to. What is offered via his spectrum of functional specialties is a generally valid point of entry for critical discussion. The specialties provide a helpful means of examining the presuppositions that go into and sometimes unnecessarily flow from the specific methods of literarily, artistically, historically, and systematically conscious persons. Where I see him getting a little "nervous," if affected at all, is in the criticism of the general structure that he sees his specific though generalist venture pointed the way to.

In "Philosophy and Theology" Lonergan is very brief about the development instilling the need for something like his philosophy of religion.[35] The figures mentioned are largely from the nineteenth century: classicist Friedrich Wolf (1759–1824), theologian Friedrich Schleiermacher, their student classicist August Boeckh (1785–1867), the eminent historian Leopold von Ranke (1795–1886), the historian-politician Johann Gustav Droysen (1808–1884), and the philosopher-historian Wilhelm Dilthey (1833–1911). Chapters 7 and 9 of *Method* provide a more detailed account. Pride of place is given to the eminent philosopher-historian R. G. Collingwood (1889–1943), his posthumously published *The Idea of History* (1946), and philosopher Hans-Georg Gadamer (1900–), his *Wahrheit und Methode* (1960). Collingwood stands out in Lonergan's list as one of the few English contributors to this development. Others include Christopher Dawson (1889–1970) and Arnold Toynbee (1889–1975). Dawson and Toynbee were a strong influence in the early Lonergan. He attributes, for instance, the initiating correction of his views on culture as normative to a reading of Dawson's *The Age of the Gods* (1928) (*2C*:264). He read Toynbee's six-volume work, *A Study of History* (1934–), very closely in the 1940s, making notes of them which are available at the Lonergan Research Institute in Toronto. The work of the famous theologian and historian Ernst Troeltsch (1865–1923) does not figure prominently in Lonergan, although he is aware of it. Sparse references to him appear, accordingly, in Lonergan's 1959 lectures on "History" and in a section titled "Historical Consciousness" in "The Human Good as Object: Differentials and Integration" (*CWL* 10:77, 234). It is somewhat odd that Troeltsch does not receive any mention in the chapter on "History and Historians" in *Method*. One suspects that the reputed relativism of Troeltsch's historicism vitiated Lonergan's interest in it, other than providing a foil for the development of his own thinking on history. Troeltsch's appearance in the concluding section of "Philosophy and Theology" seems an indirect confirmation of this. There Lonergan distances himself from the "thorough-going relativism" of Troeltsch. He sides with colleagues who view it as one of the unfortunate results of hermeneutics and critical history. We might understand Troeltsch as something of a prototype for the critical functioning, the "dialectics," of Lonergan's philosophy of religion. One of its principal aims is to reverse the philosophic inadequacies of purportedly counterpositional stances like Troeltsch's based on a sound analysis and epistemological critique of hermeneutics and critical history (*2C*:207).

This brings me back to the contention of Philip Boo Riley that Lonergan's philosophical contribution to religious studies and theology is found in his philosophy of religion ("philosophy of") and not in his model of religion per se. Nor, I would add, is it to be found in the specifics of his generally valid spectrum of functional specialties. This is hinted at or is an unwitting suggestion in a paper by Vernon Gregson delivered to a symposium held in 1980 at Marquette University in honor of Lonergan on his seventy-fifth birthday.[36] Gregson does not address the viability of the functional specialties, particularly the first and last three, in the work of religion scholars and theologians. He takes for granted that the questions raised by religion scholars is proper to the mediating specialties in their fact-seeking enterprise and those raised by theologians to the mediated specialties in their value-seeking enterprise.[37] The former prescind from questions aroused by religious sentiment or commitment, the latter see their task as founded upon it. Where I see Gregson as more or less anticipating Riley's and my contention is in his accentuation of dialectic as the "evaluative discipline necessary both for the historian of religion and the theologian in order to mediate between their horizons."[38] Neither Gregson nor I asserts that dialectic constitutes Lonergan's sole contribution to this area of discussion. Since interpretation was brought up earlier, I might mention it here again. Although much has changed in hermeneutics since Lonergan penned chapter 7 of *Method*—in fact, contemporary hermeneutical theory challenged the chapter's basic claims—some continue to see a wider philosophical relevance to Lonergan's view of interpretation.[39] My point is that the issue for philosophy of religion, as conceived by Lonergan, is principally dialectical in character, whether the aim is to mediate between different horizons or to pronounce on the methodological aspects of religious studies. The latter Lonergan explicitly identifies as the main objective of philosophy of religion (*PRP*:128). Dialectic is all about engaging implicit and explicit assumptions (cognitional, metaphysical, ethical, and religious) that shape methodical and methodological inquiry and their horizons. In so far as "philosophy of religion is the foundational methodology of religious studies," dialectics is its key operational function. The model of religion is incidental to that objective. It is a working concept, if you will, for addressing the presuppositions of methods contrived to probe deeper into the particularities of the religious phenomenon.[40]

Lonergan's model of religion and his philosophy of religion are separate though obviously related issues. Indications of this are gleaned from the papers already mentioned by Lonergan that initiate his program. We gather this as well from his Donald Mathers "Lectures on Religious Studies and Theology" (1976), which divide into three: "Religious Experience," "Religious Knowledge," and "The Ongoing Genesis of Methods." In "Religious Experience" Lonergan is basically filling out further the model he has been sketching since the late 1960s in deference to such notables in psychology as Karen Horney (1885–1952), Carl Gustav Jung (1875–1961), and Carl R. Rogers (1902–1987), and in religion as Mircea Eliade (1907–1986) and Wilfred Cantwell Smith (1916–2000). The lecture builds up to an *infrastructural* element of his model (i.e., religious consciousness), a term he introduced the year before in an article that sets the stage for much of what he outlines in "Religious Experience," namely, the article "Prolegomena to the Study of the Emerging Religious Consciousness of Our Time" (1975). Another element introduced in the same article, which Lonergan picks up on in "Religious Experience" and extends into his second lecture, "Religious Knowledge," is *suprastructure*. Infrastructure is a reference to inner experience, "consciousness as distinct from self-knowledge" (*3C*:57). Its religious instantiation is being-in-love in an unrestricted fashion, "a conscious content without an apprehended object" (*3C*:71). Suprastructure is objectifying response to infrastructural experience. It "supposes an ordinary language, through which one advances to a grasp of scientific terminology, and a commonsense style of knowledge, through which one advances to scientific knowledge" (57). It encompasses what in *Method* is described as the realms of common sense and theory. Philosophy of religion consists in scrutinizing "scientific" suprastructural accounts of infrastructural reality. Lonergan's model qualifies as such a suprastructure, but its aim is not in the scrutiny of suprastructures in the fashion of philosophy of religion. It is merely a generalized account of significant infrastructural and suprastructural aspects of religion as Lonergan sees it. Because Lonergan's model is a superstructure in its own right, it may be seen as based upon the kind of scrutiny demanded by philosophy of religion. Still, it is not one with its purpose. Hence, I am puzzled by Riley's suggestion that the chapter on religion in *Method* be construed as a philosophy of religion relevant not only to theology, but also to religious studies as well.[41] As I read that chapter, and its close textual and ideational affinities with "Faith and Beliefs" and "Religious Commitment," it consists of an outline of Lonergan's model of religion, and not philosophy of religion as he conceives its function. The distinction is a technical one.

The proper task of philosophy of religion enters in when Lonergan starts discussing religious knowledge and the proliferation of methods given to disentangling its meaning and infrastructure. In connection with the Donald

Mathers Memorial Lectures, it emerges in the middle lecture, "Religious Knowledge," beginning with the section "General Empirical Method." The obvious parallel is in *Method*, except that where general empirical method and the model are deemed background to method in theology (i.e., the functional specialties), general empirical method becomes the foreground of philosophy of religion. The model, which Riley describes in terms of Lonergan's generalized theory of religion, remains background. Put otherwise, the material component of philosophy of *religion* is neither religious experience nor religious expression as articulated in Lonergan's superstructural model. It is religious studies, the methods it employs to understand religious experience in its various aspects. The shift, then, is from articulating his own model to scrutinizing the philosophical assumptions of models proposed by religion scholars.

It is important to make these distinctions when trying to determine Lonergan's thought on the question. His model is integral to his philosophy of religion and also to his philosophy of God; it is not equivalent to it, however. This contention is further substantiated upon closer inspection of the papers in which Lonergan sketches the programmatic of philosophy of religion. For example, in "Philosophy and the Religious Phenomenon"[42] aspects related to the model are mentioned in passing as the dialectical relevance of foundational methodology ("philosophy of") comes to the fore. The same applies to "Post-Hegelian Philosophy of Religion" (1980). In both articles sparse references are made to his model and the figures from whom he gleans some relevant information for it. Actually he shares some of their basic convictions about religious experience (e.g., Heiler and Panikkar). The relevance of the model for philosophy of religion is in the elucidation of the primary task of philosophy of religion, what it is about, what one does when one is doing it.

What Is It? What Does It Do?

I have been delineating what precisely Lonergan means to include in philosophy of religion without giving too much thought to what it is about. As we turn our attention to this now, what I have been saying about Lonergan's philosophy of religion being distinct from his model of religion should come into clearer focus.

A clear statement appears in "Method: Trends and Variations" (1974). Lonergan is contrasting method to static logic, "its elder sister" (*3C*:15). Unlike logic, method is progressive and dynamic. Its goal is discovery. In logic conclusions are known before they are drawn, being implicit in their premises. The goals of logic include clarity, coherence, and rigor, not gratuitous goals in Lonergan's opinion—hence his continued support of it, but as secondary to method. Lonergan then turns to what he seems to have no problems referring to as "the basis" for the development of learning and discovery. Husserl names it one's horizon, Heidegger one's world, Richard M. Hare one's blik.[43] A horizon circumscribes three classes of objects. Lonergan is quite cryptic about what he means by these objects. Presumably he understands them in terms of the objects of experience (general) patterned commonsensically or theoretically. He is talking about the former pattern when he describes the first class as pertaining to the familiar, having their place within a horizon already. Because of this, adverting to them is thought otiose, their discussion boring. To many, a desk is just a solid body made to support things in the daily affairs of life, one's books, food, work, some flowers perhaps. Notwithstanding the objections of the interior decorator, the architect, or the designer, for whom a desk is never just a desk, there is the desk of near-empty space, of colorless wavicles, evoked by questions turning an otherwise mundane object into an interesting one.[44] This object is of the second class, of course. The third class seems to be a heightening of the second in that its cognizing takes one from interest, the enrichment and expansion of one's mental store, to expertise. It marks the transition from objects that are apprehended commonsensically to objects that are apprehended scientifically, which is quite demanding and often uneventful. Hence, about these objects "one knows little and cares less. Talk about them is met with incomprehension. Books about them get no more than a passing glance" (*3C*:16).

Knowledge of these objects is fundamentally a question of horizons. A horizon is our preunderstanding inclining us in certain ways toward what we understand and what we are to understand. As a question of understanding and of method, it is dynamic for understanding is always on the move. As a question of horizon it is dialectical, for the notion of horizon "speaks both of development and of limitation, of enrichment but also of failure or distortion or stunted growth" (*3C*:18). These are the two elements that are constitutive of Lonergan's philosophy of religion. They are documented in the statement I alluded to earlier but deferred until now:

> [T]he dynamic and dialectical account [which Lonergan is offering us in his "philosophy of"] is relevant not only to correct anticipations about the object of religious studies but also to confronting the student of religion with what a natural scientist would call his personal equation. (*3C*:19)

As has become only too clear, Lonergan's "philosophy of" is all about the personal equation, the view that our particular outlook and experience influences our reflective or so-called objective undertakings. The premise he builds on is that the outlook influencing our undertakings is, in so far as conscious experience is concerned, largely philosophical in nature. He leaves to psychologists and analysts the task of unearthing the subconscious and unconscious factors that feed and, to a certain extent, determine our horizons. Of these he is cognizant as well, although he is wary to pronounce on them given his field of competency. Still, as long as the examination of these deeper sources are given systematic form and conducted methodically, it cannot be thought to be immune from the philosophical presuppositions that a "philosophy of" means to bring into the noontide light and then develop or reverse.

In "Method: Trend and Variations" Lonergan allows religion scholars, advancing new methods of understanding the religious phenomenon, to speak to the inadequacies of former methods. These new methods are the variations of what he perceives to be the constant "inner trend" (presumably, the operations of consciousness) "by which our grasp of method begins, develops, takes command" (*3C*:21). Needless to say, this inner trend is Lonergan's concern. Its scrutiny does not produce answers to questions that, say, the sociologist of religion raises as a sociologist of religion. Rather, what it produces answers to is the questions of the sociologist of religion as they relate to the personal equation. Moreover, as "philosophic methodology," it targets the philosophical underpinnings of the personal equation, known or unknown to one, which Lonergan takes to be foundational to methodologically guided inquiry. Sample questions are provided:

> One is told that the scientist is content to describe. But does that mean that he does not perceive? Or is perception identified with sensation? One is told that science is value-free. Does that mean that the scientist is impartial, that he has no axe to grind? Or does it mean that the psychologist reaches a scientific explanation when he can reproduce the process in a robot or at least in a rat? Can one be religious and nonetheless do scientific work in the field of religious studies? Can one be objective about one's own religion, about another's? (*3C*:21)

Lonergan notes that the questions are basic and even admit of practical solutions up to a point. They are only handled adequately, however, in Lonergan's opinion, on the level of philosophic methodology. He is doubtful, though, that a consensus can be reached on this basis since "ultimate issues rest on ultimate options, and ultimate options are existential" (*3C*:21). Philosophic methodology is about method, not existential choices. One's existential choices may be addressed by it, how one's method and consequently one's discoveries are affected by those choices. By it one may even judge the viability of a method's results *on account of those choices*, that is, the scope of their relevance for a subject matter. For example, an understanding of religion grounded in a horizon closed off to what Rudolf Otto (1869–1937) calls "the numinous" is, on this understanding, in murky waters when systematizing or communicating what it may otherwise impeccably mediate in the mediating phase. This falls in the purview of philosophy of religion, but especially when the horizon becomes explicit or theoretical, when it turns, in other words, into an -ism, a materialism, a positivism, an existentialism, a pragmatism. And yet it is not about existential choices, although it includes them. It cannot decide for one what existential choices to make or which to change because of such an engagement, only that one is so involved in one's work. The options upon which one settles are personal founded on sources other than the strictly philosophical and methodological. Through philosophic methodology these options are brought to the surface as influential to judgments. They are developed if thought not to bias one's horizon over that of which an understanding is sought. They are reversed when an investigator's horizon is over-determinative, when the understanding is more of a horizon than that of which an understanding is sought.

It is significant, then, that at a high point in his Donald Mathers Memorial Lectures Lonergan inserts two sections entitled "Dialectic" and "Praxis" just before drawing the lectures to a close with the section "Religion, Theology, Religious Studies." Again, dialectic is pivotal to philosophic methodology. It is founded upon the premise that the "age of innocence" has ended, "the age that assumed that human authenticity"—that is, vigilance to maintain what Lonergan calls the transcendental precepts (be attentive, be intelligent, be reasonable, be responsible)—"could be taken for granted" and human wickedness could be evaded (*3C*:156). There is a mixture of both in seeking that which is true and good. No method can bracket human authenticity or the lack thereof as inconsequential to its discoveries. With regard to matters of interpretation, Lonergan mentions Paul Ricoeur's distinction between a hermeneutic of suspicion and one of recovery, which addresses the objective aspect of the problem. "A hermeneutic of recovery is one that brings to light what is true and good, and a hermeneutic of suspicion, that joins Marx in impugning the rich, or Nietzsche in reviling the humble, or Freud in finding consciousness itself an unreliable witness to our motives" (*3C*:157). His own study of what he dubs the origins of Christian realism (see *CWL* 6:80–93) is also mentioned as illustrative of the way in which a philosophic horizon affects the intellectual integrity of doctrinal expression. Because, we are meant to infer, Athanasius (c. 297–373) inhabits a mental space prizing the world mediated by meaning—where meaning is the truth of the Christian kerygma—his Christological and Trinitarian doctrines are said to be more authentic intellectually than those of Origen (c. 185–c. 254) and Tertullian (c. 196–c. 212). The meaning Tertullian is after, influenced as he is by Stoicism, is of the world of immediacy. Origen's meaning, influenced by Middle Platonism, *is* of the world mediated by meaning, but the meaning of ideas. Both transcend aspects of Christian and non-Christian meaning, but are insufficient in expounding Christian truth. Doubtless Lonergan would be questioned on these points on the same grounds that his treatment of philosophical figures is.[45] Still, this is a good indication of the level at which he understands his philosophy of religion to be principally operative.

The specialty of history is another specific function that Lonergan recognizes philosophy of religion to be relevant to. He distinguishes between general and specific issues. The general issues have to do with familiar categories (i.e., progress, decline, and recovery) in his notion of history, which date back to his earliest writings.[46] It involves something of a social critique of the unfolding of historical processes, the history that happens as opposed to the history that is written about. Policies, plans, and courses of action are a hybrid of creative insight and countering oversight that usher this process we refer to as history along prosperous lines at one moment and into cycles of decline at another. The challenge, of course, is with these periods of decline, "a mixed product partly of human authenticity and partly of human obtuseness, unreasonableness, irresponsibility" (*3C*:158). A partial recovery of "progress" is possible through a process of reasoning coupled with the awareness that the source of decline is human waywardness. However, because Lonergan believes, in the good company of many a philosopher and theologian, that reason is particularly susceptible to rationalization, the solution for him is not to be found in reason but in religion.

> What will sweep away the rationalizations? More reasoning will hardly do it effectively, for it will be suspected of being just so much more rationalizing. And when reasoning is ineffective, what is left but faith? What will smash the determinisms—economic, social, cultural, psychological—that egoism has constructed and exploited? What can be offered but the hoping beyond hope that religion inspires? When finally the human situation seethes with alienation, bitterness, resentment, recrimination, hatred, mounting violence, what can retributive justice bring about but a duplication of the evils that already exist? Then what is needed is not retributive justice [presumably, a possible response of reason] but self-sacrificing love.[47]

The specific issues are more directly related to the methods employed in exegesis and historiography (the history that is written about). Earlier I described this as the species of conflict that religion scholars frequently encounter. It witnesses to the complexity of history, as Lonergan says in *Method*. The clashing of opinions to which it gives rise is sometimes resolved when new data are uncovered (*MIT*:235). If the distinction between Lonergan's philosophy of religion, his model of religion, and his method in theology is sound, his brevity on this aspect in the literature developing his philosophy of religion suggests that there it is a low priority, quite unlike in his method in theology. Perhaps this is implied in his statement in "Philosophy and the Religious Phenomenon," that philosophy of religion "can pronounce, not immediately and specifically, but only remotely and generically on the validity or viability of the results of religious studies" (*PRP*:128). Presumably that is because the particular methods employed in religious studies lie outside the primary difficult task of philosophy of religion. Nevertheless, philosophy of religion may pronounce on these special issues in so far as method (in theology) is incorporated into it and in so far as the particularities of the mediating specialties reflect what religion scholars still do. And yet the dialectical *modus operandi* of philosophy of religion is neither one of confronting religion scholars with a better understanding of their data, nor one of providing better methods by which to understand their data. Rather, it is one of providing a basis for confronting in themselves the irrational that affects their so-called objective research every bit as much as it permeates the undertakings of the nonacademic. In fact, it can be more insidious, hidden under the guise of objectivism. Lonergan also adds that philosophy of religion provides "a technique for distinguishing between authentic and unauthentic evaluations, decisions, actions" (*3C*: 159). We gather from this that the primary dialectical concern of philosophy of religion is with fundamental conflicts that arise on account of a cognitional theory, an ethical stance, or a religious outlook, and not so much with the dialectical species of conflict mentioned earlier ("perspectival").

There is a praxiological side to all of this. Lonergan contends it has become an academic subject necessitated by the end of the age of innocence. He provides a quick overview of thinkers and philosophic schools from Arthur Schopenhauer (1788–1860) to Jürgen Habermas (1929–), from pragmatism to phenomenology. These have heralded the end of the age of innocence. For Lonergan, what this involves is a sublation of the cognitional by the existential, the decisional, although he is in the habit of thinking that some of the thinkers and schools he mentions (notably, Kierkegaard and Nietzsche, pragmatism and existentialism) unnecessarily minimize the former in the process. Praxis in this context centers on what one is going to do about what one discovers through dialectic: "What use are you to make of your knowledge of nature, of your knowledge of man, of your awareness of the radical conflict between man's aspiration to self-transcendence and, on the other hand, the waywardness that may distort his traditional heritage and even his own personal life [?]" (*3C*:159). Although the form of the questions are doubtless different, many academics raise them but as entirely personal or as a subtext of what it is that they do. The feeling is that what is personal is inessential to their role as researchers. According to Lonergan, we can no longer afford this luxury if we wish to be responsible or authentic inquirers. As inquirers, then, we are to take our stance on an authenticity of intelligence and reasonableness, which helps us to decipher fact from fiction. We are also to rely on an authentic deliberating and deciding, in which judgments of value are integral to deciphering those of fact. They are like the vital organs upon which we depend to live, not the ligaments we can live without.

In "The Ongoing Genesis of Methods" Lonergan is not clear on the relation of praxis *and* dialectic to the downward movement of consciousness. Only praxis is mentioned as moving from above downwards, from decision to judgment, from judgment to understanding, from understanding to experience. Praxis is grounded on the assumption that authenticity can no longer be taken for granted in methodologically based inquiry. It incorporates an understanding that follows a hermeneutic of suspicion and of recovery. In its judgments are discerned products of human authenticity and unauthenticity. It is a method that is "a compound of theoretical and practical judgments of value" (*3C*:161). However, this seems to involve more than the praxiological issues that follow from dialectical confrontation. As he puts it earlier on in his address: What are you to *do* about the irrational in human inquiry discovered through dialectical analysis? Presumably, because he is discussing praxis, he is focusing on it as the method, and he is emphasizing the praxiological moment of dialectic in this part of his address. Dialectic takes care of the theoretical aspect of a hermeneutic of suspicion and of recovery in Lonergan's sense, praxis the practical. As a hermeneutic of suspicion, dialectic, "from above downwards,"[48] is the means by which one gauges the authenticity of the upward movement of empirical method, its cognitional constitution as well as, albeit indirectly, its existential basis and implications. As a hermeneutic of recovery, it is the means by which one develops theoretically all that is authentic in that movement. What is inauthentic in its products is reversed through a hermeneutic of suspicion. Praxis, as a hermeneutic of suspicion, is an engagement of explicit and implicit value judgments; they drive the movement in which are certain practical implications. As a hermeneutic of recovery, praxis is an implementation of the value judgements grasped as authentic in the knowledge that is delivered. The distinction is of no real consequence to the proposal. It merely lends greater precision to it.

Lonergan surmises that dialectic, in its twofold theoretic and praxiological mode, will aid theologians in their discernment of the realities to which the symbols of religious consciousness point, "whether there is any real fire," as he puts it, "behind the smoke of symbols employed in this or that religion" (*3C*:161). Echoed are his sentiments in *Insight* about mystery and myth and the importance of explanation in theology.[49] Evidently, the shifts in theology from the 1950s to the 1970s, to say nothing of the criticisms of the intellectualist bent to his work, did little to sway Lonergan on this point. The contribution of dialectic to religious studies, which at the time was conceived in predominately descriptive rather than evaluative terms, is in what Lonergan saw as its endeavor to understand "the element of total commitment that characterizes religion" (*3C*:163). Apparently Lonergan had been detecting a shift in the ethos of religious studies, from a natural-science based paradigm of research, interpretation, and history to that of "profounder historical study." By the latter he means a form of study that is not only historically critically conscious, but also one that acknowledges that the evaluative is an indispensable feature of the descriptive. In such an approach, promoting the cooperation of religions becomes as important as cataloguing their relevant data, interpreting their morphology, and studying their genesis, development, distribution, and interaction. Where and when this applies, the boundaries of a perspectival dialectic expand to include one that is involved in "the radical oppositions of cognitional theory, of ethical practise, of religious and secularist man" (*3C*:163). Lonergan imagines its concrete implications in terms of a multidimensional dialectic. At one moment it assembles all the dialectics that relate religions to organized secularism, religions to one another, and differing theologies to one another; at another moment it invites representatives of related and disparate religions to dialogue. Of course, this was done in Lonergan's day, as it is in ours. His contribution to the discussion pertains to the basis of such activity. Where others might base it on the exigencies of an appropriated ethic, a philosophic position, a revelation, Lonergan advises that we base it on a continual appropriation of the cognitional and existential exigencies we find in our experience, our authentic understanding, judging, deciding, and being-in-love. This gives us both a critical and praxiological basis for assessing the authenticity of these other sources of meaning, in conversation with which our dialectic is formed.

 An added advantage of all of this is the cordial relationship that philosophy of religion forges between religious studies and theology—more cordial, anyway, than was the case with the past Lonergan was familiar with. On this view, theology is not a subacademic pursuit lacking in "objectivity" simply because belief or faith is part of its systematic venture. If objectivity is of the virtually unconditioned grasped by reflective understanding and not a mere gaping at the given; if judgments are of fact and of value; if belief is operative at every level of inquiry, although not equivalently (yet, still, legitimately relative to that level), then the issue of theology being merely subjective is moot. Objectivity for Lonergan is a consequence of authentic subjectivity. This does not blind him to the substantial differences between the natural and human sciences. Still, he is unequivocal about each having a share in objectivity in so far as their objectivity is the fruit of attentiveness, intelligence, reasonableness, and responsibility (*MIT*:265).

On Lonergan's view, religious studies is not a valueless squelcher of the consciousness it seeks to understand. The sentiment is commonly held by freshmen and clerics, but is one that—one might be surprised to discover— has a life among theologians as well. The reaction is understandable: not only in myth does knowledge of a thing imply a certain power over it. And yet the value of religious studies is inestimable to historical consciousness that seeks an understanding of the symbols that feed its psychic life. In fact, theologians employ its many techniques in the acquisition of knowledge particular to their traditions (mediated phase). Theology needs religious studies as much as religious studies needs it. As Lonergan states, "without religious studies theologians are unacquainted with the religions of mankind; they may as theologians have a good grasp of the history of their own religion; but they are borrowing the techniques of the historian of religions, when they attempt to compare and relate other religions with their own" (*3C*:164). Conversely, "[w]ithout theology religious studies may indeed discern when and where different religious symbols are equivalent; but they are borrowing the techniques of theologians if they attempt to say what the equivalent symbols literally mean and they literally imply." Philosophy of religion would serve as something of a philosophical stand-in by which one critically yet openly appropriates the results of extrinsic primary difficult questioning in relation to one's own. It would also be a means by which one engages those results philosophically for their own merit, regardless whose primary difficult questions they stem from or are most relevant to. This raises the issue of values that provide for the momentum of, as well as result from, the search and interaction, which dialectic weeds out.

In the two remaining articles, "Philosophy and the Religious Phenomenon" (*PRP*) and "A Post-Hegelian Philosophy of Religion" (*PHPR*), in which Lonergan is most explicit about his programmatic of philosophy of religion, much of what has been covered is more or less reiterated. As we saw already, philosophy of religion is described as the foundational methodology of religious studies. "Foundational methodology" is merely a nominal variation of "philosophic methodology" mentioned earlier. Indeed, one could exchange the term with *Insight*'s "generalized empirical method" or *Method*'s "transcendental method" without affecting the meaning. Except for the changes introduced in *Method*—paramount to philosophy of *religion*, but of no real consequence to *philosophic* methodology as such—the formal component remains relatively unchanged from *Insight* to *PHPR*. However, as philosophy of *religion*, foundational methodology can only function as such by moving beyond the cognitional to the existential, beyond judgments of fact to judgments of value. "Beyond" here carries the sense of sublation discussed earlier: sublation or elevation of the cognitional into the decisional or the existential. "For every religion is involved in value judgments, and value judgments pertain to the fourth level of intentional consciousness" (*PRP*:132). What Lonergan is doing more in these articles is contrasting his concept of philosophy of religion with Hegel's. He expands on this by introducing certain hermeneutic distinctions from *Method*. This is done in order to lay out the pertinent components of a philosophy of religion whose dialectic is modeled after a hermeneutic of suspicion and recovery. Also new is the recasting of that which is relevant in the concept of the differentiations of consciousness, which Lonergan believes obtains parallel results but in a less abstruse manner.

Ironically, Lonergan spends more time discussing Hegel in *PRP* than in *PHPR*, a paper whose title includes Hegel's name. In both papers he mentions what in chapter 2 I concluded is the real difference between Lonergan and Hegel. As is clear from the nature and scope of his work, Lonergan wants to retain Hegel's comprehensiveness, which he does openly state. But he wants to do this without the emphasis Hegel places on dialectical logic. More fitting for our times, Lonergan argues, is a philosophic account of empirical method. In support of this he quotes from *The Idea of History* in which Collingwood admonishes philosophers of history to break with Hegel: "Philosophy cannot interfere with history according to the Hegelian formula of superimposing a philosophical history on the top of ordinary history.... Ordinary history is already philosophical history."[50] Lonergan quotes Collingwood, not because he supports Collingwood's contention that the methodological component within history is philosophy and not just "philosophy of." Actually, he finds it "cumbrous," although not impossible (*3C*:203). Collingwood is noted here because he is a noteworthy precedent for the response that Lonergan gives to the demand for a philosophic methodology, which evidently needs to be post-Hegelian. According to him, equating philosophy with ordinary history complicates the issue of superimposition and may actually miss another problematic inherent in it.

> It seems more expeditious to discover that the consciousness of every scientist includes a consciousness of the proper method of his subject. Just as the historian needs such a consciousness of historical method, so too do physicists, chemists, biologists, psychologists, exegetes, and so on, need to be effectively aware of the methodical exigencies of their respective fields. In this fashion we are led to recognizing as many "philosophies of...," as there are distinct sciences with appropriately differentiated methods. (*3C*:203–4)

The "problematic" is skirted in *PHPR*. Reference to Hegel in it is confined to a summary of that one major component that separates Lonergan from Hegel, namely, that Lonergan's philosophy is empirically based while Hegel's is one based on his dialectical logic of movement (see chapter 2). The problematic as such receives mention in *PRP*, which requires attention now.

In *PRP* this problematic is discussed in one paragraph, although it is related to previous paragraphs about Lonergan's concept of sublation, which is in turn related to the discussion of Hegel's logic of movement. Lonergan's proposal, of course, is that we replace logic with method. The problematic is an old one, which at least in the Christian tradition stems from the early Christian apologists' desire to think through the content and claims of biblical revelation philosophically. What is to be the relationship between an endeavor that prides itself on being autonomous and free and one that sees itself as bounded by the fundamental truths of revelatory knowledge? The distinction has been sharply defined by Christian apologists down through the centuries. What Christopher Stead has written about early Christian apologists in particular can be applied to any apologist or theologian along the stops of history who appeals to sources beyond reason as crucibles of truth. For that reason, these sources have a greater hold on them in determining the scope of truth as well as how it may be determined, at least with regard to the level of judgment that these sources presuppose. Thus, speaking of Christian antiquity, Stead states, "Its commitment to the Bible as a sacred book was far more uncompromising than the philosophers' respect for Plato; and it valued communal experience and tradition in a way which offended students accustomed to accepting the guidance of expert scholars."[51] On this basis, the negative response prompted by the very suggestion of a sublation of religion by philosophy (Hegel's proposal) is predictable. If Lonergan sides with that reaction (and he does in part), it is not for the reasons usually given. The principal reason is that it subordinates supernatural truths, which transcend reason, to those that are acquired or acquirable naturally. Tagged a tertiary response that is metaphysically based, Lonergan prefers the more primary response provided by his intentionality analysis. Thus, he conceives the subordination to be of the cognitive to the existential, knowledge to decision, and not necessarily one that involves competing truth claims. This leads him to conclude, one senses with qualification, that "Kierkegaard had a point" (*PRP*:134).

More is involved, however, in Lonergan's alternative, as Elizabeth A. Morelli has shown.[52] Lonergan is not altogether rejecting Hegel's proposal, for he too sounds the Hegelian call to sublate by thought the feeling (*Gefühl*) and representational thinking (*Vorstellung*) that religion in its basic form represents. The words that Lonergan uses are different. For instance, he would prefer to say that we sublate, through cognitive self-transcendence, the undifferentiated consciousness of religion and that we do so by a differentiated apprehension of its objects. But the intention is virtually the same. Hence, Morelli offers the very plausible suggestion that we distinguish between two kinds of sublation in Lonergan's alternative to Hegel, one that is thematic, which is more or less in agreement with Hegel's proposal, and one that is existential, where Lonergan parts ways with Hegel. She provides two senses to the thematic aspect. The first pertains to foundational methodology as applicable to the development of the heuristic structure of any given field of inquiry, including religious studies. The second follows from the first in that the advancement of theoretical and interior self-knowledge advocated by foundational methodology enables one "to situate religious myth and mystery in relation to the rest of conscious phenomena."[53] This accounts for Lonergan's thematic sublation of religion by philosophy and, consequently, theology. The sublation of philosophy by theology, which Lonergan as a theologian does advocate, is but another instance of this thematic-sublational movement.[54] Lonergan's dissatisfaction with Hegel centers on the absence of any suggestion in his work of the way in which religion sublates philosophy. "[I]nsofar as religious living involves the concern, passion, freedom and love of the religious subject, religion provides the existential sublation of philosophy and all merely cognitive pursuits."[55] While I am not in a position to verify whether this implies that Hegel's conception of religion is inadequate, which is Morelli's contention, I do agree with her that this bipolar sublational movement adequately captures Lonergan's position. It also addresses the extent to which he is indebted to and yet in basic disagreement with Hegel on this question.

Lonergan's quibbles with Hegel extend back to *Insight* and even earlier writings. They extend back to a time when charting the cognitive levels and their relevance for the work of academic inquiry consumed him. His growing appreciation for the unconscious, subconscious, and existential further distanced him from Hegel. What this also did, however, is simultaneously highlight still further their points of agreement. The contrast of his program with Hegel's soon after he discusses the "one-sidedness of an exclusive intellectualism" (*PRP*:131) strongly suggests that Lonergan thought that Hegel's proposal tends toward exclusivism, albeit as a "conceptualism." But as though in defense of Hegel—rather: the spirit of Hegel, the omnivorous drive toward differentiation that Hegel in so many ways exemplifies—Lonergan states that complaints about differentiated apprehension being "abstract" are the result of ignorance: "The so-called 'abstract' is usually the incompletely determined apprehension of the concrete, and all human apprehension is incompletely determined. Indeed, intellectualist apprehension is more complete than the apprehension of undifferentiated consciousness, and it is just the ignorance of undifferentiated consciousness that complains about the abstractness of the intellectual" (*PRP*:131–2). Here Lonergan is really defending his self-designated *intellectualist* foundation of philosophy of religion. But he is defending it at a basic level so that one could just as easily see him defending the Hegelian propensity for thematic sublation purged, of course, of its so-called conceptualist underpinnings.⁵⁶ In other words, the importance of the intellectual (broadly conceived) in the later Lonergan does not wane, although the vigor with which he earlier expressed and defended it does for several reasons. The one most fitting for a discussion of his philosophy of religion is Crowe's suggestion that this apparent wane seems to naturally accompany the kind of shift that Lonergan is trying to effect to the *Geisteswissenschaften* (human sciences). "[M]atters of the spirit will always seem less subject to rigorous analysis than those of the infrahuman world."⁵⁷ Notwithstanding this, one finds that the later Lonergan defends the need for intellectual rigor in an existential sublation of philosophy by religion every bit as much as he did early in his career when engrossed with the significance of an intellectualist-thematic sublation of religion by theology.

The meaning that Lonergan gives to this in *PRP* involves a fixation on the two "levels" preceding and following from respectively the usual conscious four. Prior to what he calls "the intellectual operator" that moves from experience to understanding, from understanding to judgment, from judgment to decision, there may well be, he suggests, a symbolic operator "that coordinates neural potentialities and needs with higher goals through its control over the emergence of images and affects" (*PRP*:134). He conceived this notion of a symbolic operator in close conversation with Robert M. Doran, now coeditor of the *Collected Works*. We have already had some contact with the symbolic in Lonergan, which as operator he merges with the psychological ruminations of chapter 6 of *Insight*. When functioning positively this involves a process of selecting and arranging symbolic materials in a perspective that often leads to insight; when functioning negatively it involves a process of rejection and exclusion that blocks the psychic representation of neural, unconscious demand functions (see *CWL* 3:215–6). At the other end of the spectrum is the operator who is in love interpersonally and religiously, who is grasped by ultimate concern—another concept not unfamiliar to the reader. In *PRP* Lonergan describes this in terms of a self-present sublation of the fourth level heading beyond judgments of value with its retinue of decisions and actions toward its transcendent goal. By this nothing different is meant from what in our discussion of Lonergan's model of religion was described as a transvaluing of creatively attained values through a healing development. Lonergan finds these two "levels" particularly relevant to religious studies. I have already indicated this in regard to the second of the two levels. With regard to the first, we might see it as pertinent to theology, to one's understanding of grace, for instance, and consequently contemporary expressions of that doctrine. An example close to home is Robert M. Doran himself, who wants to ground a theology of grace on the "psychic conversion" of inquirers who are, ideally, religiously, intellectually, morally, and socially converted.⁵⁸ Religion scholars might approach it from another angle, perhaps less therapeutically and more phenomenologically. Lonergan, the theologian, has no misgivings about this. By pointing to a symbolic operator he is merely, though cunningly, suggesting that specialists are implicated in an unconscious and subconscious process that has creative and adverse effects on the way in which they approach the religious phenomenon, let alone each other's work. A critical, methodical, suprastructural move is necessary to develop the conducive affects of the censor's positive functioning and to negotiate its adverse affects when functioning negatively. Jürgen Habermas felt he had to remind Gadamer of this very thing in the latter's hermeneutic claim to universality.[59] The type of philosophy of religion that Lonergan advances provides a foundation for gauging authentic and unauthentic outworkings of this attentiveness.

In the last sentence further reference is given to the function of Lonergan's philosophy of religion as dialectical and its reliance on, but distinction from, his model of religion. Confirmation of this is found in one of the two elements, the first element mentioned, that Lonergan chooses to outline foundational methodology's primary contribution to religious studies, as the heuristic structure of religious studies. Needless to say, it is dialectic that helps one to distinguish between the authentic and unauthentic. In *PRP* followers of a given religion are introduced into the equation so that not only are interpreters encouraged to evaluate the authentic and unauthentic in themselves as they approach the object of their professional concerns, but they also are encouraged to evaluate the notions in followers of a religion that contradict the nature of the religion under investigation. Thus, a dialectical philosophy of religion is one in which "investigators are urged both to expand what they consider authentic in the followers of a religion they are studying and, as well, to reverse what they consider unauthentic. The result will be a projective test in which interpreters reveal their own notions of authenticity and unauthenticity both to others and to themselves" (*PRP*:137–8). Presumably these notions in interpreters are qualitatively on par with the level of differentiation at which followers of a religion are functioning and at which religion is primordially manifest. Otherwise Lonergan would be subject to the same critique of Hegel that he himself attempts to overcome *vis-à-vis* his existential-sublational amendment to a process exclusively thematic and unidirectional.[60]

The second element he also deems dialectical but in a different sense. I will return to it after we look at Lonergan's development of the first element in *PHPR*, in which he draws on hermeneutic distinctions from *Method*. The distinctions are of functions of meaning, four to be exact: cognitive, efficient, constitutive, communicative. Cognitive meaning is a reference to the world of meaning compactly given at first but ever-expanding as questions are raised and answered. Cognitive meaning ever-expands as the storehouse of memories gets filled, as norms and ideals are acted upon and later cultivated or rejected. Such a world is simultaneously undifferentiated (in the sense of an adult common sense), differentiated (specialized knowledge), and postsystematic (a modified common sense greatly affected by the differentiations of consciousness). "To it we refer when we speak of the real world. But because it is mediated by meaning and motivated by value, because meaning can go astray and evaluation become corrupt, because there is a myth as well as science, fiction as well as fact, deceit as well as honesty, error as well as truth, that larger world is insecure" (*PHPR*:211). Today, of course, one would be well advised to avoid equating myth with fiction, deceit, and error, as Lonergan does somewhat carelessly here. However, we have seen in what way he means this, which is compatible with modern appreciations of myth proper.

What Lonergan means by "efficient" meaning may be understood both in the commonsense meaning of the term as productive and effective and in an Aristotelian sense, that of meaning bringing about or initiating a change through a suitable agent. "We imagine, we plan, we investigate possibilities, we weigh pros and cons, we enter into contracts, we have countless orders given and executed. Over the world given us by nature, there is an artificial, man-made world; it is the cumulative, now planned, now chaotic, product of human acts of meaning" (*PHPR*:211; *MIT*:77–78). It is a fairly straightforward reference to what results from our planning and doing as well as to its efficient cause, conscious human activity.

As sound and meaning are to language so too are cultural and social realities, such as religion and the family, literature and the state, philosophy and law, to acts of meaning: they are constitutive, though they adapt to changing circumstances, involving shifts in meaning. In conjunction with the fourth function of meaning, which is communicative, Lonergan sees constitutive meaning as yielding the three key notions of community, "existence" (in the sense of *Existenz*), and history. Communicative meaning refers to common ways in which meaning is communicated. Lonergan mentions the four that he outlines in greater detail in his chapter on meaning in *Method*: intersubjective, symbolic, linguistic, and incarnate meaning. These are forms of our being-in-the-world that are progressively differentiated through clarification, expression, formulation, and definition. Lonergan notes, as he is in the habit of doing, how meaning is "enriched and deepened and transformed" through this process of differentiation. He also notes, however—which in all fairness to his critics he does not do frequently enough—how this process often impoverishes and deforms meaning (*PHPR*:212). Discontinuity is as much a part of the function of meaning as is continuity.[61]

The concept of dialectic is introduced into Lonergan's discussion of the key notions of community, existence, and history in a variety of ways. Although not as pronounced in his treatment of the notion of community as in the notions of existence and history, dialectic nonetheless colors its four degrees of common meaning.[62] These degrees of common meaning are conceived, as with most things in Lonergan, through the grid of his levels of consciousness. As potential common meaning is of a common field of experience, "to withdraw from that common field is to get out of touch" (*PHPR*:212). As formal it is common understanding, "one withdraws from that common understanding as misunderstanding and incomprehension supervene." Common meaning becomes actual through common judgments, when things are commonly affirmed and denied; it is "diluted as consensus fails." It is realized through decisions and dedication, "in the love that makes families, in the loyalty that makes states, in the faith that makes religions" (*PHPR*:212–3). At this point something of an amalgamation occurs with the key notion of existence. It arises as the concept of dialectic is treated in less piecemeal fashion in connection with the degrees of common meaning, that is, in connection with the degree of meaning where individuals have to decide for themselves what to make of themselves. "Such," Lonergan writes, "is the existential moment."

Again, the issue becomes one of ascertaining the authenticity or unauthenticity of one's stance toward something, in this case a particular religious tradition. Moreover, it involves ascertaining the authenticity or unauthenticity of the religious, philosophical, or scientific community with which one identifies that justifies or condemns that particular tradition. Lonergan spells this out concretely in a reiteration of what he says in *Method* concerning the well-intentioned yet ever-present possibility of unauthentically appropriating meaning.

> As Kierkegaard asked whether he was a Christian, so divers men can ask themselves whether they are authentically religious, authentically philosophers, authentically scientists. They may answer that they are, and they may be right. But they may answer affirmatively and still be mistaken. On a series of points they will realize what the ideals of the tradition demand; but on another series their lives diverge from those ideals. Such divergence may be overlooked from a selective inattention, a failure to understand, an undetected rationalization. What I am is one thing; what an authentic Christian or Buddhist is, is another, and I am unaware of the difference. My unawareness is unexpressed. I have no language to express what I am, so I use the language of the tradition that I unauthentically appropriate, and thereby I devaluate, distort, water down, corrupt that language. (*PHPR*:213; *MIT*:80)

Sensitive as this issue is, the suggestion does seem compelling if not simply for its timeliness. For who would deny that this is an age given to rethinking its traditions in often unprecedented radical ways—"radical" here being understood in terms of a clean break with a tradition and not simply a creative development of some of its assumptions? Not that a break with a tradition on this or that point is necessarily uncalled for. It could prove to be requisite if meaning is to be mediated attentively, intelligently, reasonably, and responsibly. An obvious example is how the patriarchal *Weltanschauung* of the Bible has been used to oppress women through the centuries and exclude them from positions of power. And yet chances of misrepresentation are high in radical rethinkings of a tradition, even, perhaps especially, in rethinkings that happen to be systematically self-conscious. Whether they are interiorly and critically self-conscious is another question. The situation is even further complicated when that rethinking issues from what Lonergan characterizes above as unawareness and, more pointedly, when rethinking does not involve a thinking at all. This can occur on a small scale in scattered individuals or on a large scale, becoming part of the common sense of a whole society. So-called religious individuals and communities are as susceptible to this as is the scientific community that Husserl diagnosed as directed by "the conventions of a clique" (*PHPR*:213).

The key notion of history flows naturally from that of existence. The existential choices one makes informs not only one's reading of a tradition but also that of a community's. Upon that community's reading one's reading may be based, informing it as well. History is contrasted with nature. Nature unfolds in accordance with classical and statistical laws. History, on the other hand, is "an expression of meaning, and meaning is open both to enduring stationary states, to development, the fruit of authenticity, and to aberration that matches the unauthenticity of its source" (*PHPR*:214). Lonergan, throwing light on what he regards as "a repertory of ideal types" in Toynbee's study of history, describes how a creative minority, amid the pulls and tugs of the history of which it is constitutive, progresses as it hits upon a cumulative sequence of relevant insights. This is owed to communal acts of self-transcendence, based, as we have said, on a readiness to be attentive, to grow in intelligence, reasonableness, and responsibility. Conversely, such a community may jostle the wheel of history into a cycle of decline in a now calculated, now inadvertent, disregard for the good and the true. "Basic decisions are shirked. Judgments lean towards superficiality. Difficult insights are ignored. Problems are referred to committees" (*PHPR*:215). All this harks back to chapter 7 of *Insight* and Lonergan's papers and lectures on history. Readers interested in applying or critically engaging Lonergan's understanding of history and its cycles are encouraged to turn to *Insight* and to the other studies I have mentioned, which go into far greater detail than I can here. A study of Lonergan's philosophy of religion cannot fail to mention it (and other components) since it is regarded as a key notion to the formal functioning of his philosophy of religion. Anything more than that, however, is bound to sidetrack us in charting what that philosophy of religion is and how it is related to, in its difference from, his philosophy of God and other related components.

What I have described thus far, the functions of meaning and its key notions, constitutes what is Lonergan's clarification of the primary sense of dialectic in philosophy of religion. In *PRP* it is summed up largely in terms of *PHPR*'s key notion of existence. In this respect the outline provided in *PHPR* is more differentiated. However, as regards that which Lonergan sees as the second contribution of philosophy of religion to religious studies, which is dialectical but in a secondary sense, Lonergan's earlier writing, *PRP*, evidently wins on the differentiation front. In *Method* it is outlined in terms of the differentiations of consciousness in its relevant stages of meaning. The stages in *PRP* are summarized as the linguistic, the literate, the logical, and the methodical. They seem to include what Lonergan means by the stages of meaning in *Method* but cast in shorthand. Detected as well is an overlap with the third and fourth functions of meaning mentioned earlier, the constitutive and the communicative. But as with *Method*'s stages of meaning, which are more or less a global rendering of the individual realms of meaning, Lonergan's formulation of philosophy of religion's second contribution to religious studies strikes one as a global rendering of the third and fourth functions of meaning. As for its dialectical feature Lonergan surmises that it is similar in style to what Louis Mink finds operative in Collingwood.[63] "In such a dialectic there are the terms whose meaning shifts in the course of time and, further, there are the terms that denote the factors bringing about such shifts in meaning" (*PRP*:138). Lonergan would doubtless attribute these shifts in meaning fundamentally (especially when conflictual) to an explicit or implicit cognitional theory, an ethical stance, or religious outlook. But clearly the sense of dialectic that we are dealing with here is different. His ensuing sketchy account of the complex shifts and oppositions in history leads one to believe that it has more in common with what in *Method*, reluctant to describe it as dialectical, he describes as perspectival. Still, it does seem to consist in more than *Method*'s "perspectival."

The context is a broad one. It pertains to four stages that are distinguishable in social and cultural modes of human interaction. The stages have been noted already. They are the linguistic, the literate, the logical, and the methodical. The social modes are said to be already understood and accepted. He groups them under headings such as family, community, mores, state, law, education, economics, and technology. The cultural modes are areas of interest such as art, religion, science, philosophy, and history. By them "social frameworks find explanation, justification, a goal" (*PRP*:138). The extent of social and cultural differentiation, the structure of their roles, is one that moves from simplicity to greater complexity, to a role that, as in the case of Christianity in the West, becomes less comprehensive in scope. The history of Western Christianity fits nicely into Lonergan's example of ancient religion and may actually inform it. "[T]he more ancient the religion, the less sharply will its role be distinguished from other roles, and the more notable will the position it occupies in the sociocultural matrix" (*PHPR*:139). The stages, which he views as exponential in their sublational movement, are essential to this development. Thus, the literate stage, in which people read and write, adds to, by sublating, the linguistic stage, in which people speak and listen. The logical stage adds to, by sublating, the literate in the promotion of clarity and coherence, moving toward permanently valid systems. The methodical (the ideal of Lonergan) adds to the logical by preserving the validity of constructing systems, although it abandons ideals of permanently valid systems. What it truly adds is an understanding of the role of method or methodical thinking as "the discernment of invariants and variables in the ongoing sequences of systems" (*PHPR*:139).

The point is also made that these stages are not universalized, which is a contributing factor to the stratification and alienation that exists from society to society and culture to culture. Literacy and illiteracy coexist as do logicality and illogicality for various reasons. The possibility of initiating new and "perhaps" better social arrangements will vary relative to the stage at which a society finds itself. The "higher" the development, it is suggested, the more capable a society will be of providing the relevant cultural justifications for new social arrangements. The alienation said to ensue is identified with both groups—those who have advanced to the higher stages and those who have not. It is experienced by both groups. Each imposes alienation on the other, though this relationship is described quite asymmetrically. Thus, the less advanced are *alienated* by their inability to comprehend the social arrangement in which they live, "motivated by appeals to values that they do not appreciate." When taking the initiative to do so, less advanced groups *alienate* those in more advanced stages by "*simpliste* social thought and crude cultural creations" (*PRP*:140). The structural dynamic of Hegel's master-serf dialectic is evident here. Social theorists might probably find cause for complaint in this rather one-sided portrayal, and I think justifiably so. But, in all fairness to Lonergan, he does plainly state that his outline is a "bold" one, conscious, we are made to feel, that a comprehensive study would iron out details that present fewer opportunities for misunderstanding. Chapter 7 of *Insight*, for example, distributes responsibility for alienation more evenly. *PRP* is not purported to be such a comprehensive analysis. It merely provides a context for Lonergan's primary concern of religion thought out relative to the stages. The target audience is the modern philosopher of religion (in his sense). She is encouraged to view not only the evolution of religious consciousness in this light, but also, we may infer, her own relation to these stages in her analysis of religious consciousness.

Religious traditions, particularly the major religious traditions in the West, Judaism, Christianity, and Islam, are located on this conceptual map. Through the stages in their varying social and cultural context they are said to discover themselves, develop their identity, differentiate themselves from and interact with other areas of life (*PRP*:140). They manifest themselves as myth and ritual at the linguistic stage. Their identity as religions of the book is telling of their literate stage. The consequent moment of reflection locates them at the logical stage. At this stage dissension is refereed by dogmatic pronouncements and reconciliation is sought through systematic theologies. As before, the influence of Hegel is obvious and barely needs mentioning. The methodical stage is one at which religious observers confront their own history and distinguish the stages of their development. Priority is given here as well to the evaluation of initiatives, whether they are authentic or unauthentic, as religiously imbued messages are communicated in the relevant styles and forms of one's society and culture. Lonergan corroborates his role not simply as a methodologist but as a contextualist's methodologist. A thinner brush with which to paint is then chosen to demonstrate the general validity of his stages model. The portrait is better served by his theological tractates, but his identification of some of the characteristics of each stage yields a fuller view of what has gone before and so are worth mentioning.

Religion in the linguistic and literate stages consists of a peculiar form of praxis closely coupled with proclamation, an undifferentiated praxiological orthodoxy, if you will. Lonergan describes this simply as doing and saying the truth. Thus, one will find formulas in the Bible nestled between and often indistinguishable from prescriptions to live virtuously. Believing that the Messiah suffered, died, and rose again in the person of Jesus of Nazareth, for example, was as important to New Testament writers as emulating his good deeds. The clashing of opinions and the desire to get things straight engendered an economy of technical terms intended to extricate the truth from its accompanying errors caused by literalistic readings of its anthropomorphic and symbolic form. Controversy breeds logic and counterlogic, and so for centuries disputes have been waged over what precisely is implied by the incarnation. "Even though the truth expresses mystery, at least it should not involve contradiction" (*PRP*:142) is how the concern of the logical mind is formulated. In addition to the councils and the heresies countering and countered by them, Lonergan mentions medieval theology as clear examples of this stage. Protestantism represents something of a "mixed bag" with its emphasis on the scripture principle (the literate stage) and its desire to remain faithful to the Greek councils (the logical stage). In time a scholasticism of its own would develop. The methodical stage in Lonergan's précis does not find representation. It is conceived as his answer to the consciousness and problems bequeathed to us through the Reformation. The consciousness is one of historical self-awareness, historical mindedness. The problem is one of understanding, and "the problems of understanding are problems of method"

(*PRP*:143). There is a general and specific side to this. The general, covered already in chapter 2 and in early sections of this chapter, grounds the specific, namely, understanding and method as Lonergan understands them. The specific side is the application of the general pertinent to philosophy of *religion* and, more particularly, in the immediate context of the different stages. In the concluding sentence of the article it is described as a methodical "ordering of differences due to developments." The ordering is dialectical. Once one grasps all that is implied by the general, it is suggested, one will avoid going astray as Scholasticism did in having its questions arise from the conflicts between theological systems rather than scripture and tradition. Also avoided will be what Lonergan humorously identifies as sixteenth-century archaist and anachronist incomprehensions of doctrinal development. While the former denounce doctrinal development, the latter, uncritically propounding it, read later developments into early ones. Both tendencies do a disservice to the significance of doctrine.

Finally, Lonergan gets to the tendency that he saw as his vocation to reverse. It is captured in a statement that he made late in his life: "All my work has been introducing history into Catholic theology."[64] In *PRP* the connotation is more critical and double-edged. To continue our narrative, in the methodical stage resources are available to avoid the once "long sustained opposition" of Catholics to historically grounded hermeneutics. I insert the word "once" here since this no longer seems to be a problem in critical expositions of Catholic faith. The concern now in theological circles is one of communicating in fresh, culturally sensitive theological ways the historical meanings that have been critically acquired and carefully logged for decades. The fear that historical investigation compromises conciliar truth has all but disappeared as a preventive for historically based study, although many are still working through the issues of redefinition. To the extent that this is true, and the truth of culturally relative expressions of scripture and tradition are not compromised, Lonergan would say that such a mentality is what he takes to be methodical in an authentic sense. What its relation is to foundational methodology is another question.

Avoiding an uncritical merger of scholasticism with modern thought is the other side of Lonergan's donation. We might see his remarks in the above paragraph about the unhistorical nature of theological inquiry in the logical stage as especially tied to this. Scholasticism is an act of meaning, and like all other acts of meaning it is embedded in a context. Over time contexts change subtly, slowly, surely (*2C*:49). Unless it changes with these contexts, Scholasticism will find itself as hopelessly irrelevant to a context as the history it represents, a not uncommon fate. Jettisoning what is valuable in and represented by scholastic-type thinking (i.e., the logical) for something else (the linguistic or the literate) is not the answer either for Lonergan. The question is one of differentiated integration in which the various stages are affected and oftentimes radically altered by a context. According to Lonergan, this is best served by the methodical stage since in neither one of the stages, individually or in tandem, are the means available to initiate and adjudicate the process.

The examples chosen to relate the relevance of this sense of dialectic to philosophy of religion pertains largely to what historical-critical study of the religious phenomenon has contributed to theology. Lonergan is not closed to the obverse situation, regardless of his shortage of examples with the stages in mind.

A number of elements have emerged in the course of this analysis that illumine an understanding of what Lonergan means by philosophy of religion. What has become most clear, so clear in fact that no argument is needed to state it, is that his sense is not what is usually understood by the term in the field of the same name. For this reason I prefer to refer to this particular "philosophy of" as his *philosophy of religious studies*. There are advantages to this. First, it conveniently demarcates the focus of his philosophy of religion from that of his model of religion. On this basis, and the fact that the model is closely associated with his foundational methodology, one may wish to designate his model in terms of a philosophy of religious experience where "religious experience" takes on the broader colloquial sense of the word. His philosophy of religion, what I label technically and quite literally his philosophy of religious studies, is more properly a philosophical-methodological preoccupation with the individual methods by which the religious phenomenon is studied. Second, this identifier permits reserving a generic sense to the term in Lonergan that betokens his entire system of philosophizing about God and religion (i.e., religious experience, faith, belief, religious studies, and theology). Figure 4.2 provides an illustration of how one might picture it.

The diagram is a development of fig. 4.1 presented earlier in this chapter. The boldfaced text represents the formal component of Lonergan's philosophy of religion, the italicized text the material. The bilateral arrow stretching from philosophy of religious studies to religious experience indicates a reciprocity of influence, which is multidimensional. The same applies to the arrow connecting Lonergan's model and religious experience. These bilateral arrows conveniently show at least two things. First, they mark a general distinction between religious experience and the suprastructures of scholars, namely, that lived and practiced by human communities. Presumably these "models" are the objects of expert study, Lonergan's type of analysis included. Second, they mark a more specific distinction between religious experience or lack thereof in the scholarly endeavor as the religious phenomenon is expertly suprastructuralized. Within each of the models are conceptions of religious experience and its contents. As suprastructuralized, however, the models are distinct from the reality of which they are an explanation. Lonergan's philoso-

Fig. 4.2
Elements of Lonergan's Philosophy of Religion

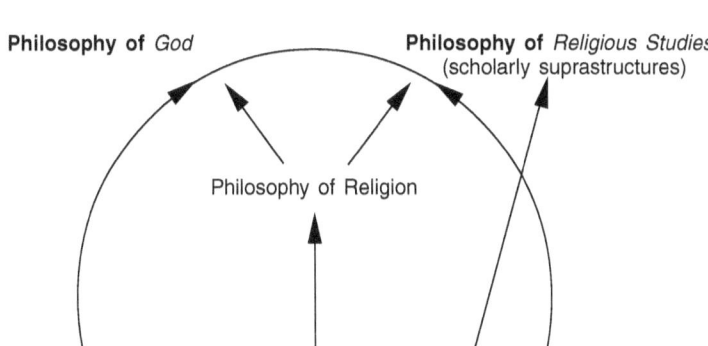

phy of religion is concerned principally with the second dynamic and so the diagram should be seen as an illustration of it rather than the larger world presupposed by the first. With regard to his philosophy of religious studies in particular, we have seen the concern to be one of scrutinizing the authentic and/or unauthentic presuppositions providing for scholarly reflection. The relationship of religious studies to theology and vice versa, we also saw, was another of its concerns. As with the various models, religious experience as infrastructure also shares a reciprocity of influence pivotal to both "philosophies of." The claim is that religious experience grounds philosophical reflection on it existentially as well as that which is grounded philosophically.

What about the role of Lonergan's model of religion? The model is the suprastructure that Lonergan has formulated informed by and as a development of his methodological suprastructure (generalized empirical method, foundational methodology, etc.). Its relation to the individual "philosophies of," in their stated purpose—not just as "philosophies of" but as philosophies of *God* and *religious studies*—is remotely connected to their function. The diagram adequately captures this by putting religious experience in a more immediate relationship with the "philosophies of." This might be interpreted as the bare recognition that religious experience "holds a fundamental place primarily in man's making of man but no less in the reflection on that making that is philosophy or, indeed, 'philosophy of...'" (*CWL* 4:187). Without conflating the intentions and/or functions of both meanings, Lonergan's model is as central to the function of his philosophy of religion as are the suprastructures of religion scholars. They provide the matter for reflecting on the authenticity or unauthenticity of this or that position, this or that utterer. They do not constitute the reflecting, however.

Conclusion

We have given form to elements of a structure that may be described as Lonergan's philosophy of religion. Complications quickly arose as our task slowly developed. To begin with, he does not use the term as it is usually understood. Indeed, even the sense I ascribe to him at the end of chapter 4 is missing from his work. Philosophy of religion fulfills a very specific task for Lonergan. Definitions have already been noted. "Philosophy of religion reveals how basic thinking relates itself to the various branches of religious studies" (*2C*:204); it "is the foundational methodology of religious studies" (*PRP*:128); and so on. Clearly one would be hard-pressed to find such definitions in the literature on the topic. Lonergan was not a card-carrying philosopher of religion. He was first and foremost a theologian who liked to think a lot, as he quaintly puts it in a letter to his provincial superior.[1] What David Burrell says is very compelling in this regard: "everything [Lonergan] did, including and especially *Insight*, is ordered to understanding the faith we have received."[2] The idea of faith as given, which philosophy of religion as a distinct discipline either prepares people for or defends, would have been as strange to Lonergan as it is, presumably, to Burrell. Issues of faith presume faith. They are expressed and thought about in traditions and the communities supporting them. Philosophy usually hones these issues through rigorous reflection. Sometimes philosophy even displaces faith, in which case a combination of some sort of pastoral counseling and life experience is needed—not more logical reasoning. For Lonergan, to ask anything more of philosophy vis-à-vis religion is to encroach upon theology.

If asked to compare Lonergan's style of philosophy of religion, I would have to settle for something comparable to Hegel's and, more recently, Ricoeur's. Lonergan is a "philosopher of religion" in the sense that these individuals are. Like Hegel and Ricoeur Lonergan thinks philosophically and comprehensively about the subjective and objective poles of religion. Also like them he is guided by structural and meta-methodological concerns. His approach, as someone whose vocation was theology, is different from theirs but no less philosophical. The closest that Lonergan comes to Anglo-American forms of philosophy of religion, which are more topical and logical in orientation, is in his early philosophy of God. His proof and his logical treatment of the problem of evil—particularly its form in *De ente supernaturali* (Thesis IV, Scholion IV), more so than in chapter 20 of *Insight*—easily fall under the familiar headings in anthologies and textbooks of philosophy of religion. I do need to enter the caveat, however, that his proof and so-called solution to the problem of evil in chapter 20 of *Insight* are meta-philosophical based on intentionality analysis.[3] At about the time reflection on religious experience enters his explicit thinking on these issues similarities begin to dwindle. The concerns shift to the relevance of method for understanding the religious phenomenon. His relation to the kind of philosophy of religion represented by Hegel and Ricoeur becomes increasingly overt as he distinguishes his empirically based contribution from the Logic of Hegel's, and as he develops Ricoeur's notion of a hermeneutics of suspicion and recovery along the lines of his dialectical and "theological" method.

This, in a nutshell, accounts for the various stages we have traced in the development of Lonergan's philosophy of religion, that is, what I want to call his "philosophy of religion." I think it is prudent to reserve the term for his whole system of philosophizing about God and religion. The reasons for this, which I offer at the end of chapter 4, pertain to the internal structure of that system. It does more than merely gather under a single term the components of his thought relevant to issues of religion. It provides, more significantly, an accurate means of demarcating his philosophy of religious studies—philosophy of religion for Lonergan—from his model of religion. Given that the terms and functions of each are easily confused, this should be duly noted. The short of it is that Lonergan's philosophy of religion comprises a philosophy of God and a philosophy of religious studies, of which theology is an integral part. These individual "philosophies of" are held together, as it were, by his model of religion, which is distinct from, though it informs, their function.

There is good reason, too, beyond that of internal relevance, to earmark the whole of Lonergan's thought on religion as philosophy of religion. This pertains to issues of comparison and are external to the system. Lonergan's choice of terms makes it incumbent upon us to distinguish carefully between his offering and that of card-carrying philosophers of religion—by which is usually meant philosophers of religion in the analytic mainstream. First, the term as I want to use it in reference to Lonergan calls attention to the fact that overlap exists. Lonergan may never have been very interested in philosophy of religion[4] but who would argue that others have not, rightly or wrongly, interpreted his work this way?[5] Remaining at the level of topics, we see this in connection with the "analytic" concern with proofs. Only moments ago I compared his philosophy of religion to so-called continental thinkers who inspire similarly classified versions of philosophy of religion. Elsewhere I attribute this taxonomy of pursuits to different patterns of thinking that I believe Lonergan's system critically accommodates.[6] The main point here, though, is that the whole of what I have outlined merits the title "philosophy of religion" not only in general terms. Lonergan's thought unequivocally qualifies as astute philosophical analysis of the religious phenomenon. What he offers merits the title technically as well for its convergence with certain aspects of the academic discipline of philosophy of religion, however accidental or unintentional. Regardless, this observation is rather humdrum compared to the more substantial issue of distinctiveness.

While much in Lonergan falls in with what passes as philosophy of religion these days, the differences are quite transparent. The most telling is his peculiar understanding of the role of logic in questions of theology and philosophy; his position on consciousness and its centrality for ascertaining the meaning and philosophical significance of proofs for God (Lonergan's in particular); and his emphasis on the personal equation in scholarly and philosophical examination of the religious phenomenon. He offers a unique perspective on these issues, which few doubt are relevant for philosophy of religion. Indeed, some might view philosophy of religion as nothing more than this. In any case, differences obtain between Lonergan's understanding of philosophy of religion and what's in vogue. In this study a means is provided for situating oneself in a comparative venture. For instance, in deciphering Lonergan's contribution to philosophy of religion one needs to determine what element or component or stage of that contribution one limits oneself to. His early or late philosophy of God? His proof? His response to the problem of evil? What also requires consideration are the relevant issues relative to the stratigraphy proposed here. How does proof function in the light of his developed understanding? What does this mean for the notion of proof in philosophical theology? What kind of response is offered to the "problem" of evil? Another issue now brought to light is why limit Lonergan's contribution to philosophy of God? His later practice seems to suggest that he himself thought philosophy of religion is more urgent, philosophy of religion, that is, which compares to Hegel's in scope and is deeply involved in issues arising from phenomenological study of religion.[7] How does this compare with philosophy of religion as it is practiced today? One's response will depend ultimately on how broadly or narrowly one defines philosophy of religion. However one is compelled to respond, the responsible comparative venture will be one that keeps distinct Lonergan's model of religion and his philosophy of religious studies. Hopefully the significance of this and other distinctions has been sufficiently impressed upon the reader.

All the foregoing presupposes that Lonergan's philosophy of religion is an important force to be reckoned with. It is startling to note how many actually have. Parse any work on philosophy of religion and Lonergan's name will seldom (if ever) appear. Outside the meager suggestions offered in the introduction, I don't know why this is. In the end, it doesn't matter much.

The point is to turn the omission into an opportunity to learn something new about something old. Lonergan's thought, like everyone else's, contains both old and new elements. As a newcomer on the philosophy and religion scene, I like to think it has something to contribute. Philosophy of religion is itself a relatively new discipline; its object (religion) is, by human standards, unequivocally old. The task of our ideal reader is to meld the new in critical interaction. The aim would be to foster the never-ending quest of valuing the thinking of that which is old. This book offers little more than a schematic; the rest is up to the reader.

Notes

Introduction

1. Stephen Toulmin, blurb on the outside cover of the 1978 paperback edition of *Insight* published by Harper and Row, Publishers.
2. David Burrell, blurb on the outside cover of the 1978 paperback edition of *Insight* published by Harper and Row, Publishers.
3. See Jim Kanaris, "The 'Ins and Outs' of Religious Love: Bernard Lonergan's Pragmatics," *Studies in Religion/Sciences Religieuses* 27/3 (1998): 295–310; "Calculating Subjects: Lonergan, Derrida, and Foucault," *Method: Journal of Lonergan Studies* 15/2 (1997): 135–50; "Engaged Agency and the Notion of the Subject," *Method: Journal of Lonergan Studies* 14/2 (1996): 183–200.
4. See works listed in chapter 1, note 1.
5. Stephen Crites, "The Pros and Cons of Theism: Whether They Constitute the Fundamental Issue of the Philosophy of Religion," in *God, Philosophy, and Academic Culture: A Discussion between Scholars in the AAR and the APA*, ed. William J. Wainwright (Atlanta, GA: Scholars Press, 1996), 39.
6. Bernard Lonergan, Preface in *The Achievement of Bernard Lonergan* (New York: Herder and Herder, 1970), xii. Schleiermacher's insight is one Immanuel Kant shared. See Kant's first *Critique* A 314 / B 370.
7. Hugo Meynell, *An Introduction to the Philosophy of Bernard Lonergan*, 2d ed. (Toronto and Buffalo: University of Toronto Press, 1991); *The Theology of Bernard Lonergan* (Atlanta, GA: Scholars Press, 1986); Joseph Flanagan, *Quest for Self-Knowledge: An Essay in Lonergan's Philosophy* (Toronto: University of Toronto Press, 1997); W. A. Stewart, *Introduction to Lonergan's Insight: An Invitation to Philosophize* (Lewiston, NY: Edwin Mellen Press, 1996); Terry Tekippe, *What's Lonergan Up To in Insight?: A Primer* (Collegeville, MN: The Liturgical Press, 1996). The following, too, provide excellent summaries: Vernon Gregson, ed., *The Desires of the Human Heart: An Introduction to the Theology of Bernard Lonergan* (New York/Mahwah: Paulist Press, 1988); Patrick Byrne, "The Fabric of Lonergan's thought," in *Lonergan Workshop*, vol. 6 (Atlanta, GA: Scholars Press, 1986).
8. Frederick Crowe, *Lonergan*, Outstanding Christian Thinkers Series, ed. Brian Davies (Collegeville, MN: The Liturgical Press, 1992). Mark D. Morelli and Elizabeth A. Morelli have also recently provided an insightful introduction in the Reader they have edited: *The Lonergan Reader* (Toronto: University of Toronto Press, 1997).

9. J. Michael Stebbins, *The Divine Initiative: Grace, World-Order, and Human Freedom in the Early Writings of Bernard Lonergan* (Toronto: University of Toronto Press, 1995).

10. One important study in this connection is Mark J. Doorley, *The Place of the Heart in Lonergan's Ethics: The Role of Feelings in the Ethical Intentionality Analysis of Bernard Lonergan* (Lanham, MD: University Press of America, 1996). Doorley does for the study of feelings in Lonergan's ethics what I do here for the study of religious experience in Lonergan's philosophy of religion. I see our work as complementary, particularly as it relates to the early Lonergan. In fact, a good chunk of this study demonstrates unwittingly a point Doorley makes about feelings but in regard to the neighboring concept of religious experience: "Lonergan's developing position on the role of feelings was gradual and consistent. It would be a mistake to posit a fundamental shift in his understanding of human understanding" (p. 38). I say "unwittingly" because Doorley's study came to my attention after this manuscript was written.

11. Jim Kanaris, "Lonergan and Contemporary Philosophy of Religion," in *Explorations in Continental Philosophy of Religion*, ed. Deane-Peter Baker and Patrick Maxwell (Editions Radopi, forthcoming).

Chapter 1: The Kehre of Philosophy of God, and Theology

1. See Gary Schouborg, "A Note on Lonergan's Argument for the Existence of God," *The Modern Schoolman* 45 (1967–1968): 243–8; Michael J. Lapierre, "God and the Desire of Understanding," *The Thomist* 33 (1969): 667–74; Ruben L. F. Habito, "A Catholic Debate on God: Dewart and Lonergan," *Philippine Studies* 18/3 (1970): 558–76; Patricia Wilson, "Human Knowledge of God's Existence in The Theology of Bernard Lonergan," *The Thomist* 35 (1971): 259–75; Joseph Martos, "Bernard Lonergan's Theory of Transcendent Knowledge" (Ph.D. diss., De Paul University, 1972); Ronald Hepburn, "Transcendental Method: Lonergan's Arguments for the Existence of God," *Theoria to Theory* 7 (1973): 46–50; Gerald A. McCool, "The Philosophical Theology of Rahner and Lonergan," in *God Knowable and Unknowable*, ed. Robert J. Roth (New York: Fordham University Press, 1973), 123–57; Jon Nilson, "Transcendent Knowledge in *Insight*: A Closer Look," *The Thomist* 37 (1973): 366–77; Ney Affonso de Sa Earp, "Love and Transcendent Knowledge" (three folders) (Rome: Gregorian University, 1974); Bernard Tyrrell, *Bernard Lonergan's Philosophy of God* (Notre Dame: University of Notre Dame Press, 1974); Ronald L. DiSanto, "Complete Intelligibility: A Study of Bernard Lonergan's Argument for the Existence of God" (Ph.D. diss., McMaster University, 1975); Edward K. Braxton, "Knowledge of God in Bernard Lonergan and Hans Küng," *Harvard Theological Review* 70 (1977): 327–41; Emil James Piscitelli, "Language and Method in the Philosophy of Religion: A Critical Study of the Development of the Philosophy of Bernard Lonergan" (Ph.D. diss., Georgetown University, 1977); B. C. Butler, "God: Anticipation and Affirmation," *Heythrop Journal* 20 (1979): 365–79.

2. As his less pedantic writings of the 1970s and early-1980s show, the ability to organize insights systematically is one of the "alluring benefits" of logic that Lonergan fortunately never outgrew.

3. J. Michael Stebbins, *The Divine Initiative: Grace, World-Order, and Human Freedom in the Early Writings of Bernard Lonergan* (Toronto: University of Toronto Press, 1995), 20. For a clear expression of Lonergan's early view of logic as systematization and ordering of answers see *UM*:6–14.

4. See Augustine, *De doctrina Christiana* 2.40.60, where he counsels that whatever truth philosophers have at their disposal should be claimed, since they are unlawfully possessed, and converted to Christian use. He legitimates this move by appealing to the despoliation of Egyptians by the Jews on the basis of God's commandment (Ex 3:22; 12:35). One could also on these grounds appeal to 2 Cor. 10:5, where Christians are counseled to "take every thought captive" to Christ. See also Aquinas, *Expositio super librum Boethii De trinitate* 2.4, ad. 5, where Aquinas writes that subjugating philosophical texts to Christian teaching is like turning water into wine.

5. See Mark D. Jordan, "Theology and Philosophy," in *The Cambridge Companion to Aquinas*, ed. Norman Kretzmann and Eleonore Stump (Cambridge: Cambridge University Press, 1993), 233, 236, 241. What Lonergan says in *Verbum* is, it seems to me, a more accurate rendering of the situation: "Because [Aquinas] conceived theology as in some sense a science, he needed Aristotle, who more than anyone had worked out and applied the implications of the Greek ideal of science. Because his theology was essentially the expression of a traditional faith, he needed Augustine, the Father of the West, whose trinitarian thought was the high water mark in Christian attempts to reach an understanding of faith. Because Aquinas himself was a genius, he experienced no great difficulty either in adapting Aristotle to his purpose or in reaching a refinement in his account of rational process—the *emanatio intelligibilis*—that made explicit what Augustine could only suggest" (*CWL* 2:9).

6. Besides the usual bickering that accompanies works of obvious genius, *Insight*, upon its publication, was heralded by Lonergan's peers as "a masterly work," offering "breath-taking intellectual liberation." *Newsweek* was quick to brand it "a philosophic classic," comparing it to David Hume's *Inquiry Concerning Human Understanding*—a comparison to Kant's First *Critique* would have made, except for the title, a better candidate. In spite of this *Insight* has, short of half a century of circulation, hardly received the attention of a classic, if by "classic" we mean something that is still widely read and not collecting dust on library storage shelves.

7. See *CWL* 3:657, 742. Use of the term "reasonableness" after that of "intelligence" is not redundant in Lonergan. Intelligence refers to the intentional predisposition of understanding, reasonableness to the intentional predisposition of judgment.

8. See Vernon Gregson, *Lonergan, Spirituality, and the Meeting of Religions* (Lanham, MD: University Press of America, 1985), particularly the section on Buddhism, pp. 67–72. Gregson's observations, however, apply more to what we discuss in chapter 4, Lonergan's model of religion, than the issue of a solution to the problem of evil.

9. This begs the larger question, of course, whether all types of immanently generated knowledge qualify *as* knowledge. Lonergan offers a cautious "yes" in so far as the conditions of such "knowledge" are met in experience. Astrological-type knowledge, for example, would not figure very high on his list.

10. See Aquinas, *Summa Contra Gentiles* I.5.

11. See Anthony Kenny, *Aquinas on Mind* (New York: Routledge, 1993), vii. The particular "book" in question is Lonergan's *Verbum: Word and Idea in Aquinas*, a series of articles that appeared in the journal *Theological Studies* between the years 1946 to 1949 later edited in book form by David B. Burrell (Notre Dame: University of Notre Dame Press, 1967). It was recently reissued as volume 2 of the *Collected Works of Bernard Lonergan*, edited by Frederick E. Crowe and Robert M. Doran (Toronto: University of Toronto Press, 1997). The eminent Yale historian Jeroslav Pelikan concludes similarly to Kenny in his *The Christian Tradition: A History of the Development of Doctrine* (Chicago: University of Chicago Press, 1985), 3:320: *Verbum*, he states, is "[o]ne of the most important studies of Aquinas."

12. See *PGT*:41. For a concise statement of his distinction between knowing complete intelligibility and intending it, the former being an impossibility this side of eternity, see Lonergan's "Response" to David Burrell in the *Proceedings of the American Catholic Philosophical Association* 41 (1967): 258–9. See *MIT*:103 for a similar statement.

13. Bernard Tyrrell, "The New Context of the Philosophy of God in Lonergan and Rahner," in *Language, Truth, and Meaning*, ed. Philip McShane (Notre Dame: University of Notre Dame Press, 1972), 305. The study alluded to in the text is Bernard Tyrrell, *Bernard Lonergan's Philosophy of God*, cited in n. 1 above.

14. See Quentin Quesnell, "What Kind of Proof is *Insight* 19?" *Lonergan Workshop* 8 (1990): 274.

15. See Lonergan, "The General Character of the Natural Theology of *Insight*," unpublished lecture given at University of Chicago Divinity School, March 1967; "Response," *Proceedings of the American Catholic Philosophical Association*; "Bernard Lonergan Responds," in *Foundations of Theology: Papers from The International Lonergan Congress 1970*, ed. Philip McShane (Notre Dame: University of Notre Dame Press, 1971), 223–34; "Bernard Lonergan Responds," in *Language, Truth, and Meaning: Papers from the International Lonergan Congress 1970*, ed. Philip McShane (Notre Dame: University of Notre Dame Press, 1972); *2C*:277–8; *PGT: passim*.

16. I borrow this section title from Charles C. Hefling, Jr., "Philosophy, Theology, and God," in *The Desires of the Human Heart: An Introduction to the Theology of Bernard Lonergan* (New York/Mahwah: Paulist Press, 1988), 121. I agree with Hefling that Lonergan brackets religious experience in chapters 19 and 20 of *Insight*. But I would add that chapter 20 presupposes a notion of religious experience ("higher *collaboration*"), while chapter 19 completely ignores it for the reason I have given.

17. The chosen theme of the congress was philosophy and religious experience. See the brief editorial remarks to the paper in *CWL* 4:294.

18. See the editors' remarks in *CWL* 4:261, n. h.

19. Lonergan, letter to Louis Roy, 16 August, 1977, quoted in Frederick E. Crowe, *Lonergan* (Collegeville, MN: The Liturgical Press, 1992), 7.

20. See *CWL* 2:102–3. See also *CWL* 4:295, n. g.

21. *CWL* 4:295, n. g. Speaking more generally, J. J. Heaney observes that "the exaggerated spread of suspicions that followed the condemnation of Modernism probably caused many scholars to avoid delicate subjects." See *New Catholic Encyclopedia*, s.v. "Modernism."

22. See Pierre Miquel, "Paul VI et la réhabilitation de l'expérience," *Collectanea Cisterciensa* 40/3 (1978): 161–70; 170.
23. *New Catholic Encyclopedia*, s.v. "Modernism."
24. See Patrick Corcoran, Foreword to *Looking at Lonergan's Method*, ed. Patrick Corcoran (Dublin: The Talbot Press, 1975), 9.
25. Lonergan, letter to Henry Keane, 22 January 1935, quoted in Crowe, *Lonergan*, p. 19.
26. Quentin Quesnell, "A Note on Scholasticism," in *The Desires of the Human Heart*, p. 149.
27. So Quesnell: "Pre-Vatican II Scholasticism in Catholic seminaries had been reduced to little more than a technique of presentation, of exposition [145] . . . It is obvious that the system was not devised to promote innovation [147]." There is more to Lonergan's comment than meets the eye in *Insight* concerning schoolboys who know the difference between parroting a definition and uttering it intelligently (*CWL* 3:31). See also in this connection his comments in *CWL* 5:35 regarding Kant's statement in the First Critique (A836/B864) about a plaster cast of a man.
28. See *CAMe*:16; Crowe, *Lonergan*, p. 23.
29. Francis Schüssler Fiorenza, "Systematic Theology: Task and Methods," in *Systematic Theology: Roman Catholic Perspectives*, ed. Francis Schüssler Fiorenza and John P. Gavin (Minneapolis, MN: Fortress Press, 1991), 1:51. Elsewhere Fiorenza points out that Lonergan's critique in *Insight* of Edmund Husserl's phenomenology as a highly purified empiricism only applies to the Husserl before 1913, "when he conceived of philosophy in a more ontological manner." He also adds that while Lonergan's critique of existentialism may apply to some it does not apply to Heidegger. See Fiorenza's Introduction to a re-issuing of Karl Rahner's *Spirit in the World*, trans. William Dych (New York: Continuum, 1994), xlv, n. 41. For dissatisfaction with Lonergan's critique in *Insight* of Hegel concerning judgment or, expressed otherwise, critical realism, see Jon Nilson, *Hegel's Phenomenology and Lonergan's Insight: A Comparison of Two Ways to Christianity* (Meisenheim am Glan: Verlag Anton Hain, 1979). With regard to Kant, Giovanni B. Sala feels that Lonergan had it right. See Sala, *Das Apriori in der menschlichen Erkenntnis: Eine Studie über Kants Kritik der reinen Vernunft und Lonergans Insight* (Meisenheim am Glan: Verlag Anton Hain, 1971); *Lonergan and Kant: Five Essays on Human Knowledge*, trans. Joseph Spoerl, ed. Robert M. Doran (Toronto: University of Toronto Press, 1994). More will be said about Lonergan's relation to Kant and Hegel in chapter 2.
30. See *CAMe*:123. This hermeneutical predisposition is in keeping with the counsel of St. Ignatius of Loyola (1491–1556), the founder of Lonergan's brotherhood, the Jesuits: " . . . it is necessary to suppose that every good Christian is more ready to put a good interpretation on another's statement than to condemn it as false" (*Spiritual Exercises* 22). See also Crowe, *Lonergan*, p. 136; Mark D. and Elizabeth A. Morelli, Introduction to *The Lonergan Reader*, ed. Mark D. Morelli and Elizabeth A. Morelli (Toronto: University of Toronto Press, 1997), 10.
31. This is practically a word for word rephrasing of a statement in Quesnell, "A Note on Scholasticism," 149, who emphasizes Lonergan's disposition in relation to "the

narrow conservative Catholic mind of pre-Vatican II Scholasticism." Reformulating it in the way in which it appears in the text seems only appropriate.

32. Lonergan has Gabriel Marcel and Karl Jaspers here in mind, although he knew Rudolf Bultmann and others were doing something more exegetically based.

Chapter 2: The Philosophical Aspect of the Concept of Experience

1. For Lonergan's most general definition of experience see *CWL* 3:407.

2. See *CAMe*:107. See also Fred Lawrence, "The Fragility of Consciousness: Lonergan and the Postmodern Concern for the Other," in *Communication and Lonergan: Common Ground for Forging the New Age*, ed. Thomas J. Farrell and Paul A. Soukup (Kansas City, MO: Sheed and Ward, 1993), 186–7.

3. Bruce Duffy, *The World as I Found It: A Novel* (Boston and New York: A Mariner Book/Houghton Mifflin Company, 1995), 24.

4. W. V. O. Quine identifies the conceptual side of epistemology as concerned with meaning, the doctrinal with truth. See W. V. O. Quine, "Epistemology Naturalized," in W.V. O. Quine, *Ontological Relativity and Other Essays* (New York and London: Columbia University Press, 1969), 69: "The conceptual studies are concerned with clarifying concepts by defining them, some in terms of others. The doctrinal studies are concerned with establishing laws by proving them, some on the basis of others."

5. Lonergan is in basic agreement with Charles Taylor who concludes that Edmund Husserl's hope for a final foundation (*Endstiftung*) is overstated. See Charles Taylor, "Overcoming Epistemology," in *Philosophy: End or Transformation?* ed. Kenneth Baynes, James Bohman, and Thomas McCarthy (Cambridge, MA: MIT Press, 1987), 480. For Lonergan's thoughts on Husserl see *LoE*:33–58. For a comparison of Lonergan and Husserl see William F. Ryan, "Passive and Active Elements in Husserl's Notion of Intentionality," *The Modern Schoolman* 55 (1977): 37–55; "The Transcendental Reduction according to Husserl and Intellectual conversion according to Lonergan," in *Creativity and Method: Essays in Honor of Bernard Lonergan*, ed. Matthew L. Lamb (Milwaukee, WI: Marquette University Press, 1981), 401–10; "Edmund Husserl and the '*Rätsel*' of Knowledge," *Method: Journal of Lonergan Studies* 13/2 (1995): 187–219. For a comparison of Lonergan and Taylor see Jim Kanaris, "Engaged Agency and the Notion of the Subject," *Method: Journal of Lonergan Studies* 14/2 (1996): 183–200.

6. John Angus Campbell, "Insight and Understanding: The 'Common Sense' Rhetoric of Bernard Lonergan," in *Communication and Lonergan: Common Ground for Forging the New Age*, ed. Thomas J. Farrell and Paul A. Soukup (Kansas City, MO: Sheed and Ward, 1993), 8. Campbell is specifically discussing the contributions of Adam Smith, George Campbell, Hugh Blair, Richard Whately, and Thomas de Quincey.

7. Campbell, "Insight and Understanding," p. 7.

8. Ibid., p. 4.

9. Ibid., p. 7.

10. See Jim Kanaris, "The 'Ins and Outs' of Religious Love: Bernard Lonergan's Pragmatics," *Studies in Religion/Sciences Religieuses* 27/3 (1998): 295–310.

11. Both specific and general meanings have their correlative contents. To hear is to hear something, to touch is to touch something, and so on. Also, experience, understanding, and judging are of "bodies" and "things" (not equivalent terms in Lonergan) that are experienced, understood, and judged to be or not to be the case.

12. The story is found in Plato's *Theaetetus* (174a), to which Lonergan often appeals in his discussion of the patterns of experience. See *CWL* 3:96, 205.

13. On the relation of "must" to insight see *CWL* 5:24–26.

14. David J. Chalmers, *The Conscious Mind: In Search of a Fundamental Theory* (Oxford: Oxford University Press, 1996), 10.

15. Chalmers, *The Conscious Mind*, p. 9.

16. David J. Chalmers, "The Puzzle of Conscious Experience," *Scientific American: Mysteries of the Mind*, special issue 7/1 (1997): 30.

17. Chalmers, "The Puzzle of Conscious Experience," p. 34.

18. Eliminativists like Paul Churchland discard commonsensical conceptions of consciousness in favor of neurobiological ones. "On this view, there are no positive facts about conscious experience. Nobody is conscious in the phenomenal sense" (Chalmers, *The Conscious Mind*, p. 161).

19. Chalmers, *The Conscious Mind*, p. 127.

20. Chalmers, *The Conscious Mind*, p. 11.

21. Chalmers, "The Puzzle of Conscious Experience," p. 36.

22. One gets a sense of this in chapter 6 of *Insight*, where the individual, whose consiousness is patterned intellectually, is spoken of in terms of "the seasoned mathematician" or, more generally, "the trained observer." His or her "selective alertness . . . keeps pace with the refinements of elaborate and subtle classifications" (*CWL* 3:209).

23. Perhaps we should recall Lonergan's disclaimer as to the difficulty of being dogmatic with regard to distinct patterns in the continuum of life. It should be remembered that the notion is of analytic distinction, and only provides one with "suggestions, arrows, pointing to possible points of reference which in different combinations may give one some approximation to what the pattern of experience at any given moment in any given individual may be" (*CWL* 5:106).

24. Laurence Olivier, *Confessions of An Actor* (London: Weidenfeld and Nicolson, 1982), 211.

25. Susanne K. Langer, *Mind: An Essay on Human Feeling*, 3 vols. (Baltimore and London: The John Hopkins University Press, 1967–1982).

26. In his analysis of aesthetic and artistic meaning Lonergan often relies on Langer, namely, her *Feeling and Form: A Theory of Art Developed from "Philosophy in a New Key"* (New York: Charles Scribner's Sons, 1953). See *CWL* 3:208, 567 (n. 5); *CWL* 6:102, 118, 144, 191; *CWL* 10:211, 222, 224; *MIT*: 61, 64. For an analysis and critique of Langer's *Mind: An Essay on Human Feeling* from a Lonergan scholar see Richard M. Liddy, *Art and Feeling: An Analysis and Critique of the Philosophy of Art of Susanne K. Langer* (Ann Arbor, MI: University Mircofilms, 1970), and his review of volume 1 of *Mind: An Essay on Human Feeling* in the *International Philosophical Quarterly* 10 (1970): 481–4. Liddy summarizes his understanding of the basic incompatibility between Langer's later strong tendency toward materialism and Lonergan's critical realism. Langer's *Mind*

consists in "the reduction of all 'higher' human activities to feelings and feelings to electro-chemical events. Langer represented the whole empiricist tradition in philosophy. As I studied her work, I gradually discovered that there was an unbridgeable gulf separating what Langer was saying about science and human consciousness and what Lonergan was saying" (Liddy, *Transforming Light: Intellectual Conversion in the Early Lonergan* [Collegeville, MN: The Liturgical Press, 1993], xv). Liddy's observations serviceably counterbalance Lonergan's wholesale endorsement of *Feeling and Form*.

27. Every thinker indebted to the Greek discovery of mind, the *zoon logon echon*, acknowledges the existence of reason. Contrary to popular opinion, it is also a point shared by radical critics of reason such as Jacques Derrida and Michel Foucault. See Jim Kanaris, "Calculating Subjects: Lonergan, Derrida, and Foucault," *Method: Journal of Lonergan Studies* 15/2 (1997): 135–50. In 1964 Lonergan was willing to go on record stating that for him Kant continued to be fundamental. The problems he raised and the problems incipient in his position had not generally been thought through. He mentions Karl Jaspers as "an extremely rich writer and penetrating" whose work, nevertheless, is fraught with Kantian limitations. Among those wishing to get around these limitations he pinpoints Martin Heidegger who "contains potentialities of getting beyond Kant, but he can't push through. He's never written the second part of his *Sein und Zeit*" (*CWL* 6:242). Paul Ricoeur levels a similar criticism against Heidegger. See Paul Ricoeur, "The Task of Hermeneutics," in *Paul Ricoeur: Hermeneutics and the Human Sciences: Essays on Language, Action and Interpretation*, ed. John B. Thompson (Cambridge: Cambridge University Press, 1981), 59. Many would argue, though, that the reason Heidegger was unable to begin what Ricoeur describes as "the movement of return which would lead from the fundamental ontology to the properly epistemological question of the status of the human sciences" owes itself to a more fundamental ontological task begun yet left unanswered by *Sein und Zeit*. Frederick A. Olafson, arguing rather unconventionally for the unity of Heidegger's thought, deems this task one of guarding *Sein* against those features of *Dasein* endangering its unity, singularity, and commonness. See Frederick A. Olafson, "The Unity of Heidegger's Thought," in *The Cambridge Companion to Heidegger*, ed. Charles B. Guignon (Cambridge: Cambridge University Press, 1993), 110. See also Olafson, *Heidegger and the Philosophy of Mind* (New Haven, CN: Yale University Press, 1987), of which his article intends to be a summary. All of this is to say that for Lonergan "Kant is still a problem" (*CWL* 6:242) for which, incidentally, he believes his cognitional theory provides a solution. For the thoughts of a Kant scholar, formerly a student of Lonergan, who agrees with him, see chapter 1, n. 29. Shedding further light on this issue is William Mathews, "Kant's Anomalous Insights: A Note on Kant and Lonergan," *Method: Journal of Lonergan Studies* 14/1 (1996): 85–98.

28. This is reminiscent of W. V. O. Quine's insight that defining something ("a sign" being his immediate referent) is to show how to avoid it. See Quine, *Mathematical Logic* (New York: W. W. Norton, 1940), 47.

29. See Jim Kanaris, "Engaged Agency and the Notion of the Subject," p. 193–9.

30. *2C*:70, n. 2. Lonergan invokes the important study of James Brown, *Subject and Object in Modern Theology* (London: SCM Press, 1955), which provides a careful survey of this history and its ambiguities.—We might also understand Lonergan's

statement about Kant making minimal concessions to the reality of the subject in connection with his earlier thoughts on Emerich Coreth's metaphysics. It builds further upon the cognitional element in the interpretation I provided in the text. In "Metaphysics as Horizon" (1963), for instance, Lonergan contrasts the context of Coreth's way of thinking with that of Kant's. Coreth emphasizes performance, not content, that is, the de facto raising of questions as *An-sich-Sein* (in Lonergan's terms, the notion of being instantiated in the raising and answering of questions). The Kantian context is said, by contrast, to be one of "contents that does not envisage performances.... [W]hile Kant envisages an *Ich denke* as a formal condition of the possibility of objective contents being thought, still he cannot find room for a concrete reality intelligently asking and rationally answering questions. In brief, phenomena appear, but they do not perform; and transcendental conditions of possibility within a transcendental logic do not transcend transcendental logic" (*CWL* 4:193). This anticipates our discussion of that which distinguishes Lonergan from Hegel.

    31. *CWL* 6:233; *CWL* 4:218. Hegel states something similar: "[T]he distinction between the in-itself [noumenon] and knowledge [phenomenon, cognition] is already present in the very fact that consciousness knows an object at all" (*Phenomenology of Spirit*, trans. A. V. Miller [Oxford: Oxford University Press, 1977], 54 (Intro. ¶85).—Lonergan uses the words "apparent" and "real" instead of the Kantian "phenomenal" and "noumenal," which can be seen as problematic. The former pair mean different things to philosophers, particularly analytic philosophers, though Lonergan means them in the Kantian sense.

    32. *CWL* 3:447–8.—In his Halifax lectures on *Insight* Lonergan mentions approvingly a gibe that Hegel once took at Kant in his *Lectures on the Philosophy of History*. For Kant, Lonergan paraphrases Hegel, experience and observation of the world are a matter of determining the ontological constitution of a candlestick here and a snuffbox there. "Preoccupation with Kant runs the risk of reducing metaphysics to the question of whether the candlestick here is a real candlestick, and whether the snuffbox there is a real snuffbox" (*CWL* 5:188). See Hegel, *Lectures on the Philosophy of History*, trans. Elizabeth S. Haldane and Frances H. Simpson (New York: The Humanities Press, 1955), 3:444–5.

    33. *CWL* 6:71.—As the editors of the *Collected Works* point out, this flies in the face of the usual interpretation, supported by the overwhelming yet partial evidence of *Insight*. Kant was not Lonergan's primary dialogue partner. With regard to the subject at least, "the evidence keeps mounting that Kant is second to Hegel here" (72, n. 27). Lonergan himself, the editors add, makes a point of saying that Kant for him "was an afterthought" (*CAMe*:10).

    34. See *CWL* 5:119: "the idea of the virtually unconditioned connects judgment with the absolute."

    35. Hugo Meynell, *An Introduction to the Philosophy of Bernard Lonergan*, 2d ed. (Toronto and Buffalo: University of Toronto Press, 1991), 49.

    36. Michael Inwood, "Concept," in Michael Inwood, *A Hegel Dictionary* (Cambridge, MA: Basil Blackwell Inc., 1992), 60.

    37. Inwood, *A Hegel Dictionary*, p. 59. What is "other" here can be either the understanding or its objects.

38. See Alvin Plantinga, "The Reformed Objection to Natural Theology," in *Faith and Rationality*, ed. Alvin Plantinga and Nicholas Wolterstorff (Notre Dame, IN: University of Notre Dame Press, 1983), 63–73. Plantinga (rightly, I think) finds grounds for this proper-basicality position in Calvin. See, in addition to the famous passages from the *Institutes* (i.e., I.1–3; II.2; III.2.14–17), Calvin's *Commentary on the Epistle to the Romans* I.20–23.

39. Étienne Gilson, *Réalisme thomiste et critique de la connaissance* (Paris: Vrin, 1939), 203, as quoted in *CWL* 4:196. Translation provided by the editors of *CWL* 4, who also footnote the original: "Ainsi, de quelque manière et à quelque profondeur de plan que nous lui posions la question: comment savoir qu'une chose existe? le réalisme répond: en la percevant."

40. Gilson, *Réalisme thomiste*, p. 197, as quoted in *CWL* 4:197. Translation provided by the editors of *CWL* 4, who also footnote the original: "C'est pourquoi, en fin de compte, on ne prend rien du réalisme tant qu'on ne le prend pas tout entier."

41. Kant, *Prolegomena to Any Future Metaphysics*, Section 13, Remark 2, as quoted in Frederick Copleston, *A History of Philosophy*, vol. 6, pt. 4: *Wolff to Kant* (New York: Doubleday, 1960), 270.

42. We shall soon see that Hegel means "mediate immediacy" differently. Here I am drawing the reader's attention to a mediate immediacy at the level of sensation, between the in-itself and intuition.

43. Hegel, *Phenomenology of Spirit*, p. 54 (Intro., ¶85). See also 104 (¶166): "consciousness makes a distinction, but one which at the same time is for consciousness *not* a distinction."

44. Robert B. Pippin, "You Can't Get There from Here: Transition Problems in Hegel's *Phenomenology of Spirit*," in *The Cambridge Companion to Hegel*, ed. Frederick C. Beiser (Cambridge: Cambridge University Press, 1993), 62 (first italics mine).

45. Pippin, *"You Can't Get There,"* p. 62–63.

46. Charles Taylor, *Hegel* (Cambridge: Cambridge University Press, 1975), 298.

47. Taylor, *Hegel*, p. 298.

48. Sala, *Lonergan and Kant: Five Essays on Human Knowledge*, p. 13.

49. Indirect support for this reading of Kant can be found in Heidegger, whom Sala also invokes: "To understand the *KRV* at all, one must, as it were, hammer into one's head the principle: Knowledge is primarily intuition." He qualifies this but reaffirms it by stating that it must "be kept firmly in mind that intuition [for Kant] constitutes the true essence of knowledge and, despite all reciprocity in the relation between intuition and thought, the former possesses the real weight" (Heidegger, as quoted in Sala, *Lonergan and Kant*, p. 6, 46).

50. Greg Hodes, *Foundations and Aporiai: The Intellectual Realism of Bernard Lonergan* (Ann Arbor, MI: University Microfilms, 1997), 23. Hodes thinks that Lonergan's inability to argue for such a position is due to his underestimating the difficulty of the problem and his precritical views of the extramental or the nature of raw data. My understanding is that Lonergan's position is consistent with his view that cognitional theory precedes epistemological questions about the extramental. Someone like him cannot view claims about the extramental as anything other than judgments about what is thought to be raw.

51. *CWL* 5:152.—I exchange the text's word "utter" for "formulate," which is how Lonergan puts it in *Insight*. In this way we can keep separate that other aspect of the concept Lonergan identifies with the "outer word," namely, the written or spoken word, the concept as brought to expression (see *CWL* 2:14; *CWL* 3:576–81). I commend to the reader the explanation the editors of *CWL* 5 offer for the apparent discrepancy: "'utter' is perhaps an unconscious carry-over from Lonergan's Trinitarian theology, where he speaks of the Father 'uttering' the Word—he would hardly speak of the Father 'formulating' the Word" (*CWL* 5:413, n. d).

52. "What is it?" and "Why?" are, in Lonergan's estimation, the guiding questions of classical heuristic structures, while "How often?" is that of statistical heuristic structures. They are questions for intelligence raised on the second level of consciousness (understanding). "What is it? leads to a grasp and formulation of an intelligible unity-identity-whole in the data as individual. The question, Why? leads to a grasp and formulation of a law, a correlation, a system. The question, How often? leads to a grasp and formulation of an ideal frequency from which actual frequencies nonsystematically diverge" (*CWL* 3:298).

53. Lonergan offers a fuller list of possibilities in *CWL* 3:340.

54. J. Nilson, *Hegel's Phenomenology and Lonergan's Insight*, p. 117. The problem is understandably skirted in David Tracy's classic work, *The Achievement of Bernard Lonergan* (New York: Herder and Herder, 1970). Tracy's interest lies "with Lonergan's interpretation of Hegel, not with Hegel himself" (94). He adds that "[i]f the latter were attempted a book at least as long as the present one would be necessitated." Although Nilson's book is not as long as Tracy's, he does offer good reasons for being baffled by Lonergan's interpretation from the perspective of someone reading Hegel himself.

55. Nilson, *Hegel's Phenomenology and Lonergan's Insight*, p. 118.

56. Ibid., p. 118.—Nilson invokes this interpretation as evidence against Lonergan's claim that fact is grasped only in the virtually unconditioned judgment. My own approach to this evidence from the *Phenomenology* is simply to show that Hegel's reversal of the bogus claims of self-consciousness, hence, his affirmation of the factual, is done from the perspective of spirit grasping what is important in the denial of finite consciousness. In other words, it doesn't have to serve as evidence against Lonergan's claim, unless, of course, one wants to pivot two different ways to something similar (Nilson, 119) against each other. I am in the habit of calling this kind of maneuver a "dialectics of superiority."

57. See Thomas E. Wartenberg, "Hegel's Idealism: The Logic of Conceptuality," in *The Cambridge Companion to Hegel*, p. 105. I owe my present exposition to Wartenberg's excellent analysis of Hegel's idealism and its various interpreters, both Hegel's contemporaries and our own.

58. *CWL* 5:298—In *Method in Theology* he makes similar concessions with regard to analysis, analysis of the preconceptual. "Without analysis, it is true, we cannot discern and distinguish the several operations" (*MIT*:17). Related to this, and a possible reason for the integral relation (though the issue involved is different) is what Lonergan says about the interpenetration of knowledge and language in *Insight*. Again, he emphasizes their distinctness but acknowledges that "they run so much together that they are inseparable" (*CWL* 3:579). In this connection see *MIT*:255–7.

59. See Inwood, *A Hegel Dictionary*, p. 125; Wartenberg, "Hegel's Idealism," p. 106–7. The point here is that the emphasis is on the unity *in* and *of* the whole, what is other than the self, and not that which the subject determines.

60. Nilson, *Hegel's Phenomenology and Lonergan's Insight*, p. 119. See *CWL* 3:117–25, 126–62.

61. This distinction will become clearer as I come to differentiate the various components of Lonergan's philosophy of religion (in the generic sense) in chapter 4.

62. Elizabeth A. Morelli, "Post-Hegelian Elements in Lonergan's Philosophy of Religion," *Method: Journal of Lonergan Studies* 12/2 (1994): 219.

63. It could be argued that the issue of the progressions of consciousness *is* a question of method for Lonergan. I mean "method" here much more generally as a description of a particular characteristic of method such as in the present case where a method is logically, metalogically, constituted and the other is heuristically so.

64. See *CWL* 4:190, 202–4.—In the terms of *Insight*, what Emerich Coreth wants to do is make explicit metaphysics primary, a *Gesamt- und Grundwissenschaft*. According to Lonergan, it is implicit metaphysics, the subject as subject raising and answering questions, that is primary (i.e., cognitional theory).

65. See Hans-Georg Gadamer, "The Universality of the Hermeneutical Problem," trans. David Linge, in *Contemporary Hermeneutics: Hermeneutics as Method, Philosophy and Critiques*, ed. Josef Bleicher (London, Boston and Henley: Routledge and Kegan Paul, 1980), 128–38.

66. See Jürgen Habermas, "The Hermeneutic Claim to Universality," in *Contemporary Hermeneutics: Hermeneutics as Method, Philosophy and Critiques*, p. 181–211.

67. To the surprise of many, the major controlling factor in Lonergan's choice of work was of a moral, social, cultural, political, and economic nature. This is often lost sight of because of the attention philosophy and theology receives in his writing. See Frederick E. Crowe, "Lonergan's 'Moral Theology and the Human Sciences': Editor's Introduction," *Method: Journal of Lonergan Studies* 15/1 (1997): 2–3. For example, out of the twenty-two volumes of the *CWL* only two treat nontheological and nonphilosophical topics, though one has to be careful not to infer from this that Lonergan writes anything nonphilosophically. He was ruthless in his criticisms of common sense approaches to the very intricate problems presented by common sense.

68. Lonergan's rejection of introspection is a qualified one. Although he shares the objectivist's rejection of unaided observation of one's experience as that which mediates reality, his reasons for doing so are far more philosophical than they are scientific. What he rejects is subjectivist and objectivist notions that observation is mere observation, namely, a looking at what is "in here" or "out there" to be looked at. This applies whether the object of observation is one's own experience or so-called objective facts.

Chapter 3: Religions Experience, Reflection, and Philosophy of God

1. See *CWL* 3:76–92, 109–62. For an excellent exposition of the complementarity of classical and statistical heuristic structures in Lonergan see Joseph Flanagan, *Quest for Self-Knowledge: An Essay in Lonergan's Philosophy* (Toronto: University of Toronto Press, 1997), 65–68, 95–103.

2. See Frederick E. Crowe, "The Genus 'Lonergan and . . .' and Feminism," in *Lonergan and Feminism*, ed. Cynthia S. W. Crysdale (Toronto: University of Toronto Press, 1994), 21.

3. Crowe, discussing this in terms of the difference between *Method* and *Insight*, which are usually taken to represent two main stages in Lonergan's career, attributes this to the different subject-matter of the volumes. "[W]here *Insight* made mathematics and the natural sciences the favoured arena for wrestling with intentionality analysis, *Method* takes the human sciences and human studies as the field for a similar struggle (a new Dilthey, perhaps, complementing a new Kant), and matters of the spirit will always seem less subject to rigorous analysis than those of the infrahuman world" (*Lonergan*, 107). Crowe grants that "*Method* does suffer in comparison with *Insight*," but that this is due to a lack of comprehensiveness, not rigor: "*Method* does not fail us in respect to its own proper standard of rigour." Crowe feels that the events surrounding the surgical removal of Lonergan's cancer-infected lung contributed to this. Speaking about various chapters in *Method*, which he describes as "laconic," he writes: "one feels that the Lonergan of pre-surgery times would have greatly expanded them [i.e., chapters 1–5], perhaps devoting separate chapters to categories for research and history, as he did for interpretation (ch. 3) and dialectic (ch. 2), as well as a chapter to show how transcendental method operates descending through the four levels, and not just in the ascent from experience to value" (107–9). For a recent biographical discussion touching on the effects of this trauma in Lonergan see William Mathews, "A Biographical Perspective on Conversion and the Functional Specialties in Lonergan," *Method: Journal of Lonergan Studies* 16/2 (1998): 142–60.

4. *CWL* 5:66.—Although Lonergan is discussing here the notion of similarity presupposed in classical heuristic structures, the example he chooses and his explanation of it are wholly applicable.

5. This is nicely demonstrated by the character Bertrand Russell in Bruce Duffy's novel, *The World as I Found It: A Novel*. Annoyed by Wittgenstein's "disingenuous, Tolstoyan fantasy that philosophy can be conducted solely with *ordinary* language," Russell exclaims: "As if an ordinary person would bother to read—let alone comprehend—a word Wittgenstein has written!" (12).

6. *CWL* 4:117.—The book in question is Johannes Beumer, *Theologie als Glaubensverständnis* (Würzburg: EchterVerlag, 1953).

7. *CWL* 4:117; Aquinas, *Summa Theologiae*, I, q. 1, a. 7 c. One might also refer to Aquinas' famous statement in *Summa Theologiae*, II–II, q. 1, a. 2, ad 2: "Actus autem credentis non terminatur ad enuntiabile, sed ad rem" (The act of the believer ends not in a statement but in 'res').—As far as I can see Lonergan uses the terms "reality" and "being" interchangeably. He does not draw on, although he is aware of, Kant's categorical distinction between the quality of reality and the modality of existence (*Dasein*). The reason for this goes deeper than simply rejecting the logic of Kant's position. It is a question of starting points. Kant infers the categories from the judgments in which they occur and consequently goes on to determine appropriate and inappropriate usage of categorical terms. Lonergan scrutinizes "the generative principles of the categories," the decisive one for knowing being rational judgment (*CWL* 3:364–5; *CWL* 5:156–7, 179, 389). In other words, he regards judgment as basic and constitutive rather than merely regulative, as in Kant. Hence, his argument

against what Kant saw as Descartes' error of confusing a logical with a real predicate would be fought on quite different grounds. As with Aquinas, Lonergan's position regarding reality is strongly semantic in structure. Maurice Boutin contextualizes this as expressing a matter of fact, that "it is more important to know and talk about something than to know and talk about our knowing and talking and categories of mind" ("Conceiving the Invisible: Joseph C. McLelland's Modal Approach to Theological and Religious Pluralism," in *The Three Loves—Philosophy, Theology, and World Religions: Essays in Honour of Joseph C. McLelland*, ed. Robert C. Culley and William Klempa [Atlanta, GA: Scholars Press, 1994], 7). Lonergan would concede this in so far as we understand that his thinking about knowing is a thinking about something that is not merely in the mind or any less real than what is "out there." When one understands that knowing is *knowing being* the subject-object dichotomy, what we spontaneously take to be in-here-now and out-there-now-real, breaks down. *Ens iudicio rationali cognoscitur*. For an illuminating discussion of the notions of "existence" (being) and "reality" in philosophical discourse see Boutin, "Conceiving the Invisible," p. 4–10.

    8. See *UM*:40: "The difficulty with [Aquinas's] work lies in the fact that he never explains what he is doing, but simply does it, and what he did we can only discern through a systematic analysis of his work."

    9. On this see particularly Michel Corbin, *Le chemin de la Théologie chez Thomas d'Aquin*, Bibliothèque des Archives de Philosophie, Nouvelle Série, 16 (Paris: Beauchesne, 1974).

    10. See *UM*:9.

    11. *De ente supernaturali: Supplementum schematicum* ("On Supernatural Being: A Schematic Supplement") will be published as volume 16 (*Early Latin Theology*) of the *Collected Works of Bernard Lonergan*.

    12. I mean the latter as to the way in which Lonergan's role as a theologian persists even in his later, more overt appreciation of *Religionswissenschaft* and its diverse methods of approaching the religious phenomenon.

    13. *CWL* 4:123—Johannes Beumer himself sees this as a problem inherent in *Glaubensverständnis*. Judging from Lonergan's reaction, though, he is skeptical that Beumer contributes to the mitigation of that problem. The whole article is built on the premise that Beumer's program would have been better served by paying closer heed to Aristotle's and Aquinas's grasp of the relation of understanding to science.

    14. Of course, I mean the terms "descriptive" and "communicative" in the context of Lonergan's later thought, his method in theology, although they may be found in his earlier works as well. A descriptive theology is one that investigates the expressions of religious experience through textual research, interpretation, historical analysis, and dialectic. A communicative theology is one that relates the doctrines of the previously mentioned fourfold theological specialization to a cultural reality.

    15. Religion or religious experience in *Method in Theology* is defined as a being-in-love unrestrictedly. "Being in love with God, as experienced, is being in love in an unrestricted fashion" (*MIT*:105).

    16. *CWL* 4:18.—The work Lonergan refers to by J. C. Ford, published the year before Lonergan's article appeared in *Theological Studies* (1942), is "Marriage: Its

Meaning and Purposes." Lonergan contrasts positive theological approaches to more speculative ones, the former being pastoral and practical in nature. See *CWL* 4:128. I will elaborate on this further when I come to treat "the two modes of thought" more explicitly as they are laid out in *De Intellecto and Methodo* and *Insight*.

17. The conclusions are those of Aquinas, that is, his transposition of Aristotle's naturalistic notion of finality in a theological context.

18. This is a paraphrase of Romans 5:5, which Lonergan clearly alludes to in the article (*CWL* 4:27). It is significant to mention it here because this passage becomes a favorite of Lonergan as a description of religious experience. It is a favorite of Augustine as well.

19. *CWL* 4:22.—Michael Shute detects that the germ of emergent probability is already contained in Lonergan's early writings of the 1930s on history. See his *The Origins of Lonergan's Notion of the Dialectic of History: A Study of Lonergan's Early Writings on History* (Lanham, MD: University Press of America, 1993). See also his own thoughts on emergent probability and the problematic of hierarchy ecofeminists have been drawing our attention to: "Emergent Probability and the Ecofeminist Critique of Hierarchy," in *Lonergan and Feminism*, ed. Cynthia Crysdale (Toronto: University of Toronto Press, 1994), 146–74.

20. These are the terms of *Insight*, excluding that of "dispositions." In "Finality, Love, Marriage" Lonergan speaks of this coincidental manifold in terms of tensions and contradictions, selfishness and unreasonableness, egoism and altruism *(CWL* 4:24–26). It falls in line with our discussion of the existential aspect of self-appropriation. See p. 57–9; *CWL* 3:244–63.

21. It must not be assumed from this, however, that Lonergan accepted the contours of the argument. For instance, in Lonergan's 1947–1948 course on grace, he spent an entire session outlining what he believed to be serious flaws in Henri de Lubac's *Surnaturel* (1946). For more details see J. Michael Stebbins, *The Divine Initiative*, p. 179–80.

22. Hans Küng, *Does God Exist? An Answer for Today*, trans. Edward Quinn (New York: Vintage Books, 1978), 522.

23. Küng, *Does God Exist?*, p. 522.

24. Stebbins, *The Divine Initiative*, p. 182.

25. Ibid., p. 176.

26. Ibid., p. 176.

27. *CWL* 4:30.—For a fuller statement Lonergan refers the reader to his study of operative grace in the thought of Aquinas, which was originally published in *Theological Studies* 2 (1941), and 3 (1942). It was edited in book form three decades later by J. Patout Burns. *Grace and Freedom: Operative Grace in the Thought of St. Thomas Aquinas*, ed. J. Patout Burns (London: Darton, Longman and Todd, 1971), 142–3.

28. See Aristotle, *Nicomachean Ethics*, 8.3–7; *CWL* 4:25.—Lonergan relies on segments of Aristotle's *Ethics* in mapping out the progression of love from nature to reason (i.e., Aristotle's notion of true friendship). But for a grounding of that progression in, as it reaches toward, God he turns to Aquinas. As mentioned earlier, Lonergan finds fault with Aristotle's methodology that precludes what is implicit in it, an absolute

good luring one beyond egoism and altruism. It is in Aquinas where this implicit element becomes an explicit one. Revelation expresses this element in compact form on the level of grace.

29. Later Lonergan will come to distinguish a bilateral movement with reference to the levels of consciousness. The movement from below upwards regards the creative process of human understanding and the movement from above downwards regards the healing process of transforming love, human and divine. See *3C*:100–14. Although there is no reference in "Finality, Love, Marriage" to a downward movement, what that spatial metaphor implies is nonetheless present in it. Thus, the aspects of love in the upwardly intensifying movement are a response to and outworking of motive good, which is "either God himself or else some manifestation of divine perfection" (*CWL* 4:30).

30. See *Gaudium et spes* 50; *Catechism of the Catholic Church* 1654.

31. One wonders whether the condemnation of Pope John Paul II in *Evangelium Vitae* (23), regarding materialist approaches to sexuality and procreation, would not equally apply to the faithful who, in their actions, also appear to be closed to "the richness of life which the child represents."

32. The statement is that of Pope Leo XIII (1878–1903) in *Aeterni Patris*, a program to which Lonergan was happy to contribute. See *CWL* 3:768–9.

33. See Hans Küng, *Theology for the Third Millennium: An Ecumenical View*, trans. Peter Heinegg (New York: Doubleday, 1988), who writes of Erasmus, "In no way could he, or would he, the highly educated, reserved, sensitive, and ultimately unaggressive intellectual type, identify himself with that intemperate religious fanatic. Where Luther was right, he agreed with him; but where Luther was wrong, one could not expect agreement from him. Thus, in the end Erasmus preferred to stick to the pope and the emperor" (1988, 28). I prefer with Lonergan to see these distinctions less evaluatively as differentiations of consciousness. The differentiations that apply between Lonergan and Erasmus may be seen as those applying between Aquinas and Calvin. See Jim Kanaris, "The Role of Reason in Aquinas and Calvin," *ARC: The Journal of the Faculty of Religious Studies, McGill University* 27 (1999): 37–65, especially 51–57.

34. Andrew Louth, *Discerning the Mystery: An Essay on the Nature of Theology* (Oxford: Oxford University Press, 1983), 3.

35. In opposition to theologians who would construct a systematic theology based on Augustinian categories, Lonergan states that the problem is that Augustinian terminology is often that of rhetoric, "in which terms are not always used in the same sense; literary usage cannot provide a consistent and firm foundation for systematic theology" (*UM*:19).

36. David M. Wulff, *Psychology of Religion: Classic and Contemporary*, 2d ed. (New York: John Wiley and Sons, 1997), 609.

37. I am indebted to Tad Dunne for the reference, who relies on a prepublished version of a paper Lonergan delivered in the fall of 1973 at Trinity College in the University of Toronto titled "Variations in Fundamental Theology." The paper was part of a series given the general title "Revolution in Roman Catholic Theology?" "Variations in Fundamental Theology," the second of Lonergan's talks, along with the fourth, "The Scope of Renewal," appear in *Method: Journal of Lonergan Studies*

16/1 (1998): 1–24, and 16/2 (1998): 83–102 respectively. In neither one of these published versions have I been able to find the important statement Dunne cites: "'We adverted to a topmost level of interpersonal relations and total commitments, a level that can be specifically religious'" (Dunne, "Being in Love," *Method: Journal of Lonergan Studies* 13/2 [1995]: 168).

38. Commenting several years later on the context-specific nature of myth in *Insight* Lonergan states: "... in chapter seventeen my usage of the word 'myth' is out of line with current usage. My contrast of mystery and myth was between symbolic expressions of positions and counterpositions. It was perhaps justifiable in the context of *Insight*, but it is not going to be understood outside of it, so another mode of expression is desirable" (*2C*:275). In what follows I consider the concept in a broader context while adhering to the terminology and ideas of *Insight*.

39. David M. Rasmussen, "From Problematics to Hermeneutics: Lonergan and Ricoeur," in *Language, Truth, and Meaning: Papers from The International Lonergan Congress 1970*, ed. Philip McShane (Notre Dame: University of Notre Dame Press, 1972), 265.

40. Rasmussen, "From Problematics to Hermeneutics," 270–1 (emphasis his).

41. *CWL* 3:557—Interpretations of the image as symbol (i.e., the aspect of image as sign) are dealt with in works like Mircea Eliade's three volume *Histoire des croyances et des idées religieuses* (Paris: Payot, 1976–1983). A genetic, cognitionally based account of myth and mystery prescinds from this kind of analysis. Even so, the type of analysis proposed by scholars as Eliade is itself an interpretive move removed from the consciousness interpreting the image as symbol. Regardless, the purpose of a genetic account is to concentrate on the structure of the mind, the way in which it approaches its contents and the implications of this in the light of such a concentration.

42. Garrett Barden, "The Intention of Truth in Mythic Consciousness," in *Language, Truth, and Meaning*, p. 25.

43. See Jacques Derrida, "Faith and Knowledge: The Two Sources of 'Religion' at the Limits of Reason Alone," in *Religion*, ed. Jacques Derrida and Gianni Vattimo (Stanford, CA: Stanford University Press, 1998). Derrida breaks with "dogmatic faith" in so far as it claims to know. This is to ignore, in his opinion, the difference between faith and knowledge (1998, 10).

44. The closest Lonergan thinks mythic consciousness can come to a self-critical utilization of myth ("mystery purified of myth") is through the language of allegory. But because allegory cannot be accompanied by an explanation of what is meant by parables and myths, thoughtful persons are left to ponder the riddles of wise persons (*CWL* 3:569). Allegorical language is transitional in a genetic account of consciousness. It does not provide the means or the language for an adequate self-knowledge, nor does it provide an understanding of what it presents. For this one needs to turn to a different, not necessarily better, set of questions, guided by a different set of rules.

45. Quentin Quesnell, "What Kind of Proof is *Insight* 19?" p. 276.

46. See chapter 1, pp. 12–14 above.

47. *CWL* 3:187.—It is clear that Lonergan is describing the enlarged horizon of the beatific vision, hence my distinction between a limited and ultimate sense to

openness as gift. Lonergan is more explicit about the latter, although he does touch on the former as implied in the quotation immediately preceding this one.

48. Mathews, "A Biographical Perspective on Conversion and The Functional Specialties in Lonergan," p. 144–5.

49. Mathews, "A Biographical Perspective," p. 137.

50. Fred Crowe, "An Exploration of Lonergan's New Notion of Value," in *Appropriating the Lonergan Idea*, ed. Michael Vertin (Washington, DC: The Catholic University of America Press, 1989), 56.

51. Another paper is the "The General Character of the Natural Theology of *Insight*" given at the Chicago Divinity School in 1967, just one year before "Natural Knowledge of God" was presented to the Catholic Theological Society of America at its twenty-third annual convention. But it is more or less a commentary on chapter 19 of *Insight*, how it is to be understood and what it accomplishes. In other words, *Insight*'s argument is not treated in the light of the expanded viewpoint of the fourth level as is done in "Natural Knowledge of God."

52. John O'Donnell, "Transcendental Approaches to the Doctrine of God," *Gregorianum* 77/4 (1996): 662.

53. An important point mentioned by Quesnell, "What Kind of Proof is *Insight* 19?", p. 276. See *CWL* 3:705: "But just as our knowing is prior to an analysis of knowledge and far easier than it, so too our knowledge of God is both earlier and easier than any attempt to give it formal expression."

54. See O'Donnell, "Transcendental Approaches," p. 662.

55. *2C*:132.—In "Natural Knowledge of God" Lonergan focuses on intellectually, morally, and religiously differentiated consciousness. In *Method* he notes that one could list up to thirty-one different types of differentiated consciousness (*MIT*:272). Lonergan would certainly not object to the discovery of more.

56. Bloom is known for his highly controversial thesis that "J" was a woman and the now equally controversial though traditional thesis that "J" was written in the tenth century B.C.E. or is even a separate source. Regardless, the element apropos to our concern is that a sophisticated form of writing is not necessarily a differentiated form in Lonergan's sense. For Bloom's thesis see his popular *Book of J*, translated from the Hebrew by David Rosenberg and interpreted by Harold Bloom (New York: Grove Weidenfeld, 1990).

57. Wolfhart Pannenberg, *Systematic Theology*, trans. Geoffrey W. Bromiley (Grand Rapids, MI: Wm. B. Eerdmans Publishing Co., 1991), 1:93.

58. In chapter 1, I look at this in terms of his wariness of the modernist movement. I also look at how others (i.e., officials), having neither the time nor the patience to work through these issues, might have misjudged him had he started talking about the basic importance of religious experience in general transcendent knowledge. Time was required for suspicions to subside. Time was also required for him to bring a needed delicacy to controversial issues to which his cognitionalist slant had something to contribute.

59. *PGT*:13. He refers to this as the "classist notion of culture" against which he posits his own "empirical notion." See *2C*:47–52, 55–67, 87–99; *MIT*:xi, 124, 301.

60. Elsewhere I have explained this as the pragmatics of Lonergan's position. See Jim Kanaris, "The 'Ins and Outs' of Religious Love: Bernard Lonergan's Pragmatics," *Studies in Religion/Sciences Religieuses* 27/3 (1998): 295–310.

61. Reference to this specifically in connection with grasping Lonergan's argument for the existence of God is made in "The General Character of the Natural Theology of *Insight*" 9; *2C*:133; and somewhat less emphatically in *PGT*:55.
62. David B. Burrell, "Lonergan and Philosophy of Religion," *Method: Journal of Lonergan Studies* 4/1 (1986): 1.
63. *CWL* 3:754–5—Again, this is not to say that there is no development from Lonergan's stance in *Insight* to *Philosophy of God, and Theology*. It is only in literature following *Insight* where we see the unprecedented development of the way in which these two orders of truth impinge upon one another in *general* transcendent knowledge.

Chapter 4: From Philosophy of God to Philosophy of Religion

1. Louis Dupré, *A Dubious Heritage: Studies in the Philosophy of Religion After Kant* (New York: Paulist Press, 1977), 146.
2. Among his several interests, Lonergan's substantial contribution to macro-economics is perhaps the clearest example of this. See the recently released volumes in the *Collected Works*, *CWL* 15, and 21. The literature on Lonergan's economics has been growing steadily. Notable contributions include: Peter S. Burley, "Lonergan as a Neo-Schumpeterian," *Australian Lonergan Workshop* (1998): 249–57; Philip McShane, *Economics for Everyone: Das Jus Kapital* (Edmonton: Commonwealth Press, 1996); Eugene L. Donahue, "Bernard Lonergan's Contribution to Social Economics," *Forum For Social Economics* 22/2 (1993): 45–60; Kenneth Melchin, "Economics, Ethics, and the Structure of Social Living," *Humanomics* 10 (1993): 21–57; Peter S. Burley and Laszlo Csapo, "Money Information in Lonergan-von Neumann Systems," *Economic Systems Research* 4/2 (1992): 133–41; William Zanardi, "Consumer Responsibility from a Social Systems Perspective," *International Journal of Applied Philosophy* (Spring 1990): 57–66; Eileen de Neeve, *Bernard Lonergan's "Circulation Analysis" and Macrodynamics* (Ann Arbor, MI: University Microfilms,1990); Peter S. Burley, "A von Neumann Representation of Lonergan's, Model," *Economic Systems Research* 1 (1989): 317–30; Vicente Marasigan, "Economic Dysfunctions," *Landas* 2 (1988): 194–203; Patrick Byrne, "Economic Transformations: The Role of Conversions and Culture in the Transformation of Economies," in *Religion and Culture: Essays in Honor of Bernard Lonergan*, ed. Timothy P. Fallon and Philip Boo Riley (Albany, NY: State University of New York Press, 1987), 327–48; Eileen de Neeve, "The Possibility of A Pure Cycle of the Productive Process: The Potential for Decline in Economic Growth," in *Religion and Culture: Essays in Honor of Bernard Lonergan*, p. 349–64; William Mathews, "Lonergan's Economics," *Method: Journal of Lonergan Studies* 3/1 (1985): 9–30.
3. I am alluding here to the particular hermeneutics of Sean McEvenue for scrutinizing the "elemental meanings" of biblical texts and their systematic mediation in theology. See Sean McEvenue, *Interpreting the Pentateuch* (Collegeville, MN: The Liturgical Press, 1990); *Interpretation and Bible: Essays on Truth in Literature* (Collegeville, MN: The Liturgical Press, 1994). He describes these elemental meanings as fundamental stances in particular "realms of meaning." These he identifies

broadly as the family, liturgy, politics, sports, and so forth. Each function according to the dictates of particular rules and within a particular horizon. Putting it somewhat crassly, in the Bible, he argues, God is expected to intervene, salvation is expected to occur, in particular realms of meaning. It is the job of theologians to communicate what those meanings are and how to adequately mediate them systematically and communicatively to their culture. This is more or less Lonergan's definition of theology (*MIT*:xi). McEvenue's contribution centers on his specialized knowledge of the Bible for the elucidation of its elemental meanings. As he points out in a recent paper delivered at the 1999 Lonergan Workshop in Boston, Lonergan's contribution, besides his generalized empirical method and his method in theology, is in the area of doctrinal development in Christianity. In the area of biblical studies, little can be gleaned from Lonergan. In any case, to avoid confusion with Lonergan's use of the term "realms of meaning," which has a technical significance, I have replaced McEvenue's with a more general yet doubtless no less wanting designation, "specific domains" of meaning.

4. McEvenue, *Interpreting the Pentateuch*, p. 14.

5. Hopefully it is recognized that by a consciousness that is converted intellectually Lonergan does not mean the difference between a consciousness that is stupid and one that is astute. As with most things intellectual, Lonergan means the operations of consciousness exclusive to knowing (experiencing, understanding, and judging). An intellectually converted consciousness would be one that has appropriated itself as such critically self-consciously, consequently objectifying that experience. As regards a consciousness that is religiously converted Lonergan means a consciousness grasped by what Paul Tillich calls "ultimate concern," and not a consciousness converted to any one particular religious tradition. It is a general concept meant to include what fundamental theologians and philosophers of religion discuss when discussing things of a religious nature.

6. I owe this reading of Anselm to Maurice Boutin. Boutin contends that Anselm's so-called ontological proof does not pertain to the being of God as it does to our thinking. Anselm, he says, provides us with a rule of thought, not a definition of God per se. Human beings can never think of anything greater than God, defined as that than which nothing greater can be conceived. If they can, it is clear that what they have in mind is not God. Anselm's whole argument is set in the context of belief, belief that God is and that God is that than which nothing greater can be conceived. Anselm is not after a proof of God's existence but an understanding of it. In doing so, he discovers a certain dignity to the human mind as well as an inescapable limit. The mind can think an awful lot of things. What it cannot think, however, is something greater than that which nothing greater can be conceived. It is an elucidation of Aristotle's discovery that the essence of human being is something rational. What Anselm is saying, in other words, is that the apex of the Greek discovery of mind is expressed by the understanding that God is that than which nothing greater can be conceived. To think this is to be fully rational. To reject this is to reject our nature as rational beings. Ruben L. F. Habito is among the few I have encountered who has made intimations toward such an understanding in a brief comparison of Lonergan and Anselm on the notion of God. He has not, however, exploited the relationship

in a way that a Lonergan scholar might appreciate in the consideration of interpretations like Boutin's. See Habito, "A Catholic Debate on God: Dewart and Lonergan," p. 564–5. The usual reading of Lonergan and Anselm is to view them as offering something completely different and in certain respects opposed. This is based on the typical distinction between ontological and cosmological arguments, the first being Anselm's means of argumentation, the second Lonergan's, albeit at a metacritical level. It is a reading of the situation Lonergan himself follows, leading him to conclude that the Anselmian argument is fallacious for the presumably obvious reason that it argues "from the conception of God to his existence. But our conceptions yield no more than analytic propositions" (*CWL* 3:693). Boutin's interpretation is based on a contemporary reading of Anselm that clearly distinguishes between what Anselm is doing and what Descartes is in his own, more suitably described ontological argument. See Marco Maria Olivetti, ed., *L'argomento ontologico* (Padova: Cedam, 1990). In my opinion, this newer reading brings out a dimension of Lonergan's argument that is Anselmian, albeit unintentionally so, even though it is more fittingly described as a cosmological argument.

7. In his summary of Lonergan's course notes "Analysis Fidei," written during the spring semester of 1952 while teaching a course "On Faith" at Regis College, Toronto, Ulf Jonsson notes that Lonergan "approaches the question of assent to faith in an abstract and rather rationalistic fashion, in a manner typical of the Scholastic kind of thinking in which he himself had received much of his education." As we observed in reference to other early writings of Lonergan, Jonsson also notes forays of an understanding that Lonergan would only later develop, to wit, that "the assent of faith is never a purely intellectual enterprise," that it is not only logical, but psychological as well. See Ulf Jonsson, *Foundations for Knowing God: Bernard Lonergan's Foundations for Knowledge of God and the Challenge from Antifoundationalism* (Frankfurt am Main: Peter Lang, 1999), 127.

8. "Belief: Today's Issue" is in *2C*:87–99; "Faith and Beliefs" has yet to be published but is available from the Lonergan Research Institute in Toronto; "Religious Commitment" was published in *The Pilgrim People: A Vision With Hope*, ed. Joseph Papin (Villanova, PA: The Villanova Press, 1970), 45–69.

9. This is how Lonergan frames the question in "Faith and Beliefs." In "Religious Commitment" it is framed somewhat differently. The insights of Abraham Maslow on "peak experiences" are incorporated into it as a psychological contribution to Smith's comparativist concerns. Lonergan's verdict as regards peak experiences and his concept of being in love with God is that "being in love with God, if not a peak experience, at least is a peak state, indeed, a peak dynamic state" (*RCo*:57). This more or less confirms what I was saying earlier about the concept in connection with the mystical pattern of experience.

10. Lonergan relies noncommittally on the depth psychology of Ludwig Binswanger as a useful introduction to his own work on consciousness, its more properly cognizing levels. See Ludwig Binswanger, "Traum und Existenz," in Ludwig Binswanger, *Ausgewählte Vorträge und Aufsätze* (Bern: A. Francke, 1947), 1:74–97.

11. Lonergan is not blind to the precarious nature of self-transcendence, cognitional, moral, and religious. "It involves a tension between the self as transcending

and the self as transcended. Hence it is never some pure and serene and secure possession. Authenticity is ever a withdrawal from unauthenticity, and every successful withdrawal only brings to light the need for still further withdrawals. Our advance in understanding is also the elimination of our oversights and misunderstandings. Our advance in truth is also the correction of our mistakes and errors. Our moral development is through repentance for our sins. Genuine religion is discovered and realized through redemption from the many traps of religious aberration. So we are bid to watch and pray, to make our way in fear and trembling" (*RCo*:53).

12. *MIT*:32—I am indebted to Robert M. Doran for this very handy term, "integral scale of values." It captures the interrelatedness of the scale of values that Lonergan outlines in *Method*. See Doran, *Theology and the Dialectics of History* (Toronto: University of Toronto Press, 1990), 93–107.

13. *RCo*:66—This understanding is summarized in very colloquial terms by Lonergan in an interview: "When you learn about divine grace you stop worrying about your motives; somebody else is running the ship" (*CAMe*:145).

14. *RCo*:61; *MIT*:109.—The outline is of Friedrich Heiler's work "The History of Religions as a Preparation for the Cooperation of Religions," in *The History of Religions*, ed. M. Eliade and J. Kitagawa (Chicago: University of Chicago Press 1959), 142–53.

15. See George A. Lindbeck, *The Nature of Doctrine: Religion and Theology in a Postliberal Age* (Philadelphia: The Westminster Press, 1984), 32.

16. See Charles C. Hefling, Jr., "Lonergan on Development: *The Way to Nicea* in Light of His More Recent Methodology" (Ph.D. diss., Andover Newton Theological School—Boston College, 1982).

17. See Hefling, "Turning Liberalism Inside-Out," *Method: Journal of Lonergan Studies* 3/2 (1985): 51–69.

18. Hefling, "The Meaning of God Incarnate According to Friedrich Schleiermacher; *or*, Whether Lonergan is Appropriately Regarded as 'A Schleiermacher for Our Time,' and Why Not," *Lonergan Workshop* 7 (1988): 126, see also 153, and 107.

19. Philip Boo Riley, "Religious Studies Methodology: Bernard Lonergan's Contribution," *Method: Journal of Lonergan Studies* 12/2 (1994): 241.

20. Riley, "Religious Studies Methodology," p. 242–3.

21. In the final analysis, even Lonergan's generalized terminology about religious experience betrays a characteristically Christian emphasis. Love, transcendent or otherwise, is espoused in most, if not, all world religions as fundamentally important. But it has become a means of earmarking the Christian religion in particular, just as submission to the will of Allah has for Islam and spiritual enlightenment has for Buddhism. Nor is this strange since it is a religion that judges love to be the greatest of all theological virtues (1 Cor. 13:13), that defines the very essence of God to be love (1 John 4:8).

22. Lonergan is particularly explicit about this in "Faith and Beliefs." As Wilfred Cantwell Smith notes in his response to Lonergan's paper, "he speaks of the Christian theologian"—presumably he means as the Christian theologian conceives the matter—"and I guess I've been asked to comment not in that capacity but as a comparativist."

23. The connection of judgment with objectification does seem a little strange, since Lonergan holds that we judge prior to objectifying our judgments. However, the informal nature of the discussion doubtless contributes to the fluidity of his terms.

24. See Tad Dunne, *Lonergan and Spirituality: Towards a Spiritual Integration* (Chicago: Loyola University Press, 1985), 118–9. Compare this with *RCo*:64.

25. Belief is not, nor need it be, blind trust. Joseph Flanagan tags it "the reasonable assessment of whether the other person has carried out the required steps to reach a true judgment," the "required steps" being, of course, experience, understanding, and reflective understanding (*Quest for Self-Knowledge*, p. 229). This is fine, as far as general definitions go. And yet each of us can recount countless instances when that upon which we relied in a structurally reasonable assessment has proven faulty. See *CWL* 3:735–9.

26. Method is meant here in the particular, not generalized empirical, sense.

27. For an interesting article on the basic trust philosophers put in reason see Adriann Theodor Peperzak, "Philosophia," *Faith and Philosophy: Journal of the Society of Christian Philosophers* 14/3 (1997): 321–33.

28. The distinction between faith and beliefs is meant to facilitate ecumenical and interreligious dialogue. This is particularly the case with regard to the distinction between beliefs in general, which is most relevant to us in tracking the development of Lonergan's philosophy of religion (in the generic sense), and beliefs in particular, which pertain to that which make traditions distinctive. The former is most relevant because it is the focal point of Lonergan's fundamental theology, of which his philosophy of God is an integral part, and his philosophy of religion.

29. By "philosophy of" Lonergan means the generalized empirical method outlined in *Insight* and augmented in *Method*.

30. It is crucial to remember that, more often than not, when Lonergan discusses philosophy of God, particularly negatively, he has Scholastic philosophy of God in mind. Also, more often than not, the intended audience is Catholic, which Scholastic philosophy of God has greatly impacted. Thus, it must not be thought that I am in any way extending these terms and sentiments to the fields of the same name today.

31. Gibson Winter, *Elements for a Social Ethic: Scientific and Ethical Perspectives on Social Process* (New York: The Macmillan Company, 1966), 280, 166–7.

32. The origins of Lonergan's preoccupation with history as a distinct area of study is traced back to his earliest extant writings on the subject, from around 1933 to 1938. For a detailed study of these writings see Michael Shute, *The Origins of Lonergan's Notion of the Dialectic of History: A Study of Lonergan's Early Writings on History* (1993).

33. The question of the relation of Lonergan's philosophy of religion to, say, Asian habits of study is an interesting one. As he states in *Insight*, "the argument from the cultural differences of East and West does not seem to touch our position," that is, his "philosophy of." "For while those differences are profound and manifest, they are not differences that lie within the intellectual pattern of experience.... When an Easterner inquires and understands, reflects and judges, he performs the same operations as a Westerner" (*CWL* 3:758). In other words, the differences, methodological

or otherwise, pertain to the content of consciousness, not to its operations. The claim is contentious. But to challenge or defend it here would take us too far afield.

34. I am indebted to Sean McEvenue for these valuable points. They come from the same unpublished and untitled paper mentioned in note 3 above. It was delivered at the 1999 Lonergan Workshop, Boston College.

35. A similar brief overview that contains the figures about to be listed can be found in the last of Lonergan's Donald Mathers Memorial "Lectures on Religious Studies and Theology" (1976) (*3C*:152–5).

36. See Vernon Gregson, "The Historian of Religions and the Theologian: Dialectics and Dialogue," *Creativity and Method*, p. 141–51.

37. The aspect of dialectic that one comes to expect from the religion scholar is to a species of conflict and opposition that Lonergan names "perspectival." It pertains to differences that "merely witness to the complexity of historical reality" and are "eliminated by uncovering fresh data" (*MIT*:235). Gregson's analysis assumes the more properly dialectical quality of Lonergan's functional speciality that pertains to "fundamental conflicts stemming from an explicit or implicit cognitional theory, an ethical stance, a religious outlook."

38. Gregson, "The Historian of Religions," p. 151.

39. Recent examples include Patrick H. Byrne, "Lonergan on Objective and Reflective Interpretation" and Jerome Miller, "Hermeneutics and Self-Transcendence in Lonergan: A Response to Patrick Byrne" (papers presented at the annual meeting of the Lonergan Philosophical Society, Pittsburgh, 1998); Ivo N. Coelho, *Hermeneutics and Method: A Study of the Universal Viewpoint in Bernard Lonergan* (Rome: Pontificiae Universitatis Gregorianae, 1994). See also Sean McEvenue and Ben Meyer, eds., *Lonergan's Hermeneutics: Its Development and Application* (Washington: Catholic University of America Press, 1989); Peter Vincent Conley, "The Development of the Notion of Hermeneutics in the Works of Bernard Lonergan, S.J." (Ph.D. diss., Catholic University of America, 1972).

40. What Lonergan says in "Faith and Beliefs" is apropos here: "I must point out that my model is just a skeleton. To apply it to any particular religion further parts may need to be added. Moreover, because religions can differ in fundamental ways, one must have different sets of parts to add and even one may have to add them in quite different ways" (*FBe*:20).

41. Riley, "Religions Studies Methodology," p. 249.

42. The date for this article is uncertain. Crowe dates it around early 1978 or late 1977. See Crowe, "Lonergan's 'Philosophy and the Religious Phenomenon': Editor's Preface," *Method: Journal of Lonergan Studies* 12/2 (1994): 121–4.

43. Lonergan notes the analyst in reference to blik. The term was coined by Richard M. Hare in his contribution to the famous falsification debate between himself, Basil Mitchell, and Antony Flew about God's existence. See *New Essays in Philosophical Theology*, ed. Antony Flew and Alasdair MacIntyre (London: SCM Press, 1955), 96–108. Blik is a nonpropositional, nonrational, term that Hare proposes as the proper basis of an assertion. As such it regards the basic attitude of utterers, shifting the attention from the logic and the verifiability of their utterances. Hence, there are sane and insane bliks that transcend issues of verification and observation.

44. This is an application of one of Lonergan's favorite examples to point out the difference between objects as conceived commonsensically (*quoad nos*) and scientifically or theoretically (*quoad se*). The example is that of Sir Arthur Eddington's (1882–1944) two tables. See *MIT*:84, 258, 274; *3C*:39, 241.

45. See chapter 1, p. 20–1 and n. 29.

46. See Michael Shute, *The Origins of Lonergan's Notion of the Dialectic of History*, especially pp. 135–57.

47. *3C*:158—As a Christian theologian, Lonergan develops this in terms of our response to and participation in the law of the cross, which is God's solution to the so-called problem of evil. See Lonergan, *De Deo Trino*, Part 5, Thesis 17, "The Law of the Cross." As a "philosopher of religion," he leaves it wide open, although "self-sacrificing love" bears unequivocal Christian connotations. Chapter 20 of *Insight*, "Special Transcendent Knowledge," is a philosophical articulation of God's revelatory response to the problem, which is consistent with a naturalist view of the universe as conceived in *Insight*. This comprises Lonergan's response to the problem of evil from the perspective of his philosophy of God. It is handled differently from the usual course taken in philosophy of religion, which tends to bracket the nature of evil as mystery to which revelatory knowledge is the appropriate response.

48. I am basing this primarily on Lonergan's connection of dialectic, the fourth functional specialty, with the level of decision (see *MIT*:141). It uncovers the theoretical roots of a conflict, not necessarily the existential ones, which is the task of foundations.

49. See chapter 3, pp. 81–6.

50. R. G. Collingwood, *The Idea of History* (Oxford: Clarendon Press, 1946), 201, as quoted in *3C*:203.

51. See Christopher Stead, *Philosophy in Christian Antiquity* (Cambridge: Cambridge University Press, 1994), 79.

52. See E. Morelli, "Post-Hegelian Elements in Lonergan's Philosophy of Religion," p. 230–7.

53. Morelli, "Post-Hegelian Elements," p. 237. Both aspects have been discussed throughout the course of our investigation. For a discussion of the first sense see chapter 4, p. 119–21. With regard to the second sense see chapter 3, p. 81–86.

54. Although this is not a point made by Morelli, it does not contravene her proposal. I base it on the quotation that she provides from Lonergan: "Theology is the sublation of philosophy. For philosophy [conceived as generalized empirical method] is the basic and total science of human living. The Christian religion as lived is the sublation of the whole of human living. Hence the Christian religion as thematized is the sublation of the basic and total science of human living" (Lonergan, "Questionnaire on Philosophy: Responses by Bernard J. F. Lonergan, S.J.," *Method: Journal of Lonergan Studies* 2/2 [1984]: 8, as quoted in Morelli, 237).

55. Morelli, "Post-Hegelian Elements," p. 237.

56. For my opinion about what I think is Lonergan's unfair assessment of Hegel as a conceptualist see chapter 2, p. 53–7.

57. Crowe, *Lonergan*, 107.

58. See Doran, *Theology and the Dialectics of History*, especially 42–63, 139–76. See also his "Consciousness and Grace," *Method: Journal of Lonergan Studies*

11/1 (1993): 51–75, which represents Doran's first public effort following *Theology and the Dialectic of History* to express his contribution in terms of a theology of grace. See also Michael Vertin's response to Doran in "Lonergan on Consciousness: Is There a Fifth Level?" *Method: Journal of Lonergan Studies* 12/1 (1994): 1–36, and Doran's subsequent reformulation of his thesis in "Revisiting 'Consciousness and Grace,'" *Method: Journal of Lonergan Studies* 13/2 (1995): 151–9.

59. See Jürgen Habermas, "The Hermeneutic Claim to Universality," in *Contemporary Hermeneutics: Hermeneutics as Method, Philosophy, and Critiques*, p. 181–211, especially 190–203. Lonergan's emphasis on the symbolic operator, all that is implied in the concept, removes him from the type of critique Habermas levels against "philosophers of consciousness." The upshot of Habermas's critique is that philosophers of consciousness ignore the effects of the unconscious and subconscious on consciousness.

60. Doubtless Lonergan's existential-sublational amendment would do little to move someone like Jean-François Lyotard or his followers in the conviction that inherent in any process that "lifts itself up" (*hebt sich auf*) is the tendency to constrict, whatever amendments may be made to it. There is much in Lonergan's concept that resonates with the problematic Lyotard emphasizes. See Lyotard, *The Postmodern Condition: A Report on Knowledge*, trans. Geoff Bennington and Brian Massumi (Minneapolis, MN: University of Minnesota Press, 1984), 33–34, 38, 81, 73. Still, this is not to deny that fundamental and perhaps irreconcilable differences exist in their respective appreciations of the "existential."

61. See Nicholas Lash, "Method and Cultural Discontinuity," in *Looking at Lonergan's Method*, ed. Patrick Corcoran (Dublin: The Talbot Press, 1975), 127–43. The most thorough treatment of this aspect from a methodological standpoint is Michel Foucault, *The Archaeology of Knowledge*, trans. A. M. Sheridan Smith (London: Routledge, 1992).

62. In chapter 7 of *Insight* the dialectic of community and of history are not so sharply differentiated.

63. See Louis Mink, *Mind, History, and Dialectic: The Philosophy of R.G. Collingwood* (Bloomington, IN: Indiana University Press, 1969).

64. Lonergan in *Curiosity at the Center of One's Life: Statements and Questions of R. Eric O'Connor*, ed. J. M. O'Hara (Montreal, 1984), 427, as quoted in F. E. Crowe, *Lonergan*, 98 (see also p. 84).

Conclusion

1. Lonergan, letter to Henry Keane, 22 January 1935, quoted in Crowe, *Lonergan*, 19.

2. David Burrell, "Lonergan and Philosophy of Religion," p. 1.

3. Quesnell's remark about Lonergan's proof is particularly incisive: "[T]his is a distinctive proof. It is a meta-proof, in the sense that it spells out the pre-premises, usually ignored, that lie behind all other [formally] valid proofs. It is 'meta-' also in the sense that what it proves to the thinking subject is not just something about the

world, but something about his or her very self. What changes the knower changes everything known or to be known" ("What Kind of Proof is *Insight* 19?" 276).

4. Burrell, "Lonergan and Philosophy of Religion," p. 1.

5. A case in point is Anthony O'Hear. He includes Lonergan's philosophy of God in a book on the introduction to philosophy of religion. See his *Experience, Explanation and Faith: An Introduction to the Philosophy of Religion* (London: Routledge and Kegan Paul, 1984), 59–64.

6. See Jim Kanaris, "Lonergan and Contemporary Philosophy of Religion," in *Explorations in Continental Philosophy of Religion*, ed. D-P. Baker and P. Maxwell (Editions Radopi, forthcoming); "Calculating Subjects: Lonergan, Derrida, and Foucault," *Method: Journal of Lonergan Studies* 15/2 (1997): 135–50.

7. Phenomenology of religion refers to the discipline within the modern academic study of religion that seeks "descriptive" knowledge of religions, regardless of one's own personal beliefs and biases. A recent approach that is both accessible and hermeneutically judicious is Dale Cannon, *Six Ways of Being Religious: A Framework for Comparative Studies of Religion* (Belmont, CA: Wadsworth Publishing Company, 1996), 1–163.

Bibliography

WORKS BY BERNARD LONERGAN

Published Works

A Second Collection: Papers by Bernard J.F. Lonergan, S.J. Ed. William F. J. Ryan and Bernard J. Tyrrell. Toronto: University of Toronto Press, 1974.

A Third Collection: Papers by Bernard J.F. Lonergan, S.J. Ed. Frederick E. Crowe. New York/Mahwah: Paulist Press, 1985.

"Bernard Lonergan Responds." In *Foundations of Theology: Papers from The International Lonergan Congress 1970*. Edited by Philip McShane, 223–34. Notre Dame: Notre Dame Press, 1971.

"Bernard Lonergan Responds." In *Language, Truth and Meaning: Papers from The International Lonergan Congress 1970*. Edited by Philip McShane, 306–12. Notre Dame: Notre Dame Press, 1972.

Caring about Meaning: Patterns in the Life of Bernard Lonergan. Edited by Pierre Lambert, Charlotte Tansey, and Cathleen Going. Montreal: Thomas More Institute, 1982.

Collection. 1967. Rpt. in *Collected Works of Bernard Lonergan*. Edited by Frederick E. Crowe and Robert Doran. Vol. 4. Toronto: University of Toronto Press, 1988.

Grace and Freedom: Operative Grace in the Thought of St. Thomas Aquinas. London: Darton, Longman and Todd, 1971.

Insight: A Study of Human Understanding. 1957. Rpt. in *Collected Works of Bernard Lonergan*. Edited by Fredrick E. Crowe and Robert M. Doran. Vol. 3. Toronto: University of Toronto Press, 1992.

Method in Theology. New York: Herder and Herder, 1972.

Philosophical and Theological Papers 1958–1964. In *Collected Works of Bernard Lonergan*, Edited by Robert C. Croken, Frederick E. Crowe, and Robert M. Doran. Vol. 6. Toronto: University of Toronto Press, 1996.

"Philosophy and the Religious Phenomenon." *Method: Journal of Lonergan Studies* 12/2 (1994): 125–46.

Philosophy of God, and Theology: The Relationship Between Philosophy of God and the Functional Specialty, Systematics. London: Darton, Longman and Todd, 1973.

"Religious Commitment." In *The Pilgrim People: A Vision With Hope.* Edited by Joseph Papin, 45–69. Villanova, PA: The Villanova Press, 1970.

"Response." In *Proceedings of the American Catholic Philosophical Association* 41 (1967): 258–9.

"The Notion of Structure." *Method: Journal of Lonergan Studies* 14/2 (1996): 117–31.

"The Scope of Renewal." *Method: Journal of Lonergan Studies* 16/2 (1998): 83–101.

Topics in Education: The Cincinnati Lectures of 1959 on the Philosophy of Education. In *Collected Works of Bernard Lonergan.* Edited by Robert M. Doran and Frederick E. Crowe. Vol. 10. Rev. and aug. unpublished text James Quinn and John Quinn. Toronto: University of Toronto Press, 1993.

Understanding and Being: The Halifax Lectures on INSIGHT. 1980. Rpt. in *Collected Works of Bernard Lonergan.* Edited by Elizabeth A. Morelli and Mark D. Morelli. Vol. 5. Rev. and Aug. Fredrick E. Crowe. Toronto: University of Toronto Press, 1990.

"Variations in Fundamental Theology." *Method: Journal of Lonergan Studies* 16/1 (1998): 5–24.

Verbum: Word and Idea in Aquinas. 1967. Rpt. in *Collected Works of Bernard Lonergan.* Edited by Fredrick E. Crowe and Robert M. Doran. Vol. 2. Toronto: University of Toronto Press, 1997.—First published in *Theological Studies* 7 (1946): 349–92; 8 (1947): 35–79, 404–44; 10 (1949): 3–40, 359–93.

Unpublished Works

"Faith and Beliefs." Paper presented to the American Academy of Religion, Newton, MA, October 23, 1969.

"Lectures on Existentialism." Typewritten transcript Nicholas Graham. Boston College, 1957

"On the Ontological and Psychological Constitution of Christ." Translated by John Hochban and Michael Shields. Willowdale, Toronto: Regis College, 1987.

"On Supernatural Being: A Schematic Supplement." Montreal: College of the Immaculate Conception, 1946. Re-ed. Frederick E. Crowe. Willowdale, Toronto: Regis College, 1973.

"The General Character of the Natural Theology of *Insight*." Paper presented at the University of Chicago Divinity School, Chicago, IL, March 1967.

"Understanding and Method." [First draft.] Translated by Michael Shields. Willowdale, Toronto: Regis College, 1988. Rev. 1997.

Works Consulted On Lonergan

Affonso de Sa Earp, Ney. "Love and Transcendent Knowledge." [Three folders.] Rome: Gregorian University, 1974.

Barden, Garrett. "The Intention of Truth in Mythic Consciousness." In *Language, Truth, and Meaning: Papers from The International Lonergan Congress 1970*. Edited by Philip McShane, 4–32. Notre Dame: University of Notre Dame Press, 1972.

Braxton, Edward K. "Knowledge of God in Bernard Lonergan and Hans Küng," *Harvard Theological Review* 70 (1977): 327–41.

Burley, Peter S. "Lonergan as a Neo-Schumpeterian." *Australian Lonergan Workshop* (1998): 249–57.

Burley, Peter S., and Laszlo Csapo, "Money Information in Lonergan-von Neumann Systems." *Economics Systems Research* 4/2 (1992): 133–41.

———. "A von Neumann Representation of Lonergan's Production Model." *Economic Systems Research* 1 (1989): 317–30.

Burrell, David. "Lonergan and Philosophy of Religion." *Method: Journal of Lonergan Studies* 4/1 (1986): 1–5.

Butler, B. C. "God: Anticipation and Affirmation." *Heythrop Journal* 20 (1979): 365–79.

Byrne, Patrick. "Lonergan on Objective and Reflective Interpretation." Paper presented at the annual meeting of the Lonergan Philosophical Society, Pittsburgh, 1998.

———. "Economic Transformations: The Role of Conversions and Culture in the Transformation of Economies." In *Religion and Culture: Essays in Honor of Bernard Lonergan*. Edited by Timothy P. Fallon and Philip Boo Riley, 327–48. Albany, NY: State University of New York Press, 1987.

———. "The Fabric of Lonergan's thought." In *Lonergan Workshop*. Vol. 6. Atlanta, GA: Scholars Press, 1986.

Campbell, John Angus. "Insight and Understanding: The 'Common Sense' Rhetoric of Bernard Lonergan." In *Communication and Lonergan: Common Ground for Forging the New Age*. Edited by Thomas J. Farrell and Paul A. Soukup, 3–22. Kansas City, MO: Sheed and Ward, 1993.

Coelho, Ivo N. *Hermeneutics and Method: A Study of the Universal Viewpoint in Bernard Lonergan.* Rome: Pontificiae Universitatis Gregorianae, 1994.

Conley, Peter Vincent. "The Development of the Notion of Hermeneutics in the Works of Bernard Lonergan, S.J." Ph.D. diss., Catholic University of America, 1972.

Corcoran, Patrick. Forward to *Looking at Lonergan's Method.* Edited by Patrick Corcoran. Dublin: The Talbot Press, 1975.

Crowe, Frederick E. "Lonergan's 'Moral Theology and the Human Sciences': Editor's Introduction." *Method: Journal of Lonergan Studies* 15/1 (1997): 1–3.

———. "Lonergan's 'Philosophy and the Religious Phenomenon': Editor's Preface." *Method: Journal of Lonergan Studies* 12/2 (1994): 121–4.

———. "The Genus 'Lonergan and . . .' and Feminism." In *Lonergan and Feminism.* Edited by Cynthia S. W. Crysdale, 13–32. Toronto: University of Toronto Press, 1994.

———. *Lonergan.* Edited by Brian Davies. Outstanding Christian Thinkers Series. Collegeville, MN: The Liturgical Press, 1992.

———. "An Exploration of Lonergan's New Notion of Value." In *Appropriating the Lonergan Idea.* Edited by Michael Vertin, 51–70. Washington: The Catholic University of America Press, 1989.

de Neeve, Eileen. *Bernard Lonergan's "Circulation Analysis" and Macrodynamics.* Ann Arbor, MI: University Microfilms, 1990.

———. "The Possibility of A Pure Cycle of the Productive Process." In *Religion and Culture: Essays in Honor of Bernard Lonergan.* Edited by Timothy P. Fallon and Philip Boo Riley, 349–64. Albany, NY: State University of New York Press, 1987.

DiSanto, Ronald L. "Complete Intelligibility: A Study of Bernard Lonergan's Argument for the Existence of God." Ph.D. diss., McMaster University, 1975.

Donahue, Eugene L. "Bernard Lonergan's Contribution to Social Economics." *Forum For Social Economics* 22/2 (1993): 45–60.

Doorley, Mark J. *The Place of the Heart in Lonergan's Ethics: The Role of Feelings in the Ethical Intentionality Analysis of Bernard Lonergan.* Lanham, MD: University Press of America, 1996.

Doran, Robert M. "Revisiting 'Consciousness and Grace.'" *Method: Journal of Lonergan Studies* 13/2 (1995): 151–9.

———. "Consciousness and Grace." *Method: Journal of Lonergan Studies* 11/1 (1993): 51–75.

———. *Theology and the Dialectics of History*. Toronto: University of Toronto Press, 1990.

Dunne, Tad. "Being in Love." *Method: Journal of Lonergan Studies* 13/2 (1995): 161–75.

———. *Lonergan and Spirituality: Towards a Spiritual Integration*. Chicago, IL: Loyola University Press, 1985.

Flanagan, Joseph. *Quest for Self-Knowledge: An Essay in Lonergan's Philosophy*. Toronto: University of Toronto Press, 1997.

———. "Knowing and Language in the Thought of Bernard Lonergan." In *Language, Truth and Meaning: Papers from the International Lonergan Congress 1970*. Edited by Philip McShane, 49–78. Notre Dame: University of Notre Dame Press, 1972.

Gregson, Vernon. "The Desire to Know: Intellectual Conversion." In *The Desires of the Human Heart: An Introduction to the Theology of Bernard Lonergan*. Edited by Vernon Gregson, 16–35. New York/Mahwah: Paulist Press, 1988.

———. *Lonergan, Spirituality, and the Meeting of Religions*. Lanham, MD: University Press of America, 1985.

———. "The Historian of Religions and the Theologian: Dialectics and Dialogue." In *Creativity and Method: Essays in Honor of Bernard Lonergan*. Edited by Matthew Lamb, 141–51. Milwaukee: Marquette University Press, 1981.

Habito, Ruben L. F. "A Catholic Debate on God: Dewart and Lonergan." *Philippine Studies* 18/3 (1970): 558–76.

Hefling, Charles C. "The Meaning of God Incarnate According to Friedrich Schleiermacher; *or*, Whether Lonergan is Appropriately Regarded as 'A Schleiermacher for Our Time,' and Why Not." *Lonergan Workshop* 7 (1988): 105–77.

———. "Philosophy, Theology, and God." In *The Desires of the Human Heart: An Introduction to the Theology of Bernard Lonergan*, 120–43. New York/Mahwah: Paulist Press, 1988.

———. "Turning Liberalism Inside-Out." *Method: Journal of Lonergan Studies* 3/2 (1985): 51–69.

———. "Lonergan on Development: *The Way to Nicea* in Light of His More Recent Methodology." Ph.D. diss., Andover Newton Theological School—Boston College, 1982.

Hepburn, Ronald. "Transcendental Method: Lonergan's Arguments for the Existence of God." *Theoria to Theory* 7 (1973): 46–50.

Hodes, Greg. *Foundations and Aprioriai: The Intellectual Realism of Bernard Lonergan*. Ann Arbor, MI: University Microfilms, 1997.

Jonsson, Ulf. *Foundations for Knowing God: Bernard Lonergan's Foundations for Knowledge of God and the Challenge from Antifoundationalism.* Frankfurt am Main: Peter Lang, 1999.

Kanaris, Jim. "Lonergan and Contemporary Philosophy of Religion." In *Explorations in Continental Philosophy of Religion.* Edited by D-P. Baker and P. Maxwell. Editions Radopi. Forthcoming.

———. "The Role of Reason in Aquinas and Calvin." *ARC: The Journal of the Faculty of Religious Studies, McGill University* 27 (1999): 37–65.

———. "The 'Ins and Outs' of Religious Love: Lonergan's Pragmatics." *Studies in Religion/Sciences Religieuses* 27/3 (1998): 295–310.

———. "Calculating Subjects: Lonergan, Derrida, and Foucault." *Method: Journal of Lonergan Studies* 15/2 (1997): 135–50.

———. "Engaged Agency and the Notion of the Subject." *Method: Journal of Lonergan Studies* 14/2 (1996): 183–200.

Lapierre, Michael J. "God and the Desire of Understanding." *The Thomist* 33 (1969): 667–74.

Lawrence, Fred. "The Fragility of Consciousness: Lonergan and the Postmodern Concern for the Other." In *Communication and Lonergan: Common Ground for Forging the New Age.* Edited by Thomas J. Farrell and Paul A. Soukup, 173–211. Kansas City: Sheed and Ward, 1993.

———. " 'The Modern Philosophic Differentiation of Consciousness' or What is the Enlightenment?" *Lonergan Workshop* 2 (1981): 231–79.

Liddy, Richard M. *Transforming Light: Intellectual Conversion in the Early Lonergan.* Collegeville, MN: The Liturgical Press, 1993.

Marasigan, Vicente. "Economic Dysfunctions." *Landas* 2 (1988): 194–203.

Martos, Joseph. "Bernard Lonergan's Theory of Transcendent Knowledge." Ph.D. diss., De Paul University, 1972.

Mathews, William. "A Biographical Perspective on Conversion and the Functional Specialities in Lonergan." *Method: Journal of Lonergan Studies* 16/2 (1998): 142–60.

———. "Kant's Anomalous Insights: A Note on Kant and Lonergan." *Method: Journal of Lonergan Studies* 14/1 (1996): 85–98.

———. "Lonergan's Economics." *Method: Journal of Lonergan Studies* 3/1 (1985): 9–30.

Melchin, Kenneth. "Economics, Ethics, and the Structure of Social Living." *Humanomics* 10 (1993): 21–57.

Meynell, Hugo. *An Introduction to the Philosophy of Bernard Lonergan.* 2d ed. Toronto and Buffalo: University of Toronto Press, 1991.

———. *The Theology of Bernard Lonergan.* Atlanta, GA: Scholars Press, 1986.

McCool, Gerald A. "The Philosophical Theology of Rahner and Lonergan." In *God Knowable and Unknowable.* Edited by Robert J. Roth, 123–57. New York: Fordham University Press, 1973.

McEvenue, Sean. *Interpretation and Bible: Essays on Truth in Literature.* Collegeville, MN: The Liturgical Press, 1994.

———. *Interpreting the Pentateuch.* Collegeville, MN: The Liturgical Press, 1990.

McEvenue, Sean and Ben Meyer, eds. *Lonergan's Hermeneutics: Its Development and Application.* Washington: Catholic University of America Press, 1989.

McShane, Philip, *Economics for Everyone: Das Jus Kapital.* Edmonton: Commonwealth Press, 1996.

Miller, Jerome. "Hermeneutics and Self-Transcendence in Lonergan: A Response to Patrick Byrne." Paper presented at the annual meeting of the Lonergan Philosophical Society, Pittsburgh, 1998.

Morelli, Elizabeth A. "Post-Hegelian Elements in Lonergan's Philosophy of Religion." *Method: Journal of Lonergan Studies* 12/2 (1994): 215–38.

Morelli, Mark D. and Elizabeth A. Morelli. Introduction to *The Lonergan Reader.* Edited by Mark D. Morelli and Elizabeth A. Morelli. Toronto: University of Toronto Press, 1997.

Nilson, Jon. *Hegel's Phenomenology and Lonergan's Insight: A Comparison of Two Ways to Christianity.* Meisenheim am Glan: Verlag Anton Hain, 1979.

———. "Transcendent Knowledge in *Insight*: A Closer Look." *The Thomist* 37 (1973): 366–77.

O'Donnell, John. "Transcendental Approaches to the Doctrine of God." *Gregorianum* 77/4 (1996): 659–76.

Piscitelli, Emil James. "Language and Method in the Philosophy of Religion: A Critical Study of the Development of the Philosophy of Bernard Lonergan." Ph.D. diss., Georgetown University, 1977.

Quesnell, Quentin. "What Kind of Proof is *Insight* 19?" *Lonergan Workshop* 8 (1990): 265–77.

———. "A Note on Scholasticism." In *The Desires of the Human Heart: An Introduction to the Theology of Bernard Lonergan*, 144–9. New York/Mahwah: Paulist Press, 1988.

Rasmussen, David M. "From Problematics to Hermeneutics: Lonergan and Ricoeur." In *Language, Truth and Meaning: Papers from The International Lonergan Congress 1970*. Edited by Philip McShane, 236–71. Notre Dame: University of Notre Dame Press, 1972.

Riley, Philip Boo. "Religious Studies Methodology: Bernard Lonergan's Contribution." *Method: Journal of Lonergan Studies* 12/2 (1994): 239–49.

Ryan, William F. "Edmund Husserl and the '*Rätsel*' of Knowledge." *Method: Journal of Lonergan Studies* 13/2 (1995): 187–219.

———. "The Transcendental Reduction according to Husserl and Intellectual Conversion according to Lonergan." In *Creativity and Method: Essays in Honor of Bernard Lonergan*. Edited by Matthew L. Lamb, 401–10. Milwaukee: Marquette University Press, 1981,.

———. "Passive and Active Elements in Husserl's Notion of Intentionality." *The Modern Schoolman* 55 (1977): 37–55.

Sala, Giovanni B. *Lonergan and Kant: Five Essays on Human Knowledge*. Trans. Joseph Spoerl. Ed. Robert M. Doran. Toronto: University of Toronto Press, 1994.

———. *Das Apriori in der menschlichen Erkenntnis: Eine Studie über Kants Kritik der reinen Vernunft und Lonergans Insight*. Meisenheim am Glan: Verlag Anton Hain, 1971.

Schouborg, Gary. "A Note on Lonergan's Argument for the Existence of God." *The Modern Schoolman* 45 (1967–1968): 243–8.

Shute, Michael. "Emergent Probability and the Ecofeminist Critique of Hierarchy." In *Lonergan and Feminism*. Edited by Cynthia S.W. Crysdale, 146–74. Toronto: University of Toronto Press, 1994.

———. *The Origins of Lonergan's Notion of the Dialectic of History: A Study of Lonergan's Early Writings on History*. Lanham, MD: University Press of America, 1993.

Stebbins, J. Michael. *The Divine Initiative: Grace, World-Order, and Human Freedom in the Early Writings of Bernard Lonergan*. Toronto: University of Toronto Press, 1995.

Stewart, W. A. *Introduction to Lonergan's Insight: An Invitation to Philosophize*. Lewiston, NY: Edwin Mellen Press, 1996.

Tekippe, Terry. *What's Lonergan Up To in Insight?: A Primer*. Collegeville, MN: The Liturgical Press, 1996.

Tracy, David. *The Achievement of Bernard Lonergan*. New York: Herder and Herder, 1970.

Tyrrell, Bernard. *Bernard Lonergan's Philosophy of God*. Notre Dame: University of Notre Dame Press, 1974.

———. "The New Context of the Philosophy of God in Lonergan and Rahner." In *Language, Truth and Meaning*. Edited by Philip McShane, 284–305. Notre Dame: University of Notre Dame Press, 1972.

Vertin, Michael. "Lonergan on Consciousness: Is There a Fifth Level?" *Method: Journal of Lonergan Studies* 12/1 (1994): 1–36.

Wilson, Patricia. "Human Knowledge of God's Existence in The Theology of Bernard Lonergan." *The Thomist* 35 (1971): 259–75.

Zanardi, William. "Consumer Responsibility from a Social Systems Perspective." *International Journal of Applied Philosophy* (Spring 1990): 57–66.

Other Works Consulted

Beumer, Johannes. *Theologie als Glaubensverständnis*. Würzburg: Echter Verlag, 1953.

Binswanger, Ludwig. *Ausgewählte Vorträge und Aufsätze*. 2 Vols. Bern: A. Francke, 1947.

Bloom, Harold. *Book of J*. Translated from the Hebrew by David Rosenberg and interpreted by Harold Bloom. New York: Grove Weidenfeld, 1990.

Boutin, Maurice. "Conceiving the Invisible: Joseph C. McLelland's Modal Approach to Theological and Religious Pluralism." In *The Three Loves—Philosophy, Theology, and World Religions. Essays in Honour of Joseph C. McLelland*. Edited by Robert C. Culley and William Klempa, 1–18. Atlanta, GA: Scholars Press, 1994.

Brown, James. *Subject and Object in Modern Theology*. London: SCM Press, 1955.

Burley, Peter S. "Lonergan as a Neo-Schumpeterian." *Australian Lonergan Workshop* (1998): 249–57.

Cannon, Dale. *Six Ways of Being Religious: A Framework for Comparative Studies of Religion*. Belmont, CA: Wadsworth Publishing Company, 1996.

Chalmers, David J. "The Puzzle of Conscious Experience." *Scientific American: Mysteries of the Mind*, 7/1 (1997): 30–37, special issue.

———. *The Conscious Mind: In Search of a Fundamental Theory*. Oxford: University of Oxford Press, 1996.

Collingwood, R. G. *The Idea of History*. Oxford: Clarendon Press, 1946.

Copleston, Frederick. *Wolff to Kant*. Vol. 6: pt. 4 of *A History of Philosophy*. New York: Doubleday, 1960.

Corbin, Michel. *Le chemin de la Théologie chez Thomas d'Aquin*. Bibliothèque des Archives de Philosophie, Nouvelle Série, 16. Paris: Beauchesne, 1974.

Crites, Stephen. "The Pros and Cons of Theism: Whether They Constitute the Fundamental Issue of the Philosophy of Religion." In *God, Philosophy, and Academic Culture: A Discussion between Scholars in the AAR and the APA*. Edited by William J. Wainwright, 39–45. Atlanta, GA: Scholars Press, 1996.

Derrida, Jacques. "Faith and Knowledge: The Two Sources of 'Religion' at the Limits of Reason Alone." In *Religion*. Edited by Jacques Derrida and Gianni Vattimo, 1–78. Stanford: Stanford University Press, 1998.

Duffy, Bruce. *The World as I Found It: A Novel*. Boston and New York: A. Mariner Book/Houghton Mifflin Company, 1995.

Dupré, Louis. *A Dubious Heritage: Studies in the Philosophy of Religion after Kant*. New York: Paulist Press, 1977.

Eliade, Mircea. *Histoire des croyances et des idées religieuses*. 3 Vols. Paris: Payot, 1976–1983.

Fasold, Ralph. *The Sociolinguistics of Language*. Oxford: Blackwell, 1990.

Fiorenza, Francis Schüssler. Introduction to *Spirit in the World*, by Karl Rahner. Trans. William Dych. New York: Continuum, 1994.

Flew, Antony and Alaidair MacIntyre, eds. *New Essays in Philosophical Theology*. London: SCM Press, 1955.

Ford, J. C. "Marriage: Its Meaning and Purposes." *Theological Studies* 3 (1942).

Foucault, Michel. *The Archaeology of Knowledge*. Translated by A. M. Sheridan Smith. London: Routledge, 1992.

Gadamer, Hans-Georg. "The Universality of the Hermeneutical Problem." In *Contemporary Hermeneutics: Hermeneutics as Method, Philosophy, and Critiques*. Edited by Joseph Bleicher and translated by David Linge, 128–40. London, Boston and Henley: Routledge and Kegan Paul, 1980.

Gilson, Étienne. *Réalisme thomiste et critique de la connaissance*. Paris: Vrin, 1939.

Habermas, Jürgen. "The Hermeneutic Claim to Universality." In *Contemporary Hermeneutics: Hermeneutics as Method, Philosophy, and Critiques*. Edited by Joseph Bleicher, 181–211. London, Boston and Henley: Routledge and Kegan Paul, 1980.

Hegel, G. W. F. *Phenomenology of Spirit*. Translated by A. V. Miller. Oxford: Oxford University Press, 1977.

———. *Lectures on the Philosophy of History*. 3 Vols. Translated by Elizabeth S. Haldane and Frances H. Simpson. New York: The Humanities Press, 1955.

Heiler, Friedrich. "The History of Religions as a Preparation for the Cooperation of Religions." In *The History of Religions*. Edited by M. Eliade and J. Kitagawa, 142–53. Chicago: University of Chicago Press, 1959.

Inwood, Michael. *A Hegel Dictionary*. Cambridge, MA: Basil Blackwell Inc., 1992.

Jordan, Mark D. "Theology and Philosophy." In *The Cambridge Companion to Aquinas*. Edited by Norman Kretzman and Eleanore Stump, 232–51. Cambridge: Cambridge University Press, 1993.

Kenny, Anthony. *Aquinas on Mind*. New York: Routledge and Kegan Paul, 1993.

Knowles, David. *The Evolution of Medieval Thought*. London: Longmans and Green, 1962.

Küng, Hans. *Theology for the Third Millennium: An Ecumenical View*. Translated by Peter Heinegg. New York: Doubleday, 1988.

———. *Does God Exist? An Answer for Today*. Translated by Edward Quinn. New York: Vintage Books, 1978.

Langer, Susanne K. *Mind: An Essay on Human Feeling*. 3 Vols. Baltimore and London: The John Hopkins University Press, 1967–82.

———. *Feeling and Form: A Theory of Art Developed from "Philosophy in a New Key."* New York: Charles Scribner's Sons, 1953.

Lash, Nicholas. "Method and Cultural Discontinuity." In *Looking at Lonergan's Method*. Edited by Patrick Corcoran, 127–43. Dublin: The Talbot Press, 1975.

Liddy, Richard M. *Art and Feeling: An Analysis and Critique of the Philosophy of Art of Susanne K. Langer*. Ann Arbor, MI: University Microfilms, 1970.

———. Review of *Mind: An Essay on Human Feeling*. Vol. 1. By Susanne K. Langer. *International Philosophical Quarterly* 10 (1970): 481–4.

Lindbeck, George A. *The Nature of Doctrine: Religion and Theology in a Postliberal Age*. Philadelphia: The Westminster Press, 1984.

Louth, Andrew. *Discerning the Mystery: An Essay on the Nature of Theology*. Oxford: Oxford University Press, 1983.

Lyotard, Jean-François. *The Postmodern Condition: A Report on Knowledge*. Translated by Geoff Bennington and Brian Massumi. Minneapolis, MN: University of Minnesota Press, 1984.

Mink, Louis. *History and Dialectic: The Philosophy of R. G. Collingwood*. Bloomington: Indiana University Press, 1969.

Miquel, Pierre. "Paul VI et la réhabilitation de l'expérience." *Collectanea Cisterciensa* 40/3 (1978): 161–70.

O'Hear, Anthony. *Experience, Explanation and Faith: An Introduction to the Philosophy of Religion*. London: Routledge and Kegan Paul, 1984.

Olafson, Frederick A. "The Unity of Heidegger's Thought." In *The Cambridge Companion to Heidegger*. Edited by Charles B. Guignon, 97–121. Cambridge: Cambridge University Press, 1993.

———. *Heidegger and the Philosophy of Mind*. New Haven, CN: Yale University Press, 1987.

Olivetti, Marco Maria, ed. *L'argomento ontologico*. Padova: Cedam, 1990.

Olivier, Laurence. *Confessions of An Actor*. London: Weidenfeld and Nicolson, 1982.

Pannenberg, Wolfhart. *Systematic Theology*. Translated by Geoffrey Bromiley. Vol. 1. Grand Rapids, MI: Wm. B. Eerdmans Publishing Co., 1991.

Pascal, Blaise. *Pensées*. Translated by A. J. Krailsheimer. London: Penguin Books, 1966.

Pelican, Jeroslav. *The Growth of Medieval Theology (600–1300)*. Vol. 3 of *The Christian Tradition: A History of the Development of Doctrine*. Chicago: University of Chicago Press, 1985.

Peperzak, Theodoor. "Philosophia." *Faith and Philosophy: Journal of the Society of Christian Philosophers* 14/3 (1997): 321–33.

Pippin, Robert B. "You Can't Get There from Here: Transition Problems in Hegel's *Phenomenology of Spirit*." In *The Cambridge Companion to Hegel*. Edited by Frederick C. Beiser, 52–85. Cambridge: Cambridge University Press, 1993.

Plantinga, Alvin. "The Reformed Objection to Natural Theology." In *Faith and Rationality*. Edited by Alvin Plantinga and Nicholas Wolterstorff, 63–73. Notre Dame: University of Notre Dame Press, 1983.

Quine, W. V. "Epistemology Naturalized." In W. V. Quine, *Ontological Relativity and Other Essays*, 69–90. New York and London: Columbia University Press, 1969.

———. *Mathematical Logic*. New York: W. W. Norton, 1940.

Ricoeur, Paul. "The Task of Hermeneutics." In *Paul Ricoeur: Hermeneutics and the Human Sciences: Essays on Language, Action and Interpretation*. Edited by John B. Thompson, 43–62. Cambridge: Cambridge University Press, 1981.

Stead, Christopher. *Philosophy in Christian Antiquity*. Cambridge: Cambridge University Press, 1994.

Taylor, Charles. "Overcoming Epistemology." In *Philosophy: End or Transformation?* Edited by Kenneth Baynes, James Bohman, and Thomas McCarthy, 464–88. Cambridge, MA: MIT Press, 1987.

———. *Hegel*. Cambridge: Cambridge University Press, 1975.

Wartenberg, Thomas E. "Hegel's Idealism: The Logic of Conceptuality." In *The Cambridge Companion to Hegel*. Edited by Frederick C. Beiser, 102–29. Cambridge: Cambridge University Press, 1993.

Winter, Gibson. *Elements for a Social Ethics: Scientific and Ethical Perspectives on Social Progress*. New York: The Macmillan Company, 1966.

Wulff, David M. *Psychology of Religion: Classic and Contemporary*. 2d ed. New York: Wiley and Sons, 1997.

Index

abstraction, 55–57
allegory, 167n. 44
Anschauung. *See* intuition
Anselm, 78, 104–5, 170–1n. 6
Aquinas, 11–2, 14, 63, 65–6, 69–70, 73, 79–80, 92, 95, 97, 153nn. 4, 5, 10, 154n. 11, 163n. 7, 164nn. 7, 8, 13, 165nn. 17, 27, 28, 166nn. 28, 33
Aristotle, 1, 12, 28, 65, 69, 73, 95, 153n. 5, 164n. 13, 165n. 17, 165n. 28, 170n. 6
Athanasius, 20, 126
Aufhebung. *See* sublation
Augustine, 12, 78, 153nn. 4, 5, 165n. 18, 166n. 35
authenticity, authentic, 89–90, 126, 128–30, 136, 138, 142, 145–6, 172n. 11. *See also* unauthenticity, unauthentic, inauthentic

Baius, Michael, 69
Baker, D-P., 177n. 6
Barden, Garrett, 84–5, 167n. 42
Baynes, Kenneth, 156n. 5
beatific vision, 68–9, 79, 167n. 47
Begriff. *See* concept
being, 163–4n. 7 (*see also* reality); notion of, 159n. 30
Beiser, Frederick C., 160n. 44
belief(s), 13–4, 15, 105, 109, 113–6, 130, 144, 170n. 6, 173nn. 25, 28
Bennington, Geoff, 176n. 60
Berkeley, George, 46, 54

Beumer, Johannes, 65, 163n. 6, 164n. 13
bias, 58–60
Binswanger, Ludwig, 171n. 10
Blair, Hugh, 156n. 6
Blayone, Todd, ix
Bleicher, Josef, 162n. 65
blik, 124, 174n. 43
Bloom, Harold, 93, 168n. 56
Boeckh, August, 120
Bohman, James, 156n. 5
Boutin, Maurice, ix, 164n. 7, 170–1n. 6
Braxton, Edward K., 152n. 1
Bromiley, Geoffrey, 168n. 57
Brown, James, 158n. 30
Buber, Martin, 42
Bultmann, Rudolf, 156
Burke, Kenneth, 28
Burley, Peter S., 169n. 2
Burns, J. Patout, 165n. 27
Burrell, David, 2, 96, 147, 151n. 2, 154nn. 11, 12, 169n. 62, 176n. 2, 177n. 4
Butler, B.C., 152n. 1
Byrne, Patrick, ix, 6, 151n. 7, 169n. 2, 174n. 39

Calvin, John, 93, 160n. 38, 166n. 33
Campbell, George, 156n. 6
Campbell, John Angus, 27, 156nn. 6, 7, 8, 9
Cannon, Dale, 177n. 7
categories, 163–4n. 7

Chalmers, David J., 5, 32–4, 157nn. 14, 15, 16, 17, 18, 19, 20, 21
Christianson, Eric, ix
Christology, 112, 126
Churchland, Paul, 157n. 18
Coelho, Ivo N., 174n. 39
cognition: acts of, 52, 60 (*see also* consciousness, operations of; levels of, 108, 134); phenomenology of, 27, 56
Collingwood, R.G., 120, 132, 140, 175n. 50
common sense, 58, 82, 87, 122, 124, 137, 162n. 67, 175n. 44
concept, 44–5, 47–51, 53–5, 88, 96, 161n. 51
conceptualism, 49, 56, 71–2, 134–5
Congar, Yves, 18
Conley, Peter Vincent, 174n. 39
consciousness, 5, 47, 52–53, 98, 158n. 26, 159n. 31, 160n. 43, 161n. 56, 170n. 5, 176n. 59; classical, 69; cognitional, 108–9, 131, 133; creative development of, 111, 166n. 29; differentiated, 93–4, 98, 134, 137, 144, 168n. 55; differentiation(s) of, 5, 37–9, 92–4, 98, 115, 132, 136–7, 140, 166n. 33; existential, 2, 22, 108–9, 114, 133, 135 (*see also* decision; existential); functionalist notion of, 32–3; healing development of, 111, 166n. 29; historical, 69, 117, 120, 131; levels of, 52, 89, 105, 108, 163n. 3, 166n. 29, 171n. 10; mythic, 81, 83, 167n. 44; operations of, 49, 52, 54, 56, 106–7, 173n. 33; philosophers of, 60, 176n. 59; post-systematic, 137; religious, 81, 87, 107, 117, 122, 129, 141; symbolic, 83; undifferentiated, 92–4, 98, 133–4, 137
conversion: intellectual, 104, 135, 170n. 5; moral, 135; psychic, 135; religious, 15, 102, 135, 170n. 5; social, 135
Copleston, Frederick, 160n. 41
Corbin, Michel, 164n. 9
Corcoran, Patrick, 155n. 24, 176n. 61

Coreth, Emerich, 56, 159n. 30, 162n. 64
Crites, Stephen, 3, 151n. 5
Croken, Robert, ix
Crowe, Frederick E., ix, 3, 89, 135, 151n. 8, 154nn. 11, 19, 155nn. 25, 28, 30, 162n. 67, 163nn. 2, 3, 168n. 50, 174n. 42, 175n. 57, 176nn. 64, 1
Crysdale, Cynthia S.W., 163n. 2, 165n. 19
Csapo, Laszlo, 169n. 2
Culley, Robert C., 164n. 7
culture: classicist notion of, 168n. 59; empirical notion of, 168n. 59

Daniélou, Jean, 18
Dasein, 158n. 27, 163n. 7
Davies, Brian, 151n. 8
Dawson, Christopher, 120
decision, 6, 81, 89–90, 92, 98, 103, 105, 107–10, 113, 116, 128–31, 133, 135, 168n. 51, 175n. 48. *See also* consciousness, existential; existential
Derrida, Jacques, 85, 158n. 27, 167n. 43
Descartes, René, 1, 31, 43, 164n. 7, 171n. 6
description, 86, 164n. 14
dialectic, 121, 126, 128–30, 132, 136–7, 140, 144, 163n. 3, 174n. 37, 175n. 48, 176n. 62
Dilthey, Wilhelm, 120, 163n. 3
DiSanto, Ronald L., 152n. 1
doctrines, 112
Donahue, Eugene L., 169n. 2
Doorley, Mark J., 152n. 10
Doran, Robert M., 135, 154n. 11, 155n. 29, 172n. 12, 175–6n. 58
Droysen, Johann Gustav, 120
Duffy, Bruce, 26, 156n. 3, 163n. 5
Dunne, Tad, 113, 166–7n. 37, 173n. 24
Dupré, Louis, 101, 169n. 1
Dych, William, 155n. 29

ecofeminism, 165n. 19

Index   195

Eddington, Sir Arthur, 175n. 44
Einstein, Albert, 36
Eliade, Mircea, 82, 122, 167n. 41,
   172n. 14
emergent probability, 68, 165n. 19
empiricism, 53
epistemology, 27, 156n. 4
Erasmus, Desiderius, 77, 166n. 33
essentialism, 71–2
evil: mystery of, 175n. 47; problem of,
   9–11, 13, 16, 148–9, 153n. 8, 175n.
   47
experience, 156n. 1, 163n. 3; epistemic,
   32; general (structure of), 24, 29–30,
   35, 49, 53, 57, 60, 157n. 11, 162n.
   68; high-plateau, 78, 80; noetic,
   noematic, 24, 52, 87; pattern(s) of,
   5–6, 29, 36–9, 62–4, 67, 77, 81, 83,
   92, 115, 124, 157nn. 12, 22, 23,
   173n. 33; peak, 68, 78, 80, 171n. 9;
   philosophy of religious, 88, 118, 144;
   reader's, 22, 24–9; religious, 4–5, 10,
   13, 15, 16–7, 19, 21, 23, 61–4, 67–8,
   77–81, 84, 86–9, 96, 98–9, 101, 104,
   107–9, 112–3, 118, 123, 144–5, 148,
   152n. 10, 154nn. 16, 17, 164n. 15,
   168n. 58, 172n. 21; sensate, 32;
   specific (aspect of), level of, 24, 29–
   30, 35, 42, 50, 52–4, 90, 101, 104,
   106, 108, 114, 129–30, 135, 153n. 9,
   157n. 11, 173n. 25
existential, 89–92, 107–8, 114–8, 125–
   6, 128, 131, 134, 136, 138, 145,
   165n. 20, 175n. 48, 176n. 60. See
   also consciousness, existential;
   decision
Existentialism, 22, 87–8, 97–8, 155n. 29
explanation, 85–87, 94, 97, 129

faith, 22, 66, 70, 79, 97, 99, 103, 105,
   109, 111, 113–4, 130, 144, 147,
   153n. 5, 167n. 43, 171n. 7, 173n. 28;
   science of, 65; truths of, 65–6, 133,
   164n. 13
Fallon, Timothy P., 169n. 2

Farrell, Thomas J., 156nn. 2, 6
feelings, 152n. 10
finality, 165n. 17; absolute, 69; horizontal, 68–9, 73–5; vertical, 67–9, 73–6
Fiorenza, Francis Schüssler, 20, 155n. 29
Flanagan, Joseph, 3, 151n. 7, 162n. 1,
   173n. 25
Flew, Antony, 174n. 43
Ford, J.C., 67, 164n. 16
Foucault, Michel, 158n. 27, 176n. 61
foundational method. See method,
   foundational; method, philosophic
foundations, 103–4, 175n. 48
Freud, Sigmund, 126
functional specialties, 89, 102–3, 112,
   119–21, 128, 164n. 14, 174n. 37

Gadamer, Hans-Georg, 57–8, 120, 136,
   162n. 65
Galileo, 64
Gaudet, Stephen, ix
Gavin, John P., 155n. 29
German Historical School, 49, 119,
   164n. 12
Gilson, Étienne, 45–7, 160nn. 39, 40
God: natural knowledge of, 89–90, 92–
   4, 98 (see also knowledge, of God);
   philosophy of, 2–7, 9, 16, 23, 55, 78,
   84, 86–7, 89–90, 93, 99, 101–2, 107–
   9, 113, 116–8, 123, 139, 144, 147,
   173nn. 28, 30, 175n. 47, 177n. 5;
   proof(s) for the existence of, 5, 9–11,
   13, 15–7, 23, 68, 87, 91–8, 101,
   104–5, 107, 114, 116–7, 147–9,
   169n. 61, 170–1n. 6, 176n. 3. See
   also love, being in
grace, 69–71, 72–6, 79–80, 87, 93, 97–
   98, 110, 113, 135, 165nn. 21, 27,
   166n. 28; theology of, 176n. 58
Gregson, Vernon, 121, 151n. 7, 153n.
   8, 174nn. 36, 37, 38
Guignon, Charles B., 158n. 27

Habermas, Jürgen, 58, 128, 136, 162n.
   66, 176n. 59

Habito, Ruben L.F., 152n. 1, 170–1n. 6
Haldane, Elizabeth S., 159n. 32
Hare, Richard M., 124, 174n. 43
Heaney, J.J., 19, 154n. 21
Hefling, Charles C., Jr., 112, 154n. 16, 172nn. 16, 17, 18
Hegel, 5, 20, 40–50, 53–56, 97, 132–4, 136, 141–142, 147–9, 155n. 29, 159nn. 30, 31, 32, 33, 160nn. 42, 43, 161nn. 54, 56, 57, 175n. 56
Heidegger, Martin, 5, 20, 42, 124, 155n. 29, 158n. 27, 160n. 49
Heiler, Friedrich, 111–2, 123, 172n. 14
Heinegg, Peter, 166n. 33
Hepburn, Ronald, 152n. 1
hermeneutic(s), 119, 121, 136, 143, 155n. 30 (*see also* interpretation); of demystification, 82; of recollection, 82–83; of recovery, 126, 129, 132; of suspicion, 126, 129, 132
history, 127, 130–2, 139, 143, 165n. 19, 173n. 32
Hodes, Greg, 160n. 50
horizon, 95–6, 124–6
Horney, Karen, 122
Hume, David, 20, 153n. 6
Husserl, Edmund, 27, 87, 124, 139, 155n. 29, 156n. 5

idealism, 45–6, 54–5, 161n. 57
Ignatius Loyola, 155n. 30
immanentism, 18
infrastructure, 122, 145
insight, 49–55, 58, 106–7
intellectual operator, 135
intentionality analysis, 133, 148
interiority, 134, 139
interpretation, 119–21, 126, 130, 155n. 30, 163n. 3. *See also* hermeneutic(s)
introspection, 162n. 68
intuition, 42–3, 50, 160nn. 42, 49
Inwood, Michael, 159nn. 36, 37, 162n. 59

James, William, 67
Jansenius, Cornelius, 69

Jaspers, Karl, 156n. 32, 158n. 27
Jonsson, Ulf, 171n. 7
Jordan, Mark D., 12, 153n. 5
judgment, 35, 43, 45, 50–3, 81, 90–1, 101, 105, 108, 112–4, 126, 135, 153n. 7, 160n. 50, 163n. 7, 173nn. 23, 25; of fact, 110, 121, 129–31, 173n. 33; of value, 109, 121, 129, 131. *See also* understanding, reflective
Jung, Carl Gustav, 122

Kanaris, Jim, 151n. 3, 152n. 11, 156nn. 5, 10, 158nn. 27, 29, 166n. 33, 168n. 60, 177n. 6
Kant, 5, 20, 40–50, 54, 90, 151n. 6, 153n. 6, 155nn. 27, 29, 158n. 27, 159n. 30, 31, 32, 33, 160nn. 41, 49, 163n. 3, 163–4n. 7
Keane, Henry, 155n. 25, 176n. 1
Kenny, Anthony, 154n. 11
Kierkegaard, 2, 42, 44, 97, 128, 133, 138
Kitagawa, J., 172n. 14
Klempa, William, 164n. 7
knowing, 53, 59–60, 62, 77, 97, 164n. 7, 168n. 53
knowledge, 160n. 49, 167n. 43; analogical, 79; general transcendent, 13, 15, 61, 78, 168n. 58, 169n. 63; ideal(s) of, 40, 57; immanently generated, 115, 153n. 9; of God, 19, 78, 80, 168n. 53 (*see also* God, natural knowledge of); special transcendent, 13, 15, 61, 78, 175n. 47
Kretzmann, Norman, 153
Küng, Hans, 70, 165nn. 22, 23, 166n. 33

Lamb, Matthew L., 156n. 5
Langer, Susanne K., 39, 157n. 25, 157–8n. 26
Lapierre, Michael J., 152n. 1
Lash, Nicholas, 176n. 61
law of the cross, 175n. 47
Lawrence, Fred, 156n. 2
Lévi-Strauss, Claude, 82
Liddy, Richard M., 157–8n. 26

Lindbeck, George A., 111–2, 172n. 15
Linge, David, 162n. 65
logic, logical, 10–1, 55–6, 123, 132–3, 142, 148–9, 152n. 2, 153n. 3, 159n. 30, 164n. 7, 171n. 7
Louth, Andrew, 77, 166n. 34
love, 13, 67, 69, 72–5, 109, 111, 114, 115, 127, 165n. 28, 166n. 29, 172n. 21; being in, 107, 109, 113–4, 122, 130, 164n. 15, 171n. 9, 175n. 47; being not in, 114, 116; knowledge born of, 109–10, 113
Lubac, Henri de, 165n. 21
Luther, Martin, 77, 113, 166n. 33
Lyotard, Jean-François, 176n. 60

MacIntyre, Alasdair, 174n. 43
macroeconomics, 169n. 2
Marasigan, Vicente, 169n. 2
Marcel, Gabriel, 156n. 32
Martos, Joseph, 152n. 1
Marx, Karl, 44, 126
Maslow, Abraham, 78, 171n. 9
Massumi, Brian, 176n. 60
Mathews, William, 89, 158n. 27, 163n. 3, 168nn. 48, 49, 169n. 2
Maxwell, P., 177n. 6
McCarthy, Thomas, 156n. 5
McCool, Gerald A., 152n. 1
McEvenue, Sean, ix, 103–104, 169n. 3, 170n. 4, 174nn. 34, 39
McLelland, Joseph, ix, 164n. 7
McShane, Philip, 154n. 15, 167n. 39, 169n. 2
meaning, 156n. 4; aesthetic, 157n. 26; artistic, 157n. 26; common, 137–8; domains of, 170n. 3; elemental, 169n. 3; functions of, 136–40; realms of, 115, 136, 140, 169–70n. 3; stages of, 140–2, 144
mediation, 47–51, 81, 160n. 42, 162n. 68, 169n. 3
Melchin, Kenneth, 169n. 2
metaphysics, 81–4, 162n. 64
method, 55–56, 113, 124–5, 129, 132–3, 141–4, 162n. 63; foundational, 6, 11, 121, 123, 131, 134, 136, 144–5, 147, 173n. 26 (*see also* "philosophy of"; method, philosophic); generalized empirical, 119, 123, 131–2, 145, 170n. 3, 173n. 26, 173n. 29, 175n. 54 (*see also* "philosophy of"; method, foundational); in theology, 19, 81, 89, 102, 113, 119, 128, 148, 164n. 14, 170n. 3; philosophic, 125–6, 131–2; transcendental, 131, 163n. 3
Meyer, Ben, 174n. 39
Meynell, Hugo, 3, 45, 151n. 7, 159n. 35
Miller, A.V., 159n. 31
Miller, Jerome, 174n. 39
Mink, Louis, 140, 176n. 63
Miquel, Pierre, 155n. 22
Mitchell, Basil, 174n. 43
modernism, 18–21, 23, 61, 63, 154n. 21, 168n. 58
Morelli, Elizabeth A., 56, 133–4, 151n. 8, 155n. 30, 162n. 62, 175nn. 52, 53, 55
Morelli, Mark D., 151n. 8, 155n. 30
mystery, 81, 83–6, 91, 129, 134, 137, 167nn. 38, 44, 175n. 47
myth, 81–2, 84–6, 129, 134, 137, 167nn. 38, 44

natural theology. *See* God, philosophy of
nature, natural, 69–70, 72–6, 78, 97–8, 101, 165n. 28
Neeve, Eileen de, 169n. 2
Newman, John Henry, 28
Newton, Sir Isaac, 36, 37
Nietzsche, Friedrich, 42, 126, 128
Nilson, Jon, 53–5, 152n. 1, 155n. 29, 161nn. 54, 55, 56, 162n. 60
noumenon, 42–7, 159n. 31, 160n. 42
nouvelle théologie, 19, 69
numinous, 126

objectification, 173n. 23
objectivity, 130; faulty notion of, 27–8, 162n. 68. *See also* judgment; judgment, of fact; judgment, of value; reality; unconditioned; unconditioned, virtually

observation, 174n. 43
O'Donnell, John, 91, 168nn. 52, 54
O'Hara, J.M., 176n. 64
O'Hear, Anthony, 177n. 5
Olafson, Frederick A., 158n. 27
Olivetti, Marco Maria, 171n. 6
Olivier, Sir Laurence, 38–39, 157n. 24
openness, 87–8
ordo disciplinae (way of instruction), 66–7
ordo doctrinae (way of learning), 66
ordo inventionis (way of discovery), 65–6
Origen, 20, 126
Otto, Rudolf, 82, 126

Panikkar, Raimundo, 123
Pannenberg, Wolfhart, 94, 168n. 57
Papin, Joseph, 171n. 8
Pascal, Blaise, 96, 114
Paul, Saint (the apostle), 93
Pelikan, Jeroslav, 154n. 11
Peperzak, Adriann Theodor, 173n. 27
personal equation, 124–5
phenomenon, 42–3, 159nn. 30, 31
"philosophy of", 2, 16, 63, 87–8, 108–9, 117–8, 121, 123–5, 132, 144–6, 148, 173n. 29. *See also* method, foundational; method, generalized empirical; method, philosophic
philosophy of God. *See* God, philosophy of
philosophy of religion. *See* religion, philosophy of; religion, Lonergan's philosophy of
philosophy of religious studies. *See* religious studies, philosophy of
Pippin, Robert B., 47–8, 160nn. 44, 45
Piscitelli, Emil James, 152n. 1
Plantinga, Alvin, 46, 160n. 38
Plato, 1, 54, 133, 157n. 12
Popes: John Paul II, 166n. 31; Leo XIII, 166n. 32; Paul VI, 18; Pius X, 18, 20; Pius XII, 19
pragmatics, 29, 168n. 60
praxis, 128–30
prayer, 77–8

preconceptual, 49, 51, 53, 55, 161n. 58. *See also* cognition, acts of; consciousness, levels of; consciousness, operations of; experience, general (structure of); experience, specific (aspect of), levels of; insight; understanding; judgment; decision
proof(s) for the existence of God. *See* God, proof(s) for the existence of

Quesnell, Quentin, 21, 87, 154n. 14, 155nn. 26, 27, 30, 167n. 45, 168n. 53, 176n. 3
Quincey, Thomas de, 156n. 6
Quine, W.V.O., 156n. 4, 158n. 28
Quinn, Edward, 165n. 22

Rahner, Karl, 18, 21, 155n. 29
Ranke, Leopold von, 120
Rasmussen, David M., 82, 167nn. 39, 40
realism, 45–6; critical, 45, 52
reality, 51–4, 88, 106, 162n. 68, 163–4n. 7. *See also* being
reason, 70, 72–6, 79–80, 97, 99, 127, 133, 158n. 27, 165n. 28, 171n. 7. *See also* faith
religion, 105, 113, 115, 125, 127, 132–3, 135, 142, 147, 164n. 15, 172n. 11; dialectical philosophy of, 136; Lonergan's philosophy of, 2–7, 9–11, 16–7, 23, 55–56, 101–2, 108–9, 113, 117–9, 121–4, 126–8, 130–2, 135–6, 139, 144–50, 152n. 10, 162n. 61, 173nn. 28, 33; model of, 6, 107–9, 113–7, 121–3, 128, 135–6, 144–6, 148–9, 153n. 8, 174n. 40; phenomenology of, 149, 177n. 7; philosophy of, 2, 3, 6, 9, 96, 118, 144, 147–50, 175n. 47, 177n. 5; theory of, 112; word of, 114
religious studies, 9, 16, 118–9, 121, 123–4, 128, 130–1, 134, 136, 144–145, 147; philosophy of, 6, 144–5, 148–9

revelation, 65–6, 71, 73, 78–9, 81, 88, 96, 133, 166n. 28, 175n. 47; truths of, 65, 88
rhetoric, 28, 166n. 35
Ricoeur, Paul, 82, 126, 147–8, 158n. 27
Riley, Philip Boo, 112–3, 121–3, 169n. 2, 172nn. 19, 20, 174n. 41
Rogers, Carl R., 122
Rosenberg, David, 168n. 56
Roth, Robert J., 152n. 1
Roy, Louis, ix, 154n. 19
Russell, Bertrand, 163n. 5
Ryan, William F., 156n. 5

Sa Earp, Ney Affonso de, 152n. 1
Sala, Giovanni B., 155n. 29, 160nn. 48, 49
Sandburg, Carl, 11
Schleiermacher, Friedrich, 3, 111–2, 120, 151n. 6
Scholasticism, 20–21, 98, 143, 156n. 31, 171n. 7, 173n. 30
Schopenhauer, Arthur, 128
Schouborg, Gary, 152n. 1
science, 115, 153n. 5, 163n. 3, 164n. 13
Sein, 158n. 27
self, 53–5, 89–90, 118, 162n. 59, 171–2n. 11. *See also* subject
self-appropriation, 5, 26, 29, 38–9, 55, 57, 60, 81, 96, 116–7, 130; existential aspect of, 57, 59–60, 165n. 20; technical aspect of, 40, 55, 57, 60
self-consciousness, 48–9, 54, 161n. 56
self-knowledge, 1, 41, 81, 117, 134, 167n. 44
self-transcendence, 90, 105–7, 110–11, 117, 128, 133, 171n. 11; communal acts of, 139
Shields, Michael, ix
Shute, Michael, 165n. 19, 175n. 46
Simpson, Frances H., 159n. 32
Smith, Adam, 156n. 6
Smith, Wilfrted Cantwell, 105, 113, 122, 171n. 9, 172n. 22
social ethics, 118–9

Soukup, Paul A., 156nn. 2, 6
Spinoza, 43
Spoerl, Joseph, 155n. 29, 160n. 49
Stead, Christopher, 133, 175n. 51
Stebbins, J. Michael, 4, 11, 71–2, 152n. 9, 153n. 3, 165nn. 21, 24, 25, 26
Stewart, W.A., 3, 151n. 7
structures: classical heuristic, 161n. 52, 162n. 1, 163n. 4; statistical heuristic, 161n. 52, 162n. 1
Stump, Eleonore, 153n. 5
subconscious, 134–5, 176n. 59
subject, 43–4, 53, 57, 84–5, 87, 90, 92, 104, 110, 114, 116–7, 158–159nn. 30, 33, 162nn. 59, 64, 164n. 7, 176n. 3. *See also* self
sublation, 48–9, 53, 80, 105–8, 131, 133–6, 175n. 54, 176n. 60
supernatural, 66, 70–2, 76, 79, 85, 98, 101
suprastructure, 122–3, 136, 144–6
symbol, 82, 84, 86, 129, 131, 135, 137, 167nn. 38, 41
symbolic operator, 135–6, 176n. 59
systematics, 15–6, 102, 104

Taylor, Charles, 48, 156n. 5, 160nn. 46, 47
Tekippe, Terry, 3, 151n. 7
Tertullian, 20, 126
Thales, 30, 37
theology, 9, 64–7, 71–2, 80–1, 98–9, 118, 121, 129–31, 135, 144–5, 147–9, 153n. 5, 162n. 67, 169–70n. 3, 175n. 54; communicative, 164n. 14; descriptive, 164n. 14; fundamental, 173n. 28; method in (*see* method, in theology); of grace, 176n. 58; systematic, 166n. 35
theory, theoretical, 82, 84–5, 95–6, 115, 122, 124, 126, 134, 175n. 44, 175n. 48
thing-in-itself. *See* noumenon
Thompson, John B., 158n. 27
Tillich, Paul, 170n. 5
Tolkien, J.R.R., 12

Toulmin, Stephen, 1, 151n. 1
Toynbee, Arnold, 120, 139
Tracy, David, 3, 161n. 54
Trinity, 62, 65–6, 80, 126
Troeltsch, Ernst, 120–1
truth, 156n. 4, 169n. 63, 172n. 11; symbolic value of, 21; *See also* faith, truths of; judgment; reality; unconditioned, virtually
Tyrrell, Bernard, 15, 152n. 1, 154n. 13

unauthenticity, unauthentic, inauthentic, 89, 91, 128–9, 136, 138, 142, 145–6, 172n. 11. *See also* authenticity, authentic
unconditioned, 50; formally, 107; virtually, 45, 51, 53–4, 91, 130, 159n. 34, 161n. 56
unconscious, 134–5, 176n. 59
understanding, 36, 45, 50–2, 72, 90–1, 101, 104–8, 124, 126, 129, 135, 142–3, 152n. 10, 153n. 7, 161n. 52, 164n. 13, 172n. 11, 173n. 33; reflective, 51, 130, 173n. 25, 173n. 33; unrestricted act of, 14, 91–2, 104–5

value(s), 90, 108, 110, 114, 121, 131, 137, 163n. 3; apprehension of, 110; integral scale of, 110, 114, 172n. 12; judgement of, 109–10, 121, 129, 131; originating, 111; religious, 110; transvaluing of, 110–1
Vattimo, Gianni, 167n. 43
verbum (word), 63, 161n. 51
verification, 174n. 43
Vertin, Michael, 168n. 50, 176n. 58
Vico, Giambattista, 28
Virgil, ix
Vivaldi, Antonio, 37

Wainright, William J., 151n. 5
Wartenberg, Thomas E., 161n. 57, 162n. 59
Weber, Max, 119
Weinberg, Steven, 33
Whately, Richard, 156n. 6
Wilson, Patricia, 152n. 1
Winter, Gibson, 7, 118–9, 173n. 31
Wittgenstein, Ludwig, 2, 163n. 5
Wolf, Friedrich, 120
Wolterstorff, Nicholas, 160n. 38
Wulff, David M., 78, 166n. 36

Zanardi, William, 169n. 2

www.ingramcontent.com/pod-product-compliance
Lightning Source LLC
Chambersburg PA
CBHW020332240426
43665CB00043B/447